Two Chan

Prince Gortchakof and Prince Bismarck

Julian Klaczko

(Translator: Frank P. Ward)

Alpha Editions

This edition published in 2024

ISBN : 9789362510433

Design and Setting By
Alpha Editions
www.alphaedis.com
Email - info@alphaedis.com

As per information held with us this book is in Public Domain.
This book is a reproduction of an important historical work. Alpha Editions uses the best technology to reproduce historical work in the same manner it was first published to preserve its original nature. Any marks or number seen are left intentionally to preserve its true form.

Contents

TRANSLATOR'S PREFACE .... - 1 -
I. .... - 3 -
THE MISSIONS OF PRINCE GORTCHAKOF AND THE DÉBUTS OF M. DE BISMARCK. .... - 3 -
II. .... - 40 -
A NATIONAL MINISTER AND A FAULT-FINDING DIPLOMAT AT ST. PETERSBURG. .... - 40 -
III. .... - 64 -
UNITED ACTION. .... - 64 -
IV. .... - 97 -
THE ECLIPSE OF EUROPE. .... - 97 -
V. .... - 116 -
ORIENT AND OCCIDENT. .... - 116 -
VI. .... - 146 -
TEN YEARS OF ASSOCIATION. .... - 146 -
APPENDIX. .... - 158 -
THE MISSION EXTRAORDINARY OF MR. FOX. ..... - 172 -
FOOTNOTES: .... - 174 -

TRANSLATOR'S PREFACE.

In the year 1866 Carlyle said: "The only man appointed by God to be His viceregent here on earth in these days, and knowing he was so appointed and bent with his whole soul on doing, and able to do God's work," is M. de Bismarck. If this be true, then M. de Bismarck has found a most valuable ally and colleague in the present Premier of Russia. It is of these two men, Prince Bismarck, and Prince Gortchakof, the Chancellor of Germany, and the Chancellor of all the Russias, that this book treats. The author is M. Julian Klaczko, a Polish refugee, a man of cosmopolitan habits, an accomplished and able writer, thoroughly acquainted with the contemporaneous history of Europe, prejudiced against Prussia, an ardent friend of Austria, and devoted to a conservative and monarchical form of government. He was always the friend of Poland. In 1863 he defended Denmark in a series of able papers, which came out in the "Revue des deux Mondes," under the title of "Studies of Contemporaneous Diplomacy." After the battle of Sadowa, he appeared as the friend of Austria in a work entitled, "The Preliminaries of Sadowa." Count de Beust summoned him to Vienna, and attached him to the Foreign Office. Klaczko was then elected Deputy in the Polish province of Galicia. After 1870 he resigned his posts and returned to France.

In the "Two Chancellors" he has given a condensed but graphic review of the diplomatic history of Europe from 1855 to 1871, and a sketch of the lives of Prince Bismarck and Prince Gortchakof, the two most eminent men of the day. He also seeks to prove that the "disaster" of Sadowa, followed by the still greater one of Sedan, was brought about by the blind devotion of Prince Gortchakof to Prince Bismarck, aided largely, it is true, by the "inconceivable vacillations and hallucinations of Napoleon III., the Dreamer of Ham." In a word, he seeks to establish that the prodigious events of the last ten years are due to a conspiracy between Russia and Prussia. This is a one-sided, partial view, but is presented with such power as will almost persuade the reader that such may have been the case. According to Klaczko's theories, Prussia has grasped the substance and Russia the shadow, and the old chancellor of the great empire of the North has been the dupe of his pupil of Berlin.

The great changes which will undoubtedly soon take place in the East, make M. Klaczko's views as to the past and present relations between Germany and Russia of marked interest, and the student of contemporaneous history will find in the "Two Chancellors," notwithstanding the peculiar views and strong prejudices of the writer, one of the most instructive as well as interesting works that have appeared for many years. It has been issued in book form in Paris, and widely circulated in Russia, where it has caused a profound sensation.

In the translation I have endeavored to reproduce as justly as possible the words of M. Klaczko, whose style, though strong and forcible, is at times somewhat involved. With these few words in regard to the importance of the subject and the character of the author, I leave to the judgment of the reader the account of the momentous events which may be truly said to have changed the political face of Europe.

I.

THE MISSIONS OF PRINCE GORTCHAKOF AND THE DÉBUTS OF M. DE BISMARCK.

The good old Plutarch, in commencing his long and charming series of Parallels with the account of the lives of Theseus and Romulus, experiences some difficulty in justifying such an association of the two heroes; he can find in them only very vague traits of resemblance, and these by no means striking. "To strength they both joined great powers of mind, both carried off women by violence, and the one as well as the other was not exempted from domestic miseries; indeed, toward the end of their lives they both aroused the hatred of their fellow-citizens."[1] Without doubt a writer of our day, wishing to give a comparative study of the two most prominent figures of contemporaneous politics, the chancellors of Russia and Germany, would only mislead in giving prominence to such points of resemblance. The association in this case is justifiable, for it suggests itself to every contemplative mind, to whoever has meditated on the events of the last fifteen or twenty years. The modern Plutarch who would undertake to write the lives of these two illustrious men, could, as it seems to us, easily resist the temptation of searching too deeply for, or forcing analogies in a subject where similarities abound and are so striking. Perhaps he would rather have to guard against necessary and tiresome repetitions in presence of a commonalty of ideas and of a harmony of action such as history has rarely known in two ministers guiding two different empires.

It is not, the reader may be well assured, a work of this sort which the author has undertaken in the following pages. We have only given the mere sketch of a picture which, to be even in a slight degree full and satisfactory, would have required much larger proportions, and above all a much more skillful hand. Without pretending to present here new and unpublished materials, or indeed to reunite all those which are already known, we have simply chosen a few, and tried to assort and arrange them so as to afford a better perspective. We have been obliged to renounce the wish to give to the different parts an equality of design and depth of coloring, and we have not even bound ourselves to follow a very regular and methodical course in this narration. Before a subject so vast and presenting so many shades and shadows, we have thought that it was permissible, that it was indeed occasionally useful, to vary the points of observation and to present it in different aspects.

I.

Like the Odoïefski, the Obolenski, the Dolgorouki, and many aristocratic families on the banks of the Moscova and the Neva, the Gortchakof also pride themselves on their descent from the Rourik; to speak more plainly, they claim to trace their origin from one of the sons of Michael, Grand Duke of Tchernigof, put to death towards the middle of the thirteenth century by the Mongolians of Batou Khan, since proclaimed martyr of the faith, exalted, indeed, among the saints of the Orthodox Church. One meets, nevertheless, with but few illustrious bearers of the name of Gortchakof in the gloomy and exciting annals of old Russia. In the epoch which preceded the accession of the Romanof, there lived a certain Peter Ivanovitch Gortchakof, the unfortunate commander of Smolenski, who surrendered this celebrated place to the Poles after two years of energetic and desperate resistance. He was taken to Warsaw, and there, in 1611, with the Czar Vassili, the two princes Schouyski, Sèhine, and a number of powerful *boiars*, he was forced to take part in the famous "*cortége* of captives" which the grand constable Zolkiweski presented one day—*honorificentissime*, says the chronicle of the times—to the king and the senate of the most serene republic. It was only in the second half of the last century, under the reign of Catherine II., that a Prince Ivan Gortchakof succeeded (thanks especially to his marriage with a sister of the opulent and courageous Souvorof) in again raising the glory of his old house, which has never since ceased to distinguish itself in the different branches of state service, principally in the career of arms. The France of to-day has preserved the memory of two Princes Gortchakof, two old soldiers of Borodino who distinguished themselves during the war of the Orient. The one commanded the left wing of the Russian troops at the battles of Alma and Inkermann; the other, Prince Michael, was the generalissimo of the armies of the czar in the Crimea, and rendered his name imperishable by the heroic defense of Sebastopol. Afterwards he governed the Kingdom of Poland as lieutenant of the emperor, and became therefore (strange example of the vicissitudes of history!) the supreme representative of a harsh, foreign government in this same city of Warsaw, where one of his ancestors had formerly figured in a memorable procession of the vanquished. However, if this circumstance ever occurred to Prince Michael, he drew therefrom none but suggestions worthy of his character; he governed the conquered country with moderation and benevolence, and left behind him the fame of a man as just in civil administration as he was intrepid in war.

The cousin of Prince Michael and present chancellor of the empire, Alexander Mikhaïlovitch Gortchakof, was born in 1798, and was educated in that lyceum of Zarkoe-Zeloe which has its distinct place in the pedagogic history of Russia. Founded by Catherine II. as a model educational establishment for the aristocratic youth of the empire, the lyceum shone with great *éclat* under the reign of Alexander I., although the Rollin and the Pestalozzi would certainly have had more than one reservation to make with respect to a college which only moulded its scholars for the world, and thought the vigorous classical studies a burden too heavy to carry into the ethereal spheres of pleasures and elegance. Almost all the professors of the establishment were foreigners, men marked with the stamp of the eighteenth century, acute minds, slightly frivolous, and above all disciples of Voltaire. The most eminent among them, the professor of French literature, he who initiated the future chancellor into the language of Voltaire, of which he so well knew the subtleties, was a Genevese, who, under the inoffensive name of M. de Boudry, concealed another of a terrible significance. M. de Boudry was the brother of Marat, that "*sinistre conventionnel*."[2] The Empress Catherine, in order "to end a scandal," had forced this patronymic change on M. Marat, without, however, succeeding in making him change his opinions, which always remained "Jacobin." He died in final impenitence, cherishing an openly avowed admiration for *the friend of the people*, unjustly calumniated. From this education of very doubtful value, the young Gortchakof succeeded in extracting a strong and useful substance. He left Zarkoe-Zeloe with various and solid acquirements; a surprising matter, he was even a good Latinist, and this last fact has remained a cause of amazement to his fellow-scholars as well as to the generations who followed. It is certain, however, that the chancellor could quote Horace with about the same appropriateness as Louis XVIII. of sainted memory. One of his best known dispatches ingeniously borrows from Suetonius an eloquent passage on the distinction to be established between liberty and anarchy.

Next to his classical attainments, that part of his youth which the chancellor loves especially to recall is that he was the fellow-scholar, and that he remained the friend, of the great national poet, Pouchkine, a fact more to his honor inasmuch as this friendship has brought with it embarrassments at certain times. When, by the order of the Emperor Alexander I., in consequence of an offensive ode, which one is not now known, the young singer of "Rouslan" and "Loudmila" was confined in an obscure village in the far interior of Russia, only two of his former comrades at the lyceum had the courage to go to see and offer him their condolence, and one of these intrepid youths was Prince Gortchakof. One finds in the work of Pouchkine some verses written in a lively and playful style, and which only derive their interest from the name of Alexander Mikhaïlovitch, to whom they are addressed. In one of these juvenile pieces, Pouchkine wishes his friend "to have Cupid as an inseparable companion as far as the banks of the Styx, and to go to sleep on the bosom of Helen in the very boat of Charon." Thoughtless wishes, which human malignity would surely not have failed to carry out in the end, if very fortunately the chancellor had not been able to preserve his old days from every deceitful seduction, and to avoid even the appearance of an arctic Ruy Gomez. The inspiration of the poet was happier another time, when, speaking of their different vocations, he predicts for Alexander Mikhaïlovitch a splendid destiny, and calls him "the beloved child of fortune."

Fortune was nevertheless slow to recognize its child, and to give him the lot which he merited. Having early entered the department of foreign affairs, being attached to the *suite* of M. de Nesselrode at the time of the Congresses of Laybach and Verona, Prince Gortchakof had already long passed that period which Dante calls the *mezzo del cammin di vita*; and even when very near his fiftieth year, was still only a minister plenipotentiary at a little court in Germany. A fortunate event at last came to commend him to the kindness of his master, and to render him distinguished in those diplomatic circles, in those regions "free from tears, but filled with sighs," which in the language of diplomacy are called the secondary posts.

In a moment of paternal weakness, the Emperor Nicholas had one day consented to the union of his daughter, the Grand Duchess Marie, with the Duke of Leuchtenberg, "the son of a Beauharnais, a Catholic officer in the service of the King of Bavaria," as was whispered with sadness in the intimate circles of the winter palace. Nicholas was not the man to retract his given word, but not the less did he feel the sting of what his surrounding court did not cease to call a *mésalliance*; and the bitterness increased when none of the foreign members of the imperial family came to take part in the brilliant festivities which preceded or followed the nuptial ceremony. Ill-luck would have it that soon afterwards a first cousin of the new imperial son-in-law and daughter of the ex-King Jerome married a Russian grown rich in trade, a prince in the valley of the Arno but scarcely a gentleman on the banks of the Neva,—a disagreeable accident, and which, according to the amazed courtiers, made the autocrat of all the Russias *the relation of one of his subjects*! It became necessary to efface all these unpleasant impressions, and to take, by a brilliant alliance, an incontestable revenge for so many vexations. It was hoped for a moment to be able to marry the Grand Duchess Alexandra to an arch-duke of Austria, but it was necessary to fall back on a prince of Darmstadt; for the Grand Duchess Olga, the most beautiful and the most beloved of the emperor's daughters, had been chosen by the only prince royal then unengaged, the presumptive heir to the throne of Würtemberg, of the old and illustrious house of Suabia.

The plan was not easily executed. The good Suabian people had little liking for it. A Russian marriage made it tremble for its constitutional liberties; and what was a graver matter, the old King William of Würtemberg, a good, liberal sovereign, but obstinate in all things, showed himself rather reluctant, and at his own pleasure retarded the negotiation. Other objections came from other sides still; but the Russian minister plenipotentiary at Stuttgart, the old fellow-scholar of Pouchkine, knew how to overcome them all with consummate skill. By aid of art and address, he was able to establish the Grand Duchess Olga in the royal family of Würtemberg. The joy of the Emperor Nicholas was great and unreserved, and the winter palace sang the panegyrics of the wonderful diplomat. After such a success, Prince Gortchakof could well demand to be promoted in his career, having approached nearer by several strides towards that embassy of Vienna which was considered as the supreme goal of ambition. He did nothing of this sort, however, and showed an admirable patience,—the patience of the patriarch Jacob with Laban, son of Nahor. To the four years which he had already passed at Stuttgart, Alexander Mikhaïlovitch declared himself ready to add another term more prolonged if it were necessary. He promised the empress-mother to remain indefinitely by the side of the Grand Duchess Olga, to aid her as a guide and counselor in a foreign country and in the midst of surroundings entirely new to her. Barren as the soil might be, he did not despair of growing there under this ray of beauty and of grace, which came directly from the great boreal sun; and in truth he kept this post at Stuttgart for eight more long years. *Tenues grandia conamur!*

However, any point of observation is good for one who understands how to adjust his glass and question the stars. The resident minister at Stuttgart had extensive information and found means of informing his government of many things quite outside the limits of the horizon of the little kingdom of Würtemberg. Soon the year 1848 came with its terrible catastrophes, with its great revolutionary earthquakes which added to the experience of the most experienced, which lightened with a sudden glimmer the ignorant depths of human nature, and, in the words of Milton, lightened the darkness. Such a lesson of history was not without profit, one can well believe, to the former scholar of Zarkoe-Zeloe. The *salons* and the cabinets for a long time had had no secrets from him; he now knew those of the forum and of the cross-roads. The vicinity of Frankfort, seat of the famous parliament, permitted him to study closely and fully the German agitation of this memorable epoch; he understood beforehand the phases, by turns *naïve*, burlesque, and odious, and was able to predict in good time the unfailing miscarriage of a revolution, the subdued billows of which foamed for a day even in the streets of Stuttgart, ordinarily so peaceful.

It was in the month of April, 1849. Preceding by twenty years the great work of 1870, the parliament of Frankfort had just formed a German Empire to the exclusion of Austria, and offered the crown to the King of Prussia, Frederick William IV. The King of Prussia hesitated, and ended by declining; the other German princes were still less willing to assent to a decree which implied their abdication; but this was by no means the plan of the German demagogy. It suddenly fell enthusiastically in love with this constitution, which on the very eve before it had denounced as reactionary, fatal to the liberties of the people, and designed to impose by force the Prussian vassalage decreed at Frankfort on different sovereigns of Germany. In Würtemberg, the chamber of deputies voted a pressing, imperious address in order to draw from the king the recognition of the Emperor Frederick William IV. The monarch replied by a refusal. The riot thundered on the public square, and the members of the court were forced to seek refuge at Ludwigsburg, fleeing from an enraged capital. "I will not submit to the House of Hohenzollern," the old King William of Würtemberg had said to the deputation of the chamber. "I owe it to my people and to myself. It is not for myself that I speak thus; I have but very few years to live. My duty to my country, my House, my family, forces this course of action on me." Alexander Mikhaïlovitch, touched by these agitating scenes, by this pathetic protestation of the father-in-law of Olga, "for the House, for the family of Würtemberg," assuredly had then but little expectation that one day, as Chancellor of the Russian Empire, he would become the most useful auxiliary, the firmest aid of an aggressive, audacious policy, destined to realize in every particular the plan of the rioters of Stuttgart, and to make Queen Olga the vassal of Hohenzollern.

This was, however, nothing but the noisy prologue of a drama yet far distant, and the year 1850 could indeed rejoice at seeing disappear in Germany the very last traces of an agitation which had done nothing but astonish Europe, instead of illuminating and warning it. Towards the end of this year, 1850, the German Confederacy was established anew under the terms of the ancient treaty of Vienna. The *Bundestag* again commenced its peaceable deliberations, and Prince Gortchakof was quite naturally appointed to represent the Russian Government at the Diet of Frankfort. Alexander Mikhaïlovitch henceforth had his marked place in a great centre of political affairs, where the personal merit of the minister borrowed a peculiar *éclat* from the extraordinary fortune which the latest events had created for his august master. Russian influence, at all times very considerable with the ruling houses of Germany, had grown prodigiously, having reached its zenith, one will remember, after the disorders of February. Alone remaining sheltered from the revolutionary tempest which had swept over almost all the States of the Continent, the empire of the czars appeared to be at that time the firmest stronghold of the principles of order and conservatism. "Humiliate yourselves, nations, God is with us!" said the Emperor Nicholas in a celebrated proclamation; and without being too much offended at language which made God in a manner the accessory to a great human boast, monarchical Europe had only acclamations for a prince who, after all, worked with a remarkable disinterestedness for the reëstablishment of the legitimate authorities, and for the maintenance of the equilibrium of the world.

In fact, it is just to acknowledge that in these troubled years of 1848-50, the autocrat of the North used his influence, as also his sword, only to strengthen the tottering thrones and to enforce respect for the treaties. He effectively protected Denmark, towards which from this epoch the rapacious hand of Germany was stretched, and he was the most ardent in calling a meeting of the Powers, which ended by snatching from the Germans the coveted prey. He interposed directly in Hungary, and with his military forces helped put down a formidable insurrection there, which had shaken to its foundations the ancient empire of Hapsburg, undermined at the same time by intestine troubles and an aggressive war which the kingdom of Piedmont had twice stirred up against it. Little favoring by his principles and interests this united Germany, "of which the first thought was a thought of unjust extension, the first cry a cry of war,"[3] he later used all his power in bringing about the reëstablishment pure and simple, of the German Confederation on the same basis as prior to 1848. The bonds of relationship and of friendship which united him to the court of Berlin were never strong enough to make him abandon for a single instant the cause of the sovereignty of princes, and of the independence of the States; and in spite of the sincere affection which he bore "his brother-in-law, the poet," he neither spared the King of Prussia, Frederick William IV., the evacuation of the Duchies, nor the hard conditions of Olmütz. Defender of European right on the Eider and the Main, of monarchical right on the Theiss and Danube, peacemaker for Germany, and, so to say, wholesale dealer in justice for Europe, Nicholas had at this moment a true greatness, an immense *prestige*, well merited on the whole, and which allowed no reflection on the agents charged with representing away from home a policy of which no one dared contest the immovable firmness and the perfect justice.

The Emperor Nicholas, in accrediting Prince Gortchakof to the German Confederation, in an autograph letter dated 11th November, 1850, recognized in the reunion of the Diet of Frankfort "a pledge for the maintenance of the general peace," and thus characterized by an able and judicious act, the honorable and salutary mission of this Diet in ordering matters created by the treaties of 1815. However legitimate the grievances of the liberal Germans were against the internal policy of the *Bund*[4] and its tendencies, little favorable to the development of the constitutional *régime*, yet one cannot deny that, according to the European point of view, and with regard to the equilibrium and the general peace of the world, this was a marvelous conception, well fitted to preserve the independence of the States and to hinder any deep perturbation in the bosom of the Christian family. The chimerical and mercantile minds of the times, the leading men of Manchester and the rich publicists, with at least "one idea a day," imagined that this was the moment to declare "war to war," to force a universal disarmament, to abolish military slavery; and to this effect they convoked noisy congresses of peace in different parts of the world. They had, indeed, in a day of *naïveté*, convoked one at Frankfort, without suspecting that by their side, and in this very *Bundestag* of such modest appearance, had sat for a long time a true and permanent congress of peace,—a congress which would do as much good as possible, and which, moreover, would have the advantage of not being ridiculous.

Placed in the very centre of Europe, separating by its large and immovable body the great military powers which form the border, so to speak, of our old continent,—a power neutral by necessity and almost by law over those great plains, where in former times the destinies of empires were decided,— the German Confederation formed an *ensemble* of States sufficiently coherent and compact to repulse any shock from abroad, yet not strong enough to become aggressive itself and to menace the security of its neighbors. Many years later, and when chancellor of the empire, Prince Gortchakof, in a celebrated circular, rendered homage to this beneficial combination of the *Bund*, "a combination purely and exclusively defensive," which permitted the localization of a war, become inevitable, "instead of generalizing it and of giving to the struggle a character and proportions beyond all human calculation, and which in any case would pile up ruins and cause torrents of blood to flow."[5]

In truth, if in this long half century which intervened between the Congress of Vienna and the ill-omened battle of Sadowa, the frontiers of the States have changed so little in spite of so many and so great changes in their political complexion; if the revolution of July, the campaign of Belgium, and even the wars of the Crimea and Italy have been carried on without noticeably disturbing the balance of the nations, or injuring them in their independence, we are specially indebted to this *Bundestag* so unappreciated, which by its very existence, by its position, and the wheelwork of its completed mechanism, prevented any conflict from becoming a general conflagration. It is doubtful whether the cause of humanity and civilization, or the very cause which the chancellor of Russia more specially represents with such facility and *éclat*, have gained in any considerable degree in seeing this old "combination" replaced in our time by another, more simple, it is true, but, perhaps, also much less calculated to restore confidence.

While acquitting himself zealously of the duties of his office in connection with the Germanic Confederation, Alexander Mikhaïlovitch continued to occupy the post of minister plenipotentiary at Stuttgart. He held it to be a matter of honor to fulfill to the end his confidential and intimate mission by the side of the Grand Duchess Olga. He divided his time between the free city on the Main, the seat of the *Bund*, and the little capital on the banks of the Neckar, where a warm and kind interest always greeted him. At Frankfort he took especial pleasure in the society of his Prussian colleague, a young lieutenant in the *Landwehr*,[6] an entire novice in the diplomatic career, although marked out for such a prodigious destiny. There had been settled here for many years a great Russian celebrity, a poet, who was at the same time an influential courtier, and who could not be overlooked by a diplomat with a love for intellectual enjoyments, and who had been a school-fellow of Pouchkine. The good and mild Vassili Joukofski had certainly none of the genius of Pouchkine, nor his independent and ardent character. More properly a facile versifier and an ingenious translator than a creative and original mind, with a nature rather effeminate and contemplative, the formerly renowned author of "Ondine" had early made his peace with the official society which the despotic will of Nicholas had created, and had always sunned himself in th e rays of imperial favor.

During his long and pleasant career as poet at the court, he had not been without dignities and honors. He, however, had a mission much more important and honorable; he was charged with directing the education of the heir-presumptive, Alexander, the present emperor, and of his brother the Grand Duke Constantine. Joukofski devoted himself to this task with intelligence and ardor, and retained the affection of his two august pupils to the end of his life. A proof of this fact is the correspondence which ensued and which he still maintained with them while at Frankfort. These letters were published quite recently. After having finished the education of the grand dukes, he made a voyage of pleasure in Germany. At Düsseldorf he found a companion for life, much younger than himself, but sharing all his tastes, even his charming weaknesses. He finally selected a home on the banks of the Main, at Frankfort.

Thus, as it happens to more than one of his compatriots, Joukofski, living entirely in a foreign country, and being indeed manifestly unwilling to return to his native land, considered the Occident miserably sunken and corrupted, and hoped only in "holy Russia" for the renovation and safety of a world overrun and possessed by the demon of revolution. The events of February only served to confirm him in these gloomy visions and to plunge him more and more into an uneasy mysticism, at times even irritating, but more often inoffensive and not devoid of a certain unhealthy charm. The campaign of Hungary caused a momentary diversion in his sad thoughts, and filled him with joy. It was not so much the glory with which the Russian army covered itself which pleased his mind; it was not even the triumph attained by the Russian sword, the sword of St. Michael, over "the impure beast:" his prayers, his hopes went far beyond. He hoped—thus he wrote to his imperial pupil that the great czar would profit by the power which God had given him and would "solve a problem on which the crusades had stranded;" that is to say, that he should drive the infidel from Byzantium, and liberate the holy land. Mme. Joukofski, although born a Protestant, felt in unison with her melancholy husband. Her soul had need of a "principle of authority," which failed her in the reformed confession, and which she sought one day in the

Orthodox Church, to the great joy of the poet, without, however, being able to find there perfect rest.

Sometimes in the *salon* of the Joukofski the conversations were strangely varied and *bizarre*, on literature, politics, the glorious destinies of holy Russia, the inanity of modern civilization, the necessity of "a new eruption of Christianity," and on many matters invisible and "ineffable." Occasionally there fell into the midst of this *salon*, like a fantastic apparition, like a ghost from the world of spirits, a genius original and powerful in a very different way, but also tormented and troubled differently from the good court poet and former preceptor of the grand dukes. After having unveiled the hideous sores of Russian society with a vigorous, implacable hand, after having presented to his nation, in "Les Ames Mortes" and in "L'Inspecteur," a picture whose vices were appalling with truth and life, Nicholas Gogol suddenly gave up in despair civilization, progress, and liberty, and betaking himself to adore that which he had burned, valued nothing but barbarian Muscovy, saw no salvation but in despotism, thought himself in a state of "unpardonable" sin, and went in search of divine pity which always fled from him. Shortly afterwards he went from St. Petersburg to Rome, then to Jerusalem, then to Paris, everywhere seeking appeasement for his lacerated soul. Then he came from time to time to Joukofski, and passed whole weeks in his house, exhorting his friends to prayer, to repentance, and to contemplation of the divine mysteries. There were discussions without end, without a truce, on the "heathens of the Occident," on "a crusade," which was drawing near, on the redemption of sinful humanity by a race not yet defiled, and which had kept its faith. At several revivals the physicians were forced to interfere to put an end to a connection not without peril. One day Gogol was found, having died of inanition, prostrate before the holy images, in the adoration of which he had lost all thought of himself.... May we be pardoned for this short digression. It makes us acquainted with the state of the minds of a certain Russian society towards the end of the reign of Nicholas, and adds a curious stroke to the picture of the origins of the war in the Orient. One delights, however, to think of Alexander Mikhaïlovitch in this *salon* of the Joukofski, on an evening for instance, during such an intellectual conflict with the poor Gogol. The diplomat, equally cultivated and skeptical, was certainly made to recognize the bright and brilliant flashes which furrowed those driving clouds in a great, disordered mind; and he was made to unravel more than one strong and thrilling thought from the midst of those strange ramblings concerning an imminent crusade and the near deliverance of Zion.

Who would have thought it? It was these mystics, these men laboring under hallucinations, who had the true presentiment and saw the signs of the times! While Joukofski composed his "Commentary on Holy Russia," and Gogol mortified himself before the *icônes*, the Emperor Nicholas revolved in his mind the great thought of a crusade, and prepared in the most profound secrecy the mission of Prince Menchikof. The fact that the monarch who had done so much for preserving the peace and equilibrium of Europe had suddenly decided to throw such a fire-brand of war in the midst of the continent scarcely consolidated, while on the other hand the autocrat had awaited precisely this epoch of relative calm and of the reëstablishment of general order to announce his designs, in place of executing them boldly some years before during the revolutionary tempest which paralyzed almost all the Powers, his armies being already in the very heart of Hungary and commanding the banks of the Danube,—these facts will be for the impartial historian an evident proof of the good faith with which the czar undertook his fatal campaign, of the mystical blindness which guided his spirit at this time, and of the profound conviction which he had of the justice of his cause. Did Prince Gortchakof partake in the same measure of the illusions of his master? We doubt whether he did. We believe that, like the Kisselef, the Meyendorf, the Brunnow, and all the distinguished diplomats of Russia, without excepting the chancellor of the empire, the old Count Nesselrode, he was conscious of the great error toward which a proud prince, who allowed no objections and understood being "his own minister of foreign affairs," was tending. That naturally did not prevent the Russian representative to the German Confederation from fulfilling his duty with all the zeal which circumstances so critical made necessary, and from placing the various resources of his mind at the service of his country in the sphere of action which was reserved for him.

Events did not make it of much importance. In the *Bundestag* were concentrated not only all the efforts of the secondary States of the confederation, but there also were formed or conceived the projects, the preparations, and even the desires of the two principal German powers, the assistance of which Russia on the one side and France and England on the other, were equally concerned in obtaining. Prince Gortchakof could not complain of the turn affairs took in Germany. Frederick William IV. was faithful against every temptation. The czar could count in any case on "his brother-in-law, the poet;" and Alexander Mikhaïlovitch found an equally firm support in his colleague of Prussia, the young officer of the *Landwehr*. The cabinet of Berlin consented from time to time to join in the representations which the allies sent to St. Petersburg, to sign in concert with them the same note, or one analogous or concordant. But it did not take long to see that it only did this to retard their movements, and to deter them from any energetic resolution. At decisive moments it stopped short, hesitated, and pretended to preserve "*la main libre*" (*free Hand*). The other members of the *Bund* were much more sympathetic and more frankly won over to the Russian policy. They did not think the demands of the czar against Turkey at all exorbitant, and troubled themselves very little about the preservation of the "sick man." They likewise desired to preserve "*la main libre*," closed their ranks in the famous conferences of Bamberg, and were at times all ready to draw their swords. In truth, Alexander Mikhaïlovitch showed in the sequel, in the fatal year 1866, very little gratitude, very little distributive justice, for these poor secondary States, so devoted, so serviceable, so immovably attached at the time of the Oriental crisis.

While at London and at Paris vehement comments were made in the celebrated dispatches of Sir Hamilton Seymour, and the ambitious projects of Russia were denounced there, at Hanover, at Dresden, at Munich, at Stuttgart, at Cassel, nothing but censure was heard against the proceedings of the allies and their "usurpations." At Berlin they groaned all the more at seeing Christian monarchies undertake so ardently the defense of the Crescent. A single Germanic power, however, at that time the largest it is true, maintained a different attitude; a single one thought the cause of the allies just, seemed, indeed, at moments to be inclined to make common cause with them; and that power was Austria,—Austria, but lately succored by the Russian arms; saved by the strong and generous hand of the czar on the very brink of the abyss; "saved" by him from sudden dissolution. The astonishment, the stupefaction, the exasperation of the Emperor Nicholas knew no bounds. The entire Russian nation shared his sentiments,— Alexander Mikhaïlovitch like every patriotic Muscovite. "The immense ingratitude of Austria" became even then the unanimous cry,—the *siboleth* of every political faith in the vast empire of the North; and so it has remained even to our days.

It is necessary to lay stress upon this sentiment born in Russia in consequence of the Oriental conflict, and to discuss the real causes for it; for this sentiment has produced incalculable effects. It has contributed largely to the recent catastrophes; it has dictated more than one extreme resolution to the cabinet of St. Petersburg; it has made it abandon its venerable traditions,—its principles, consecrated by the experience of generations and seemingly immovable, having become, in a certain sense, the *arcana imperii* of the descendants of Peter the Great. To sum up, it has governed the general policy of the successor of Nesselrode during the last twenty years.

Assuredly Russia had the right to count on the recognition of Austria after the signal and incontestable service which it had rendered her in 1849. The armies which the czar then sent to the succor of the tottering empire of Hapsburg contributed powerfully to suppress a fatal, menacing insurrection there; and if it is true that in order to obtain this succor it was sufficient to recall to the Czar Nicholas a word given long before in a moment of confidential intimacy, the action does not become the less meritorious, and does so much the more honor to the heart of the autocrat.[7] It would be difficult to deny that this intervention in Hungary had not a generous and chivalric character which astonished the contemporaries and the clever. The clever ones, the statesmen, who, at this troubled epoch of Europe, had still preserved enough liberal spirit to cast their eyes toward the Danube,—Lord Palmerston among others,—remained for a long time incredulous, and endeavored to divine the reward paid for the aid that was lent. Should not the czar retain Galicia as a recompense for his assistance? Would he not procure some positive assurance from the side of the Principalities? was asked in the offices of Downing Street. Nothing of the sort happened, however. The Russians left Austria without a reward, as they had entered it without an *arrière-pensée*, and the troops of Paskévitch evacuated the country of the Carpathians unladen with booty. A young and ardent orator in the Prussian chambers, with the name (as yet but little known) de Bismarck,—the same who fifteen years later was to project striking a *coup au cœur* and arming the legions of Klapka,—admired at this moment the brilliant action of the czar, and only expressed the patriotic regret that this magnanimous *rôle* had not fallen to his own country, to Prussia. It was for Prussia to bring assistance to its elder brother in Germany, to "its former comrade in arms."[8] But it is allowable to suppose that, even with a king as loyal and poetic as Frederick William IV., affairs would have been conducted much less handsomely than with the barbarian of the North, and that similar aid from Prussia would have cost the empire of Hapsburg a part of Silesia or a part of its influence on the Main.

Shall we say, then, that in intervening in Hungary the Emperor of Russia acted from pure chivalry and platonic friendship, that he had no thought of personal interest and the good of his empire? Certainly not; and the czar had too much loyalty not to avow it frankly. He intervened in Hungary, not only as the friend of the Hapsburg, not only as the defender of the cause of order against cosmopolitan revolution; the most powerful motive in deciding him was the presence in the Hungarian army of Polish generals and officers, who intended to carry the war into the countries subjected to Russian rule. In his manifest of the 8th May, 1849, Nicholas expressed himself as follows: "The insurrection sustained by the influence of *our traitors from Poland*, of the year 1831, has given to the Hungarian revolt an extension more and more *menacing*.... His majesty, the Emperor of Austria, has invited us to assist against *the common enemy*.... We have ordered our army under way to quell the revolt, and to destroy the audacious anarchists, *who equally menace the tranquillity of our provinces.*" The language was clear and frank, as was fitting for a sovereign preserving the consciousness of his dignity. This sovereign intended to render himself a service as well as his ally. He was going to stifle in his neighbors' territory an incendiary fire which threatened to harm his own domains; and in the act of intervening, let it be well understood, he at the same time acted in self-preservation.

Well! it seems according to all justice that the gratitude should correspond to the service rendered, and that the law of preservation, the supreme law of nature, should have equal force for the party under obligations as for the benefactor. There is no policy in the world, were it even taken from Holy Writ which could advise voluntary servitude; there is no doctrine, however sublime one wishes to imagine it, which, among the duties of the confession, recommends suicide. Now, it was nothing less than absolute subjection, the ruin of its personality as a great European State, which the Russians demanded of Austria in demanding its assent to their pretensions against the Orient. By geography, by the spirit of races, by religion, the Russian enterprises would strike a mortal blow at the empire of the Hapsburg, if this empire allowed them to triumph. A Danubian power, Austria should take care that the Lower Danube remained neutral, and that it should not fall into the hands of a powerful neighbor, who would then become master of this great river. A Sclavic power in its Oriental provinces, it ought to guard against being placed in immediate contact with an empire pan-Sclavic by tradition and by fatality, and it could not wish it to be planted in the Principalities, in Bosnia and Herzegovania. A Catholic power, it was forbidden to recognize the influence and the protectorate which the orthodox czar claimed over the Christians of the Grecian rite, of whom it counted several millions among its subjects. "My conduct in the question of the Orient! Why it is written on a map?" said Count Buol, to his brother-in-law, M. de Meyendorf, the Russian ambassador. He added that it was also written in history. "I have made no innovation. I have only inherited the political legacy of M. de Metternich."

In fact, in a previous crisis, at the time of the Hellenic insurrection and the war of 1828, the grand chancellor of the court and of the empire had defended this principle of the integrity of the Ottoman Empire with a firmness which nothing could disturb. During eight years he had defended it, braving the storm alone, not allowing himself to be discouraged either by the unpopularity then attaching to the Turkish cause or by the desertion of France. Why should the Russians hope that Austria would now desert this principle so vital for her, that she would desert it at the very moment when it commenced to triumph over the indifference of the Occident, and counted France and England among its most earnest champions?

Placed between a sentiment of gratitude very lively and real, as we have said, and a great political necessity, the government of Vienna has certainly done for gratitude all that it owed. It lavished warnings, prayers, good offices, offers of mediation on the Emperor Nicholas. Austria pardoned Russia more than one want of respect, more than one action of ill humor; it pardoned her the more than airy tone in which it had been disposed of in the effusions with Sir Hamilton Seymour,—the manner in which a certain autograph letter of the Emperor Francis Joseph had been received at St. Petersburg,—the haughty, almost insulting attitude of Count Orlof during his mission at Vienna. It did not cease till the end to calm the irritation of the allies, to modify and alter their programme, to assert the conciliating disposition of the czar, to hope against all hope. It pleaded only for the return *in statu quo*, repudiating any idea of humiliating or weakening Russia; it demanded nothing from her but the freedom of the Danube, the renunciation of the protectorate, and refused to follow the allies in their demands concerning the Black Sea. Unfortunately, as it happens too often to him who wishes to be equitable and just towards all parties, the Austrian government, by this conduct, ended by alienating France and England and exasperating the Russians. In the summer of 1854, at the very moment when Prince Gortchakof exchanged his post at Frankfort for that at Vienna, an eminent publicist, who was then, so to speak, the mouth-piece of the Occident, and of its generous spirits, almost despaired of Austria, and cried with bitterness that over there, in the *Burg*, "the Russian alliance was something as sacred as a religion, as fixed as propriety, and as popular as a fashion!" In the spring of the following year, the cabinets of Paris and of London resisted, as too favorable to Russia, a new plan of arrangement presented by Count Buol, and the French government on this occasion reproached Austria, in the "Moniteur Officiel," with offering an expedient rather than a solution.

The solution! The Emperor Francis Joseph certainly had it in his hands, and it perhaps depended only on him to render it as decisive and as radical as the most mortal enemies of Russia could wish. Why not confess it? To see the bitter fruit *gathered* by Austria in consequence of its honorable efforts during the Oriental crisis, and to see the implacable hatred and the cruel disasters which fell to its lot because of its attitude then, one surprises one's self sometimes in regretting that the cabinet of Vienna had so many scruples at this memorable epoch. One almost reproaches it for not having given proof of that independence of heart which seems, alas! the forced, indispensable condition for the independence of states. If Austria had wished to be a little less grateful and a little less politic during this war of the Orient, she would have resolutely joined herself to France and England, she would have taken part in the struggle, and instead of letting the allies rove for years around the borders of Russia, in the Black Sea and Baltic, she would have opened for them the fields of Poland, and have entered there with them. In place of "tickling the soul of the Colossus or of filing off a nail,"—as Russian publicists said later, and not without justice,—they should then have given him a *coup au cœur*,—one of those blows that the great recluse of Varzin knows how to plan and give. The cabinet of the Tuileries would not have refused to do this. In his dispatch of the 26th March, 1855, M. Drouyn de Lhuys laid down very skillfully the question of Poland; neither would the cabinet of St. James have raised serious objections. As to the probable success of such an enterprise, it suffices to remember that Russia was at the end of its resources, and that Prussia had not yet re-formed its military organization, was not yet in possession of its "instrument," and lastly that in place of William the Conqueror, Frederick the Romantic occupied the throne of the Hohenzollern. The mind is confounded before the contemplation of the consequences which such a decision on the part of the Emperor Francis Joseph might have caused. The face of the world would have been changed; Austria would certainly not have seen Sadowa[9] in 1866; Europe would not have seen the dismemberment of Denmark, nor the destruction of the *Bund*, nor the conquest of Alsace and Lorraine.

It was in the summer of 1854, as we have said above, that Prince Gortchakof was sent to Vienna. He replaced there, first provisionally, and in the following spring, definitely, Baron de Meyendorf, whose situation had become unpleasant in consequence of his ties of very near relationship with the Austrian Minister of Foreign Affairs. Alexander Mikhaïlovitch at last held that post at Vienna to which he had so long a time aspired, the post which, with that of London, was considered, under the reign of Nicholas, as the highest in Russian diplomacy, like the *bâton* of a marshal in his career. But now how full this honor was of bitterness, and what patriotic pangs accompanied a distinction formerly ardently wished for, to-day accepted through devotion to his sovereign and his country! On this ground, formerly so pleasant and smiling, the envoy of the czar could everywhere see nothing but briers and thorns. In this capital, renowned for its boisterous gayety and too frequent frivolity, he received nothing but disastrous and distracting news. And this "Austrian ingratitude," which he had only had glimpses of and combated from afar during his mission at Frankfort, he could now look in the face—and smile at it! There is a grief greater than the *ricordare tempi felici nella miseria*; it is to see a dream of happiness turn into a reality of misery, and one can easily understand what a treasure of gall this sojourn at Vienna must have heaped up in the wounded heart of the Russian patriot.[10]

It is superfluous to lay stress upon the activity which the new envoy of the czar displayed in this unhappy mission; to mention the infinite variety of means which he placed at the service of his cause, especially during the conferences of Vienna, which were opened after the death of Nicholas and the accession of the Emperor Alexander II. That was a moving sight and one which was truly not wanting in grandeur, that of the two Gortchakof, one behind the ramparts of Sebastopol, the other before the council board of Vienna, both defending their country with an equal tenacity, only yielding each inch of ground after a desperate combat, forced into their last intrenchments, but honored even to the end by loyal and chivalrous adversaries. To-day an epoch "of iron and of blood" has accustomed us to the summary proceedings—we had almost said executions—of Nikolsburg, of Ferrières, of Versailles, and of Frankfort, and a martial law used by the diplomats in helmets has replaced that which a former Europe, full of prejudices, loved to call the right of nations. To-day it is difficult to resist a sentiment of astonishment, almost of incredulity, in re-reading the protocols of these conferences of Vienna, where everything breathes decorum, politeness, urbanity, and mutual respect. One thinks himself carried back to an idyllic age, one far from us, to a world of ancient gentlemen. M. Drouyn de Lhuys, Minister of Foreign Affairs in France, Lord John Russell, until lately President of the Privy Council of England, did not think it beneath their dignity to go in person to Vienna to discuss there with Prince Gortchakof the possible conditions of a peace. Russia had lost several great battles, the allied fleets had blockaded all its seas and even menaced its capital. That did not prevent the French and English plenipotentiaries from treating it with all deference, with all the respect which the diplomacy of this good old time could employ. They displayed a veritable art in the invention of euphemisms; they gave themselves pains to find the mildest mediums, the most acceptable terms for the representative of a vanquished power. Indeed, that excellent Lord John Russell forced kindness so far as to recall, and that in the face of M. Drouyn de Lhuys, that England had made Louis XIV. submit to conditions much harder and more humiliating.[11] That was, perhaps, the only instance of want of tact which one can find in the conferences of Vienna, and yet what was it but a courteousness from an ally to an ally? As for Austria, it exhausted itself in finding means to spare the susceptibilities of Russia, and ended by presenting a plan of arrangement which was judged inacceptable by the cabinets of London and Paris, and drew on it the reproach of the "Moniteur Officiel," of which we have already spoken.

Negotiations were broken off, and nothing could be done but to await the issue of the supreme combat under the walls of Sebastopol. The Russian plenipotentiary awaited it at his post in Vienna in the twofold anguish of a patriot and a relation. The bulwark of the Crimea fell, and Russia found itself in the most critical situation. It was exhausted,—indeed much more exhausted than Europe then thought,—and the prolongation of the war would have infallibly transported the hostilities to the plains of Poland. At this moment Austria intervened anew. It agreed to the demands made by the allies at the conference of Vienna,—even that clause concerning the neutralization of the Black Sea, which it had hitherto resisted as too wounding to Russia. It was not possible to refuse this satisfaction to the allies after the capture of Sebastopol. In reality, these were the easiest conditions which have ever been imposed on a power at the close of a war so long, so bloody, and of such incontestable victories. Austria did more; it sent these conditions under form of an ultimatum, declaring that it would make common cause with the allies if they were not accepted; and Russia accepted them. To look at it plainly, this was a service rendered to a young sovereign, who, having inherited a disastrous war, thus found the means to spare at the same time the memory of his predecessor and the pride of his people. He could say now that he had only made peace because of a new adversary, who had arisen at the side of the old ones, and whom his father did not count on. In fact, it was said in Russia,—it was believed, indeed, so much was it in their interest to believe it. The Russian people were quickly reconciled with the conquerors of Alma and of Malakof. A single power remained in their eyes responsible for their disasters,—the power which during the whole war had rested on its arms. Even at this hour every Russian heart boils with indignation at the thought of Austria, of its immense ingratitude and its great treason.

Alexander Mikhaïlovitch shared these bitternesses, these popular rancors, and became the most energetic and openly avowed representative of them. In this respect he allowed his sentiments to burst forth with a frankness which approached very nearly to ostentation. A remark uttered by him during the session of the Congress at Paris, is still cited at Vienna: "Austria is not a state, it is only a government." These words preceded him to St. Petersburg and made his fortune there. The popular voice designated him as the future avenger, as the man destined to prepare for his nation a brilliant revenge; and the acute diplomat did not trouble himself to controvert such an opinion. Already, however, at this Congress of Paris certain tendencies, certain desires were revealed, which gave hope, which even opened horizons entirely new. The name of Italy was pronounced there. Roumania itself found there an unexpected support. At this strange Congress, which definitely regulated the conditions of a peace that France, England, and Austria had imposed on Russia, Austria appeared gloomy and morose, England irritated and nervous. France and Russia alone exchanged between one another the most exquisite politeness and surprising cordialities. The sword of Napoleon III. became the lance of Achilles, healing where it had just wounded, wounding where it had healed. "There was balm of Gilead in it," and support in the sovereign of the Tuileries. The day after the Congress, in the month of April, 1856, the old Count Nesselrode asked to be retired on account of his age, and Prince Alexander Gortchakof became Minister of Foreign Affairs.

II.

During the four years which he had passed at Frankfort as representative of his government to the German Confederation, Prince Gortchakof, as we have already seen, had made the acquaintance of, and maintained the most intimate relations with a colleague, whose rare qualities of mind, as probably also those of the heart, he appreciated as no one else did. The two friends were separated in the summer of 1854, when the Russian plenipotentiary went to fulfill his painful mission at Vienna. But they did not delay in meeting anew, and found as before that perfect congeniality of ideas and of sentiments, which, established since their first meeting in Frankfort, has never been interrupted, and has lasted for twenty-five years: *grande mortalis ævi spatium*. This friend of Prince Gortchakof on the smiling banks of the Main, was no other than M. de Bismarck, the future chancellor of Germany.

Otto-Edward-Leopold de Bismarck-Schoenhausen, born the 1st of April, 1815, at Schoenhausen, hereditary estate of his family in the old Mark of Brandenburg, could not flatter himself with having, like his friend Alexander Mikhaïlovitch, blood of the Saints in his veins. His biographers even observe with visible satisfaction, that at least two of his ancestors were excommunicated by the Church and died in final impenitence. What is more serious is that the most authorized historians of the Mark of Brandenburg, M. de Riedel among others, call into question the noble origin of the family. They show that the first of the line, of whom authentic documents of the fourteenth century speak, Rulo Bismarck, was a member and on several occasions even provost of "the guild of master tailors in cloth" at Stendal, a small market town of the old Mark. The fact does not seem doubtful. But could not the citizens of Stendal, just as well as those of certain cities in Tuscany, have forced every country noble, who wished to inhabit the city, to subscribe himself in one of those guilds? This is the opinion of the tories in this curious genealogical dispute. To hear them, the good citizens of Stendal must have been on a par, in the fourteenth century, with the great citizens of Florence and of Pisa, and Rulo Bismarck must have been master tailor in cloth about as much as Dante, his contemporary, was an apothecary. The whigs, on the contrary, the biographers in national-liberal colors, take their part gayly, and one of them ingeniously concludes, that in any case the ancestor Rulo ought "to contemplate with satisfaction and pride from the high heavens the splendid imperial mantle which his descendant has made for King William out of the cloth of Europe."

In times relatively more modern, the House of Bismarck presents, like many a noble country family of Brandenburg, an unbroken succession of modest and faithful servants of the state, some soldiers, some employed in civil duties. The eighteenth century offers us two rather more curious specimens, the grandfather and great uncle of the chancellor. One was surnamed the *poet*, the other the *adventurer*. The *poet*, this painful avowal must be made, composed his verses in the French language. We have notably by him an "*Eloge ou Monument érigé à la Mémoire de Christine de Bismarck, née de Schoenfeld, par Charles-Alexandre de Bismarck*," Berlin, 1774. It was to his dead wife that the retired captain of cavalry thought necessary to elevate this mausoleum of words and of *Welche* rhymes, full of the insipid sentimentality of the time. The *adventurer* (Ludolf-August) is more deserving of his name. He killed his servant in a fit of anger or drunkenness, was pardoned, took service in Russia, became involved in political intrigues in Courland, and was forced to go to

Siberia in exile. Pardoned again, he entered into Russian diplomacy, filled several missions, and died commanding general at Poltava. Let us say in passing, that this Ludolf was not the only one of his family to serve under the Russian flag, and thus the name of Bismarck has long been well known at St. Petersburg.

The whig biographers lay much stress on the fact, that the mother of the young Otto, "an intelligent, ambitious, and rather cold woman," was a *bourgeoise*, a Miss Menken, of a family of *savans* well known at Leipsic. They love to prove in this manner that the restorer of the empire was connected by his mother with the *bourgeoisie*, that studious and cultivated *bourgeoisie* which is the great strength of Germany,—while claiming his right to the nobility and the army by his father, retired captain of cavalry, and by his grandfather the *poet*. Those profound Germans have a weakness, it is known, for all symbolism. They dignify very often with this name that which is nothing but a *jeu d'esprit*, in reality a play of words, and it is thus that they attach a certain signification to the futile circumstance that the young Otto was confirmed[12] at Berlin at the hands of Schleiermacher, the celebrated Doctor of Divinity, whose learning was much more respectable than his life; "in a manner and for a fleeting moment, it is true, but solemnly, the young man called to a life of action *par excellence*, was brought in contact with our learned theology and our romantic philosophy." Nor has it been forgotten to exalt the name of the "gray cloister" (*Grauer Kloster*), which the lyceum at Berlin bore, where the future destroyer of convents studied, or to note the French origin of one of his principal professors, Doctor Bonnet, descendant of a Huguenot family which sought refuge in Brandenburg in consequence of the revocation of the Edict of Nantes.

After having finished his studies at the lyceum of the gray cloister, Otto de Bismarck went to the University of Goettingen, to the celebrated *Georgia Augusta*, in order to study. In reality, he did nothing but lead the life of the sons of the muse, who have the good or bad fortune to be at the same time sons of family, *cavalieri*; he cultivated nothing but hunting, riding, swimming, gymnastic exercises, and fencing. He had more than twenty duels, and fully justified the glorious name of *Bursche*, which clung to him for a long time afterwards, even when he was ambassador and minister. One easily understands that the Institutes and Pandects cannot be very thoroughly studied in the midst of so many corporal exercises, and even the attempt to change the noisy *Georgia Augusta* for the most quiet and sedate University of Berlin, was a remedy heroic rather than efficacious. Has M. de Bismarck ever regularly passed this "state examination" (*Staatsexamen*) which in Prussia is the indispensable condition for an appointment to any public function? A grave question, which was discussed for a long time in Germany, and out of which a weapon has shaped itself for twenty years against the man, the deputy, the ambassador, the president of the council. A fact worthy of notice, and one which well characterizes the formal and regulative mind of the nation: M. de Bismarck had already defied all Europe, and dismembered the Danish monarchy, when in the opposition journals of Germany, there appeared from time to time, like belated rockets, malignant allusions to this problematical state examination! Since the epoch of Sadowa only have these malicious jibes entirely ceased: Sadowa caused many other irregularities to pass unnoticed, and assuredly much graver ones.

It is perhaps proper to inquire here what benefits M. de Bismarck reaped from his academic life, and to estimate, if but briefly, the cultivation and the peculiarities of his mind. It seems certain that M. de Bismarck is not a man of science and study, and that his liberal education shows more than one gap. A pleasing contrast, the two chancellors, Russian and German, of whom one knew but a single lyceum and that one of very doubtful merit, while the other attended the most renowned college (*gymnasium*) and *alma mater* of learned Germany. Certainly the pupil of Zarkoe-Zeloe, as regards classical knowledge and true *humaniora*, is far in advance of the lucky foster child of *Georgia Augusta*. Nevertheless it is well to observe that M. de Bismarck fills and more than fills a certain programme laid down one day by the *spirituel* and regretted Saint-Marc Giradin for the well educated men of the world. "I do not require, said he, that they know Latin; I only ask that they have forgotten it." From his academic youth, there has always remained to the chancellor of Germany a fund of culture of which he well knows the use on occasion, and he understands in a sufficient degree, his Bible, his Shakspere, his Goethe, and his Schiller, those four elements of all education, even the most common one, in German countries,—precious and enviable quadrivium of the children of Arminius! Prince Gortchakof has the refinements as well as the weaknesses of the man of letters; he takes care of his "*mot*," he corrects his phrase, he looks at and admires himself in his compositions; it is known that he was one day surnamed the *Narcissus of the inkstand*. By his tastes, by his exquisite sensibility, by his artistic instinct, he has a marked superiority over his former colleague of Frankfort. But the latter regains all this advantage as soon as one considers the original and personal stamp which he knows how to give to his thoughts and to his speech, as soon as one seeks the individuality, the breathing creator, the *mens agitans molem*, that something mysterious and powerful which antique sculpture rendered so ingeniously by placing a flame on the forehead of certain of its statues.

The chancellor of Germany is not a lettered man in the strict and somewhat vulgar acceptation of the world. He is, to speak correctly, neither an orator nor a writer. He does not understand developing a theme well, graduating its arguments, arranging its transitions. He does not construct his period and does not trouble himself about it. He has difficulty in expressing himself, both on the tribune and also with the pen. His style is harsh, occasionally very incorrect, as unacademical as possible. It is intricate, embarrassed, even trivial at moments. Every part guarded, and all reserve made, there is something of Cromwell in his manner of expressing himself. But in an entirely different manner than in Cromwell one is forced to admire in him those flashes of thought, those strong and unforeseen images, those penetrating words which strike, which impress themselves, and which are not forgotten. When quite lately in the midst of an argument, disconnected and embarrassed, concerning his conflict with Rome, he suddenly cried out: "Be sure of one thing, gentlemen, *we will not go to Canossa*!"[13] one should remember that he knew how to comprise there, in a sort of menacing *cæterum censeo*,[14] a whole world of memories and of passions. In a very different spirit, also in a time already far distant, it is true, speaking one day—about twenty years have since flown—of the principles of revolution and contra-revolution, he said that a parliamentary debate could never decide between these two principles: "The decision will only come from God, from the God of battles, *when he lets fall from his hand the iron dice of destiny*!" One thinks that he hears De Maistre in this last part of the phrase, and like M. de Maistre the chancellor of Germany has had his passage decried by the *hangsman*; we wish to speak of this invocation to *iron* and to *blood*, which must be replaced in its frame and put in its true light,—to settle its date,—to appreciate all the relief by the side of the incontestable brutality. The invocation was made when those national-liberals, to-day of such great servility towards him and with the *obedience of a corpse*, wished to prevent him from reforming the army, at the same time demanding him to complete the unity of Germany. The man who felt the distant thunder of Sadowa and Sedan rumble in his soul, launched at this moment to the orators the *défi* which he has only too well justified since, saying that it was not by speeches that Germany could be united: "to consummate this unity, iron and blood are necessary!" This orator does not breathe at ease in the uniform which never leaves him, and he advances only by fits and starts. He collects laboriously the clouds of his rhetoric, but the spark ends by flashing and by illuminating the whole situation. To make himself understood he employs the greatest or most familiar images, without choice, just as they come; he borrows a quotation from Shakspere and from Goethe just as well as from the Wasps of M. Alphonse Karr, or from a couplet of the vaudeville. One of his most happy, most memorable inspirations, he suddenly drew one day from the libretto of the "Freischütz."

The reader will kindly permit us to recall this last episode, even at the risk of delaying somewhat in some preliminary explanations of which a German auditory, full of souvenirs of its "Freischütz," would have no need. In this opera of Weber, Max, the good and unfortunate hunter, borrows a cartridge from Robin, the evil spirit, and immediately kills an eagle, one of whose feathers he proudly sticks in his cap. He then asks for some more cartridges, but Robin tells him that they are "enchanted balls," and that in order to obtain them he must surrender himself to the infernal spirits, and deliver his soul to them. Max draws back, and then Robin, sneering, tells him that he hesitates in vain, that the bargain is made, and that he has already committed himself by the ball he made use of: "Do you think, then, that this eagle was a free gift?" Well! when in 1849 the young orator of the Mark of Brandenburg had to implore the Prussian chamber not to accept for the King of Prussia the imperial crown which the parliament of Frankfort offered him, he ended by crying out: "It is radicalism which offers this gift to the king. Sooner or later this radicalism will stand upright before the king, will demand of him its recompense, and pointing to the emblem of the eagle on that new imperial flag, it will say: *Did you think, then, that this eagle was a free gift?*" A striking image and equally deep and ingenious! Yes, one cannot use with impunity the "enchanted balls" of revolution, and one does not make a bargain with the popular demon, without leaving it some of his soul. Sooner or later there will stand upright before you the bad genius whose aid you have accepted, Robin of the woods and the streets. He will come to receive your salute, and tell you that he did not intend to have worked for the King of Prussia. This magnificent oratorical burst of the young deputy of the Mark, the chancellor of Germany might have considered with benefit in more than one decisive circumstance, for instance on the day when he overthrew the secular throne, also the day when he gave the signal for the *combat of civilization.*

The writer does not differ much from the orator, and, in speaking of the writer, we think above all of those intimate and familiar letters which have been published in the well known book of George Hesekiel, and which have had a merited success in Germany. There is always the same obscurity, the same embarrassment of elocution, the same disorder, from time to time passages of lively and original expressions, of astonishing figures, of a bitter, harsh *humor*, which grinds and bites you with cruel pleasure. These letters are for the great part addressed to his sister, to "dear Malvina" (married to an Arnim), and we will borrow from them more than once during the course of this study. One notices in them certain descriptions of nature, of the brightness of the moon, of the North Sea, of the view of the Danube from the heights of Buda-Pesth, which are not wanting in coloring effect, and make up a picture. There is something of Heinrich Heine in these private *Reisebilder*, and it has been remarked of them, that there is perhaps something of Hamlet (and what a Hamlet!) in the following passage, the only melancholy one which we have met with in the midst of so many sanguine and robust sallies. "At the mercy of God! Everything is in reality but a question of time, peoples and individuals, wisdom and folly, peace and war. To the living, everything upon earth is but hypocrisy and jugglery, and this *mask of flesh having once fallen off*, the wise man and the fool resemble each other greatly, and it would be hard to distinguish between the Prussian and the Austrian, *their skeletons being very carefully prepared.*" These lines fell from the same hand, however, which, since then, and assuredly by a very specific patriotism, has furnished so many thousand subjects to the preparers of skeletons!

One sees by these letters that M. de Bismarck handled at an early hour and with predilection this irony, in which he is without a master; a cold, crafty irony, and which too often approaches sneering. He used it later in his speeches, in his conversations with ministers and ambassadors, and even in diplomatic negotiations, in the most important, most decisive moments of history. At such moments this irony sometimes affects a great frankness, sometimes a great politeness, but a frankness to make you fall on your knees before the first lie, however brazen, a politeness to make you implore an incivility without forms as a veritable charity. One day, on the very eve of the war of 1866, Count Karolyi, ambassador of Austria, and acting in the name of his government, summoned M. de Bismarck to declare categorically if he expected to break the treaty of peace, the treaty of Gastein.[15] "No," was the reply, "I have not that expectation; *but, if I had, would I answer you differently?*" There is an example of that frankness which disconcerts, which confounds, and seems to cry in your ear with that devil from the "Inferno":

"Tu non pensavi ch'io loico fossi!"

As to the murderous politeness, which sometimes clothes the sarcasm of M. de Bismarck, let us recall here the *mot* which he launched later at the negotiators of Versailles, coming to treat with him concerning the surrender of famished Paris, and to offer him two hundred millions in contributions. "Oh," said he, "*Paris is too great a personage* that we should treat it in such a shabby manner; let us do it the honor of a milliard." That is truly an original turn which the rival of Heine thought to give to the *maxima reverentia* which one owes to misfortune! When one is destined in a ripe age to exercise his *humor* with such ease at the cost of princes and of peoples, how is it possible when young not to jest pleasantly about that poor fellow of a peasant in Pomerania who drank too much water? In one of his letters to his dear Malvina, the young country gentleman describes with a hilarious spirit an inundation which swept over his domain which is divided by a little branch of the narrow river Hampel. This inundation severed him from all his neighbors, carried off so and so many casks of *eau-de-vie,* "introduced an anarchical interregnum from Schievelbein to Damm," and he ends by this stroke: "*I am proud to be able to say,* that in my little branch of the Hampel a wagoner was drowned with his horse and his whole load of tar!" How proud in a different degree was this gentleman one day when, Europe having become his domain, he saw disappearing in the midst of the billows, billows of blood this time, a whole army and its chief, a whole empire and its emperor,—*currus Galliæ et auriga ejus!* That did not prevent, at another time, the young country gentleman from jumping bravely into the water to rescue his groom and gaining the medal for saving life. During many years this medal was the only one to decorate the broad chest of the Prussian minister at Frankfort. Asked one day by a colleague to the *Bund* about a decoration to which the diplomatic corps is but little accustomed, he replied in the tone which he alone possesses, that he sometimes happened to rescue a man,—in his leisure moments, be it understood. Probably, if he had been further pressed, he was capable of adding that he only did it for exercise.

Thus, to resume, from the epoch of his apprenticeship at the gray cloister and *Georgia Augusta*, Otto de Bismarck carried a literary burden, which, without being either too heavy or too full, has nevertheless enabled him to make his tour of the political world with ease and honor. And also since this epoch his mind disclosed the precious qualities which still distinguish it; a vivid and powerful imagination, a rare happiness in his choice of expressions occasionally grandiose, occasionally vulgar, but always striking; and lastly, a *humor* which has no equal, and which, to speak with Jean Paul, is a true *sirocco* to the soul. With all this no grace, no charm, no distinction or delicacy,—not a generous accent, no sweet and sympathetic cord, a complete absence of that milk of human kindness of which the poet speaks, an absolute want of that charity which, according to the great Christian moralist, is like the heavenly perfume of the soul. As to the art or rather handicraft, as to the work which consists in arranging his phrases, in connecting and disposing them so as to introduce harmony and clearness in the different parts of speech, in effacing its asperities and inequalities, in one word as to the *style*, M. de Bismarck never learned it or always disdained it. If we dared to apply to this style one of those trivial but expressive images of which he himself offers us more than one example, we would willingly compare it to a certain strange drink, hardly credible, and which, according to his biographers, the German chancellor has always liked: it consists of a mixture of champagne and *porter*! The language is in imitation of the drink: one finds in it the *piquant*, the sparkling, the exhilarating of the *Aÿ* together with the heaviness, the blackness, and above all the bitterness of the *stout*.

It is a curious fact, that the man who one day was to impose on all the States of Germany the severe bureaucratic and military laws of Prussia, "to place Germany in the saddle," to use one of his *mots*, to press it into the straight jacket of obligatory service,—even to indirectly train all Europe to new exercises, and to make it leave the plow for the sword, liberal occupations for the autumn and summer manœuvres,—this man, for his part, has never been able to bind himself down to academic duties, neither to the regular work of the bureau, nor to the severe discipline of the soldier. He himself has acknowledged having heard but *two* hours of lecture during his whole stay at *Georgia Augusta*. The university course being ended, he tried several times the administrative or judiciary career; he tried it at Aix-la-Chapelle, at Potsdam, at Greifswalde, then again at Potsdam, and had to give it up every time, disgusted by the monotonous labor of the bureau, or by quarrels with his superiors. On this subject is told the *piquant* reply of the young *referendarius* to a principal who had made him wait an hour in an antechamber: "I came to request a short leave of absence; but during this long hour I have had time to reflect, and I demand my dismission." Thrice he made a trial of the military service, without arriving at a higher grade than that of lieutenant in the *Landwehr*, a rank which he appreciated, however, and of which he loved to don the uniform on solemn occasions, even at the very time when he was already minister at Frankfort. The reader knows that the day of Sadowa brought him the insignia of a general. Those ten or twelve years which had passed for M. de Bismarck since his disputed state examination to his entrance into the Prussian chamber, the German biographers call by the fine name "years of storm and trouble," which recalls one of the most brilliant epochs of their literature.[16] In truth they were stormy, filled with miscarriages of more than one kind, with travels, financial embarrassments, perhaps also with an unrequited love. At least that is the meaning one is inclined to give to the following passage from a letter addressed to his sister Malvina: "I struggle in vain, I shall end by marrying ———; the world wishes it thus, and nothing seems more natural, and then we will both be killed on the spot. She left me coldly, it is true, but they all do that. It would not be so bad, however, if one could throw off his feelings with his shirts, no matter how rarely one changes the latter."

He seems to have had a very sincere affection for this sister; he overwhelms her with the most tender names. Thus he calls her his little dear, his Malvina, his *Maldewinchen*, his good little Arnim; he even calls her once (pardon him, O divinities of Walhalla) simply *and in French*, "*ma sœur*." In all the letters of this epoch, dated for the most part from the estates of Kniephof or Schoenhausen (it was not until later that M. de Bismarck acquired the famous Varzin[17]), by the side of an always biting and harsh *humor*, one can perceive a certain disenchantment; by the side of the cares of fortune appear from time to time projects for the future, very modest, truly, and which seldom aim at politics. In 1846 he attached a certain importance at being made surveyor of dikes in the district (*Deichhauptmann*). "The position is not remunerative, but it offers some interest in regard to Schoenhausen and other estates, for we would depend on it in a great measure if we were again without water as in the past year.... Bernard (a friend) insists on my going to Prussia (to Berlin). I would like to know what he expects there. He affirms that by my disposition and my inclinations, I am made for the service of the state, and that sooner or later I will end by entering it." Suddenly, and on the very eve of the reunion of the first Prussian parliament, one is surprised by the plan of a voyage to the Indias,—probably to make his fortune and establish himself there,—and one thinks involuntarily of Cromwell wishing to embark for America on the eve of the long parliament. Do not think, however, that the days passed sadly and morosely at Kniephof and at Schoenhausen: one lives there, one overlives the life of *Juncker* (country squire) and the officers of the neighboring garrison are good and stout fellows, in whose company one hunts and dances, "one empties great bowls half filled with champagne, half with porter;" the guests are awakened in the morning by pistols fired off close to their pillows; on entering the *salon* the female cousins are frightened with four foxes, and honor is paid to the name given by the whole country to the proprietor of the domain, the name of "mad Bismarck" (*der tolle Bismarck*). They are madcaps, and blusterers, prompt to draw their swords, to fight with pistol or steel, and they do not even avoid a pugilistic scene. One day in a smoking room at Berlin, the former pupil of *Georgia Augusta* broke his beer mug on the skull of a stranger disrespectful in his language towards a member of the royal family; not, however, without having first addressed a charitable warning to the insolent speaker, nor without having afterwards, very sedately, very politely, asked of the waiter the cost of the damage.[18] This happened in 1850; M. de Bismarck had already been deputy several years, and was on the point of becoming minister plenipotentiary to the Germanic Confederation.

Der tolle Bismarck; it was not only at Kniephof and at Schoenhausen that the future chancellor of Germany was thus called. The Berlinese themselves had no other name for him for a long time, during all the parliamentary period of the young deputy of the Mark, since his maiden speech and his first appearance on the tribune,—when having provoked an indescribable tumult by a violent attack against the liberals he drew from his pocket a newspaper, and quietly commenced reading, while waiting for the storm to calm,—up to his last speech on December 3, 1850, which completed the exasperation of the chamber, but was worth a diplomatic post to the orator. Success advances a little like the aristocratic law of the Chinese: it is necessary to supply glory from the rear and to throw lustre on the obscure antecedents of the favorite of fortune. This was, however, more to mistake the time and to misplace the historical perspective, than to wish to assign to M. de Bismarck in those years (1847-50) any important *rôle* which he did not fill until fifteen years later. The truth is that this *rôle* was not in this first period either of such eminence, or, above all, sufficiently respected to be tempted to arrange itself in an abstract, inductive method. An active and restless member of the group of *Juncker* in 1847, and of the great *party of the cross* which was formed after the revolution of February, the country gentleman of Schoenhausen was far from having in the bosom of this party the authority of a Gerlach and a Stahl, or the great position of a similar feudal lord of Silesia or Pomerania. In spite of his audacity, his impetuosity, and his *sang-froid*; in spite of his exceedingly happy sallies with an eloquence unequal and embarrassed in a very different manner from to-day, M. de Bismarck was at this epoch nothing but the Hotspur, and the *enfant terrible* of the sacred phalanx which defended the throne, the altar, and the conservative principles. He was in a measure the General Temple of the ill-tempered light-horsemen, a General Temple joined with the Marquis of Piré. At any rate he only passed for a successful Thadden-Triglaff, that brave M. Thadden-Triglaff who declared that he desired the liberty of the press, on condition, however, "that there was a power by the side of each journal to hang up the pamphleteers." The speeches of M. de Bismarck, friend and neighbor of this ingenious legislator of the press, were often not more reasonable. Did he not say one day, word for word, "that all the great cities ought to be destroyed and razed to the ground, as the eternal homes of revolution?"

The Athenians of the Spree[19] laughed at these jests, repeated those words full of *humor*, and above all admired a certain argument *ad hominem* by means of a mug of beer. Occasionally also they criticised with malice the advances made to the innocent, to the democrats, and diverted themselves especially over the famous little branch of olive which the country squire of Schoenhausen showed one day to his colleague of the chamber, the very radical Doctor d'Ester. This branch, he told him, he had cut in a recent excursion to Vaucluse, from the tomb of Laura and Petrarch. He put it carefully in his cigar case and thought of presenting it one day to the red gentlemen "as a sign of reconciliation." It was in the strange destiny of this extraordinary man not to be thought in earnest until the day when he became terrible. *Der tolle Bismarck*, the Germans said in 1850; at Frankfort the good Count Rechberg called him scoffingly a *Bursche*, and he was considered a personage worthy of laughter in the eyes of the French minister, a man of mind, however, even in 1864. The year after the legendary coast of Biarritz, he pursued with his projects the Emperor Napoleon III., who, resting on the arm of the author of "Colomba," whispered from time to time into the ear of the academician senator those words: "He is crazy!" Five years later the dreamer of Ham gave up his sword to the crazy man of the Mark.

"I belong,"—such was the defiant declaration of M. de Bismarck in one of his first speeches in the chamber,—"I belong to an opinion which glories in the reproaches of obscurantism, and of tendencies of the Middle Age; I belong to that great multitude which is compared with disdain to the most intelligent party of the nation." He wanted a *Christian State*. "Without a religious basis," said he, "a state is nothing but a fortuitous aggregation of interests, a sort of bastion in a war of all against all; without this religious basis, all legislation, instead of regenerating itself at the living sources of eternal truth, is only tossed about by human ideas as vague as changeable." It is for this reason that he pronounced against the emancipation of the Jews, and repulsed, above all, with horror the institution of civil marriage, a degrading institution, and one which "made the church the train-bearer (*Schleppentraeger*) of a subaltern bureaucracy."[20] He was as *intransigeant* for the throne as for the altar: he set at defiance the principle of the sovereignty of the people; universal suffrage (which he himself was to introduce one day into the whole German empire!) seemed to him a social danger and an outrage to good sense. He denied the rights of the nation; the crown alone had rights: the old Prussian spirit knew but that,—"and this old Prussian spirit is a Bucephalus who willingly allows his legitimate master to mount him, but who will throw to the ground every Sunday rider (*Sonntagsreiter*)!"

A resolute adversary of modern ideas, of constitutional theories, and of all that then formed the programme of the liberal party in Prussia, the deputy of the Mark combated with the same energy the two great national passions of this party: the "deliverance" of Schleswig-Holstein and the unity of Germany. He deplored that "the royal Prussian troops had gone to defend the revolution in Schleswig against the legitimate sovereign of that country, the King of Denmark;" asserted that they were making a groundless quarrel with this king, that they sought a quarrel with him "for no cause" (*um des Kaisers Bart*), and he did not hesitate to declare before an angry chamber, that the war provoked in the Duchies of the Elbe was "an undertaking eminently iniquitous, frivolous, disastrous, and revolutionary."[21] As to the unity of Germany, the young orator of the ultras repulsed it in the name of Right, of the sovereignty and of the independence of princes, as well as in the name of patriotism, be it understood. He was Prussian, a *specific* Prussian, a hardened Prussian (*stockpreusse*), and cared very little to unite the good and firm substance "with the dissolved elements (*das zerfahrene Wesen*) of the South." He called on the army: Does this army wish to exchange the old national colors, black and white, for this German tricolor, which was only known to it as the emblem of revolution? Does it wish to exchange its old Dessauer march for the song of a Professor Arndt on the *German fatherland?*

We have already spoken of his speech against the imperial crown offered by the parliament of Frankfort, of the ingenious allusion borrowed from the libretto of the "Freischütz." While refusing the imperial crown, Frederick William IV. did not the less endeavor, during the years 1849 and 1850, to rescue some waifs from this wreck of unitarian ideas; he tried to group around himself, and with the aid of the liberals, a notable part of the Germanic body, to create a sort of northern confederation: "restricted union" became for a moment the *mot d'ordre* of a programme which General Radowitz was charged to place on the stage of the parliament of Erfurt. M. de Bismarck condemned without pity or weakness all these vain attempts; with the great theorician of his party, the celebrated Professor Stahl, he pleaded for the return to the *statu quo* prior to 1848. Like him he demanded "that the overturned column of right be replaced in Germany," that the *Bund* be restored on legal bases, according to the terms of the treaty of Vienna, and that no cessation should be made in placing Prussian politics on its guard against any "course of Phæton" in a region of clouds and thunder.

The thunderbolt did not in truth delay in striking, and the "course of Phæton" was brusquely arrested by the hand of that great Austrian minister, who himself only traversed, like a luminous meteor, the most elevated regions of power to disappear suddenly and to leave behind him eternal regrets. Prince Felix de Schwarzenberg recalls in some respects those statesmen of whom England lately offered the astounding example, those Peterboroughs, those Bentincks, and those like them, who knew how to interrupt, almost suddenly, a life given up to pleasures and to the frivolous follies of the world, to reveal themselves in a trice like veritable political geniuses, and to die before their time, after having exhausted the intoxication of easy good fortune and of glory, arduous in a very different degree. It is known with what a firm and steady hand the prince seized the helm of affairs in Austria, and in how short a time he succeeded in lifting up a monarchy placed on the brink of an abyss. Was his conduct in every particular irreproachable; was it even provident to the end? That is not the question for us. Let us limit ourselves in saying that rarely has a minister met with more good luck in his short career, found so much assurance in success, and spoken in a loftier or prouder tone in vexatious necessities. This time Prince Schwarzenberg spoke with all the authority which right gave him. Perhaps he spoke even too harshly, and Prussia seemed for a moment ready to pick up the glove. Frederick William IV. demanded of the chambers a credit of fourteen million thalers for the armament, and made a warlike speech. Europe became attentive, the national assembly of France was on the point of ordering a new levy of troops, and, fatidical prelude of a tragedy which was not to be played till fifteen years later, in 1850 as in 1866, Louis Napoleon thought that he ought to encourage the cabinet of Berlin, encourage it with aid, and in direct opposition to the general sentiment of the country! While the national assembly in France pronounced itself very plainly for neutrality and the minister of foreign affairs was even inclined in favor of Austria, the president of the republic sent an intimate friend to Berlin, M. de Persigny, with the mission to engage the King of Prussia as much as possible in the war. War appeared inevitable. The troops were already disposed in two parts; there had already been encounters between the advanced guards. All of a sudden, and before a menacing ultimatum from Vienna, strengthened by a friendly notice from St. Petersburg, M. de Manteuffel, president of the Prussian council, proposed to that of Austria to hold an interview at Oderberg, on the frontier of the two States. Some hours after having sent this proposition, he announced by telegraph (a proceeding then very rare), that, on positive orders from the king, he should go as far as Olmütz, without waiting for the reply. He went there, and signed (29 November, 1850) the preliminaries of peace, the famous "punctuations" by which Prussia yielded to the demands of Austria on every point.

It is not astonishing that such a profound humiliation,—preceded by a measure of distress up to that time unheard of in the annals of diplomacy, and immediately followed by an Austrian dispatch which very uselessly did nothing but irritate the wound,[22]—filled liberal Prussia with grief and indignation. It was in vain that M. de Manteuffel endeavored to justify his conduct before the national mind. He affirmed that he would rather be placed "in front of conical balls than pointed speeches" (*lieber Spitzkugeln als spitze Reden*); the chamber of Berlin expressed with passion the griefs of the country, and M. de Vincke closed one of the most vehement philippics with these words: "Down with the ministry!" A single orator dared to undertake the defense of the ministry, and to make in the same moment the apotheosis of Austria. Already in the preceding year M. de Bismarck had desired for his country the *rôle* of the Emperor Nicholas in Hungary. Since then he had never neglected an occasion to resent in behalf of the empire of the Hapsburg the insults which German liberalism had heaped on him, and he remained true to this policy even in the most extraordinary circumstances, and in the midst of the indescribable clamors of the assembly. He maintained that there could be no possible or legitimate federation in Germany without Austria. One of the greatest griefs of the Teutons against Austria has been in all times its not forming a state purely German, its containing in its bosom different populations and of an "inferior" race. This was the principal argument of the parliament of Frankfort in favor of the constitution of a Germany without the empire of the Hapsburg, and M. de Bismarck did not fail to reproduce it in 1866, in a memorable circular. In 1850 the deputy of the Mark did not share this opinion; he was convinced that "Austria was a German power in the full force of the term, although it also had the good fortune to exercise its dominion over foreign nationalities," and he boldly concluded that "*Prussia should subordinate itself to Austria* to the end that they might combat in concert the menacing democracy." Truly, in recalling that session of the Prussian chamber on the 3d December, 1850, one can, in the words of Montesquieu, observe the spectacle of the astounding vicissitudes of history; but the irony of fate commences to take its truly fantastic proportions, when one remembers that it was precisely this speech of the 3d December, 1850, which decided the vocation of M. de Bismarck and opened to him the career of foreign affairs. Forced to consent to the restoration of the *Bund*, and resigned to the preponderance of the empire of the Hapsburg, the Prussian government thought in truth that it could give no better pledges of its disposition than in choosing for its plenipotentiary to the Germanic Confederation the ardent orator whose devotion to the cause of the Hapsburg was even able to resist the proof of the humiliation of Olmütz.

And it was as the most decided partisan of Austria that the future conqueror of Sadowa made his entrance into the arena of diplomacy!

The chamber was prorogued in consequence of this stormy discussion. The rupture with the national party was consummated, and M. de Manteuffel, whose cold and bureaucratic mind sympathized in reality but very slightly with the ultras, thought it nevertheless useful to strengthen the government by making them some advances. Several prominent posts in the civil service were conferred on members of the extreme right: M. de Kleist-Retzow, among others, held the presidency of the Rhenish provinces. One could hardly dream of utilizing in the same manner the talents of the former *referendarius* of Potsdam and Greifswalde, who had shown so little disposition and taste for the administrative career: on account of the considerations already mentioned, it was first thought of sending him to Frankfort as first secretary of the legation, but with the assurance of being made real representative at the end of some time. This choice produced some surprise. It was an entirely new proceeding (they have become accustomed to it there and in other places since) to reward a deputy with a diplomatic mission for his attitude or his vote in the chamber. It was asked if the eccentric and impetuous cavalier of the Mark would be the right man in the right place in the midst of such delicate circumstances. The timid and overscrupulous M. de Manteuffel was not without apprehension on this head, and the very ardor with which M. de Bismarck accepted the position only augmented the uneasiness of the president of the council. King Frederick William IV., who personally had a very high regard for the ardent "Percy" of the *party of the cross*, had nevertheless some doubts. "Your majesty can try me," said the aspirant for diplomacy; "if matters go wrong, your majesty will be at perfect liberty to recall me at the end of six months or even before."

It was only, however, at the end of eight years that he was recalled by the successor of Frederick William IV. And still, after the first days of his mission (June, 1851) he expressed himself thus in a confidential letter concerning the men and the affairs he was charged to deal with: "Our relations here consist in distrust and mutual *espionage*. If we only had something to spy out or to hide! But these are merely silly trifles, for which these people torment their minds. These diplomats who retail with an air of importance their *bric-à-brac*, seem to me much more ridiculous than a deputy of the second chamber draping himself in the feeling of his dignity. If exterior events do not unexpectedly arise, I know from to-day exactly what we shall have done in two, three, or five years, and what we can dispatch in twenty-four hours, if we wish to be sincere and reasonable for one day. I never doubted that all these gentlemen did their cooking in water; but a soup so watery and insipid that it is impossible to find in it a trace of fat does not cease to astonish me.... I have made very rapid progress in the art of saying nothing with many words; I write several sheets of reports, plain and round, like the leading articles, and if, after having read them, Manteuffel understands a jot, he is cleverer than I am. No one, not even the most malicious of democrats can have any idea what nonsense and charlatanisms diplomacy hides."

Some years later, during the complications of the Orient, he wrote to his sister Malvina: "I am at a session of the *Bund*; a very highly honored colleague is reading a very stupid speech on the anarchical situation in Upper Lippe, and I think that I cannot better improve this opportunity than in pouring out before you my fraternal sentiments. These knights of the *round table* who surround me in this ground floor of the Taxis palace are very honorable men, but not at all amusing. The table, twenty feet in diameter, is covered with a green cloth. Think of X—— and of Z—— in Berlin; they are entirely of the calibre of these gentlemen of the *Bundestag*. I have the habit of approaching all things with a feeling of innocence which gapes. My disposition of mind is that of a careless lassitude after I have succeeded in bringing little by little the *Bund* to the desolating consciousness of its profound nothingness. Do you remember the *Lied* of Heine: *O Bund, o chien tu n'es pas sain*, etc.? Well! that *Lied* will soon, and by a unanimous vote, be raised to the rank of national hymn of Germany."

The lassitude, the disgust as well as the contempt for the *Bund* increased from year to year. In 1858 he thought of leaving the career forever. He had enough of "this *régime* of truffles, of dispatches and of grand crosses." He spoke of withdrawing "under the guns of Schoenhausen," or still better of "growing young by ten years, and once more taking the offensive position of 1848 and 1849." He wished to fight, without being hindered by relations and official courtesies, to throw off the uniform, and to "go into politics in swimming drawers (*in politischen Schwimmhosen*)."

What is there astonishing in it? Of all imaginable political men, M. de Bismarck was certainly the least fitted to have a regard and liking for a deliberative body essentially moderated and moderating, where everything was discussed in private, in elaborated speeches, thought over at length and still more freely discussed, and where the gashes and thrusts actually amounted to nothing. A great congress of peace could scarcely have any attraction for the ardent Percys whom the smallest conference of Bangor[23] caused, enraged, to jump out of their skins; and the *Bundestag*, as we have said, was a permanent congress of peace called to maintain the *statu quo* and to remove every cause for conflict. The little incidents, the little manœuvres and the little struggles for influence were not wanting, it is true, in this company, more than in any other; they served to maintain the good humor of the ordinary diplomats, and were generally considered as useful stimulants for the good management of affairs and good digestion of dinners. But they must have seemed paltry in the eyes of a man of action and of combat; they must have irritated, at times even exasperated him! To observe the affairs of the world from this post on the Main, which allowed them to be grasped in their *ensemble*; to profit by abundant information, to compose therefrom brilliant dispatches, fit to instruct and above all to amuse an august master; to utter occasionally a very *spirituel*, very malicious *mot*, and to rejoice at it; to make others enjoy it, even to carry it perfectly warm to Stuttgart, and to confide its further expedition to a gracious Grand Duchess,—that was an occupation which might content Prince Gortchakof, even charm the leisure hours of a man educated in the school of Count Nesselrode and grown old in the career. But how was it possible to make such an existence agreeable to a cavalier of the Mark, improvised into a minister plenipotentiary, or to shut up in such a narrow circle, though a pleasant one, a "*fiancé* of Bellona," still foaming from battles delivered without cessation for four years on a resounding stage! In order to find a fitting compensation in the new circle in which he was placed, he needed at least some great European combination, some great negotiation capable of exercising his faculties, and of making them known,—and they talked to him of *bric-à-brac*, of Upper Lippe! A negotiation as insignificant as that with the poor Augustenburg, brought to a happy end in 1852, could certainly not be counted among the triumphs worthy of a Bismarck,[24] and this was nevertheless the single and pitiful "bubble of fat" which he was able to discover in the soup cooked during several years at Frankfort!

It is true that the question of the Orient did not delay in breaking out, and that at first it even seemed to open vast perspectives. Prussia was well disposed towards Russia. The secondary States of Germany showed themselves still more ardent, and sometimes even went so far as to have the appearance of being willing to draw their swords; so much the worse for Austria if she persisted in making common cause with the allies; that might bring about important territorial modifications, and all to the advantage of the House of Hohenzollern! And the representative of Prussia to the Germanic Confederation ("his excellency the lieutenant," as he was then called on account of the Landwehr uniform which he liked to wear) gave a warm and firm support in this crisis to his colleague of Russia, who had become his most intimate friend. He was not, however, long in seeing that the Germanic Confederation would not desert its neutrality; that the secondary States, in spite of all the agitations in the conferences of Bamberg, would not take an active part either in one sense or in the other, and that the war would be localized in the Black Sea and the Baltic. He conceived a profound disdain for the *Bund*, was "conscious of its unfathomable nothingness," and hummed over the green cloth of the Taxis palace the *Lied* of Heine on the Diet of Frankfort. In addition, he experienced on this occasion a grief, which he never forgot, which he recalled many years afterwards in a confidential dispatch which has become celebrated. During the Oriental complications, he wrote in 1859 to M. de Schleinitz, "Austria overcame us at Frankfort in spite of all the commonalty of ideas and desires which we then had with the secondary States. These States, after each oscillation, always indicate with the activity of the magnetized needle, the same point of attraction." Nothing more natural, however; it was not from the empire of the Hapsburg that Hanover and Saxony had to dread certain annexation, as events have since proved only too clearly. But the man who can one day desire the destruction of great cities, as the hot-beds of revolutionary spirit, did not hesitate to condemn in his soul and conscience the small States as the inextinguishable hearths of the "Austrian spirit."

Austria, in truth, was not slow in taking in the thoughts and the resentments of the cavalier of the Mark the place which the revolution had lately held there, and the ardent champion of Hapsburg in the chambers of Berlin became little by little their most bitter, most implacable enemy in the *Bundestag*. Moreover, all the great men of Prussia, commencing with the great elector and Frederick II., and without excepting William I., have always had, as regards Austria, "two souls in their breasts" like Faust, or, like Rebecca, "two children conflicting with one another in her bosom;" in a word, two principles, one of which imbued them with an almost religious respect for the antique and illustrious imperial house, while the other urged them to conquest and spoliation at the cost of this very house. In the month of May, 1849, the honest and poetical King Frederick William IV. declared to a deputation of ministers from the Germanic States,[25] "that he should consider that day as the most happy one of his life when he should hold the wash basin (*Waschbecken*) at the coronation of a Hapsburg as Emperor of Germany;" that did not prevent him later from smiling from time to time at the work of the parliament of Frankfort, and from working for the "restricted union" under the auspices of General de Radowitz. And even M. de Bismarck was certainly very sincere as deputy of the Prussian parliament in his "Austrian religion," when in the name of conservative principles he undertook the energetic defense of the Hapsburg against the attacks of German liberalism; but he was now the representative of his government in the Taxis palace, encountered Austria on its way to a struggle for influence with the secondary States, to a struggle of interests concerning the affairs of the Orient, and he began to engage in an order of ideas, at the end of which he was to take up the policy of "heart blow." It was thus that on the occasion of the war in the Orient and in the very city of Frankfort there arose in the hearts of the two future chancellors of Russia and of Germany that hatred of Austria which was to have such fatal consequences, for, that the reader may not be deceived, it was the connivance of these two political men,—the fatal ideology of the Emperor Napoleon III. aiding them largely, it is just to add,—which rendered possible the catastrophes of which our days have been the witnesses: the calamity of Sadowa, and the destruction of the *Bund*, and the dismemberment of Denmark as well as of France! With Prince Gortchakof, this sentiment of hostility burst forth suddenly in consequence of an erroneous appreciation of events, but which his whole nation shared with him. With M. de Bismarck, the hatred of Austria had not an origin so spontaneous; it had not, for instance, as an origin, the grievances of Olmütz, which the deputy of the Mark had on the contrary been able to easily overcome; it was slow in forming, it developed, consolidated itself in consequence of a long and daily struggle in the heart of the *Bund*, in consequence of an experience acquired at the end of several years of vain attempts, and from the definite conviction that Hapsburg would never of its free will, abandon the secondary States, and he defended them against every effort at absorption. Resuming the instruction which his sojourn of eight years at Frankfort had given him, the representative of Prussia to the Germanic Confederation wrote in 1859, in his often quoted dispatch to M. de Schleinitz, those remarkable words: "I see in our federal relations a fault which sooner or later we must cure *ferro et igne*." *Ferro et igne!* that is the first version of the received text "iron and blood," which one day the president of the council laid down in an official manner in a speech to the chamber.

At the same time that the ancient "Austrian religion" underwent with its former ardent confessor a transformation so radical, a no less curious change was wrought in his mind in regard to several other articles of the *credo* of his party. Removed from the *mêlée* and participating no longer in the parliamentary struggles, he began to observe more coldly certain questions important in those times, and to temper more than one antipathy of past days. Since 1852, on returning from a trip to Berlin, he writes: "There is something demoralizing in the air of the chamber; the best men of the world become vain there and cling to the Tribune as a woman to her toilet.... I find parliamentary intrigues hollow and unworthy of any notice. While one lives in their midst, one has illusions concerning them, and attaches to them I do not know how much importance.... Every time that I arrive there from Frankfort, I experience the feelings of a temperate man who falls among drunken people." Many things in old times disgraceful and abhorred, take now a less repulsive aspect to the eyes of the statesmen maturing great projects for the future. "The chamber and the press can become the most powerful instruments of our external policy," wrote in 1856 the former despiser of parliamentarism and friend of M. Thadden-Triglaff, and it is thus that one finds in the correspondence of these times the vague idea of a national representation of the *Zollverein*, even a pronounced desire for universal suffrage itself, provided that these means could become the *instrumenta regni*. The example of the second empire exercised then an influence which the historian should carefully bear in mind. This system of absolutism tinged with popular passions, "spotted with red," to employ a characteristic expression of M. de Bismarck, seduced the imagination of more than one aspirant for *coups d'état* and *coups d'éclat*, and the former colleague of the Doctor d'Ester must have opened his cigar case more than once and contemplated there the little sprig of olive plucked from the tomb of Petrarch and Laura.

Yet the goal seemed distant, and how veiled was the future, still indistinctly seen! It was not under King Frederick William IV., whose mind became more and more clouded, that he was permitted to think of action; even the accession of the regent, the present King William, seemed at first to make no change in the exterior situation. The new ministers of the regent, the ministers of the *new era*, as was said then, were honest doctrinarians who spoke of the development of conceded liberties and of the strengthening of the representative *régime*. The good and *naïf*, they even allowed William I. to proclaim solemnly one day that "Prussia need only make *moral conquests* in Germany!" Evidently the *new era* was not yet the era of M. de Bismarck. During the years which passed after the war of the Orient until his embassy in Russia, one sees the representative of Prussia to the Germanic Confederation in constant motion, on continual journeys across Germany, France, Denmark, Sweden, Courland, and Upper Italy, seeking subjects for distraction, or perhaps also subjects for observation, and each time returning to Frankfort only to raise a difficulty, break some *bric-à-brac*, and to press to the utmost the nervous and bilious Count Rechberg, Austrian representative and president of the *Bundestag*. His frequent excursions to Paris caused him to have a presentiment of the events which were preparing in Italy; he only became more aggressive, and there was a time when his recall was considered at Frankfort as indispensable for the maintenance of peace. It was at this moment that he thought of definitely abandoning this career, of throwing off the uniform, and of going into politics in his "swimming drawers." He consented, however, to do it in "a bear-skin and with caviar," as he expressed himself in one of his letters; in other words called to exchange his post at Frankfort for that at St. Petersburg. One hoped thus to remove him from the burning ground, to "put him on ice" (another expression of M. de Bismarck); as for himself, he perhaps attached other hopes to this removal, and in any case found consolation in seeing his former colleague of Frankfort become principal minister of a great empire, and with whom he was always on such good terms. The 1st of April, 1859, "the anniversary of his birth," M. de Bismarck arrived in the capital of Russia.

II.

A NATIONAL MINISTER AND A FAULT-FINDING DIPLOMAT AT ST. PETERSBURG.

I.

In the prodigious development which advanced the empire of the czars after the impulse which the genius of Peter the Great had given it, one can certainly signalize more than one Russian minister of foreign affairs whose name has a right to be commemorated by history. For instance, the mind of Count Panine was not an ordinary one, who conceived and caused to be accepted by different states the idea of *armed neutrality* at sea, and this at an epoch when Russia scarcely began to be reckoned among the maritime powers of the second or third class. If in this bold conception, as well as in the still more interesting attempts of Panine to limit the absolute power of the czars by aristocratic institutions, the remote influence of an Italian origin could be seen (the Panine descended from the Pagnini of Lucca), one cannot, however, overlook the perfectly indigenous, largely, autochthonal character of another famous minister of the same century, that of the Chancellor Bestoujef, whose figure Rulhière has drawn so very originally. Bestoujef, who spoke perfectly, feigned stammering, and had the courage to simulate this defect for seventeen years. In his conversations with foreign ambassadors he stammered in such a manner as not to be understood. He also complained of being deaf, of not understanding all the *finesses* of the French language, and had the same thing repeated a thousand times. He was in the habit of writing diplomatic notes with his own hand in a manner perfectly illegible. They were sent back to him and sometimes he could decipher their meaning. Having fallen into disgrace, Bestoujef immediately recovered his speech, hearing, and all the senses.

Very different is the type which was presented during all of the first half of this century by the immediate predecessor of Prince Gortchakof, the chancellor of the emperors Alexander I. and Nicholas. Connected with Germany by origin and the interests of his family, never even having learned to speak the language of the country whose relations with other powers he watched over, Count Charles Robert de Nesselrode did not the less complete a long and laborious career to the satisfaction of his two august masters, and figured with honor in congresses and conferences at the side of Talleyrand and Metternich. Without having recourse to the too Asiatic subterfuges of a Bestoujef, Count Nesselrode knew and practiced all the allowable tricks of the profession, and few men equaled him in the art of preserving an air of dignity and ease in the midst of the most embarrassing situations. He knew how to change his conduct without too great a change of language, and among other things managed in a very delicate manner the transition between the policy of the czar Alexander I. (unfavorable to the Greeks) and the frankly philhellenic sympathies of his successor. During the last Oriental crisis he placed all the resources of a shrewd and subtle mind at the service of a cause in which he saw nothing but grave dangers, and of which he ignored the national and religious side completely. Differing from Bestoujef, and much more European in this sense than in many others, M. de Nesselrode lost in his disgrace or rather in his retreat, the greater part of his faculties and his virtues, and above all caused an immense deception by his posthumous memoirs, composed in the decline of life and of a hopeless insignificance. But perhaps this was nothing but a last trait of cleverness and diplomatic malice in order to deceive on this point profane curiosity, and to leave behind him a work as empty and uninstructive as possible of a life so well filled.

Not one, however, of the Russian statesmen who have just been named was a great minister in the Occidental acceptation of the word. No one of them (in order to make comparisons in absolute monarchies only) had the position of a Duke de Choiseul in France during the last century, the authority of a Prince Clement de Metternich in Austria in the present century, or even the notoriety and popularity which Prince Gortchakof actually enjoys in Russia itself. Bestoujef, Panine, Nesselrode were, one may say, much better known abroad than in their own country, and their contemporaries were far from attributing to them the merit which posterity later saw in them, thanks to the posthumous revelations of the archives. No one of them was raised to power by a current of opinion, nor sustained in his position by public favor; not one of them pretended to show an individuality, to impress a personal direction on the affairs, which he conducted. This is because since Peter the Great to the present government, the *éclat* of the imperial name in Russia cast into the shade every other name, and instead of being a favorite or a great captain, every state servant was only the subaltern executor of a single and absolute will. The external policy, above all, was then considered as the exclusive domain of the sovereign, and the very fixity of the system rendered in some degree secondary and unimportant the question of the persons charged with fulfilling it. In fact, from the time of Peter the Great, the Russian government has always had in its relations with Europe certain traditions approved by experience, and certain sacred principles, from which it never deviated even in a small degree. The minister of foreign affairs at St. Petersburg, whatever his name might be, always had to labor to augment Russian *prestige* among the Christian populations of the Orient, to guard the maintenance of the equilibrium of power between Austria and Prussia, and to extend the influence of his government among the secondary States of Germany. To these rules, so to speak, elementary and invariable, of the external Russian policy, there was added from the year 1815 an international principle of preservation, a superior idea of solidarity between the governments for the defense of established order, the feeling of the duties and of the common interests created in the representatives of the monarchical authority in opposition to subversive passions sprung from the revolution, and it was this *ensemble* of the views and convictions of the two emperors Alexander I. and Nicholas which Count Nesselrode had, during almost half a century, to enforce, in all the acts and documents emanating from the chancellor's office at St. Petersburg.

It has been the destiny of the successor of Count Nesselrode to break little by little with all this *ensemble* of traditions and principles, and to inaugurate for the empire of the czars, in its external relations, an entirely new policy. One may dispute the merit of this policy, and dispute it the more widely as it is still far from having borne all its fruit. What is indisputable and astonishes at first sight, is that Prince Gortchakof has been able to attach his name to a change of system which is marked in the diplomatic annals of his country, and to create for himself, as minister of foreign affairs in Russia, a situation entirely personal, an important position, such as none of his predecessors ever had. Alexander Mikhaïlovitch is not only the faithful servant of his august master, he is the veritable chief of his department, the directing minister; he accepts boldly his part of the responsibility, and above all his share of the *éclat* in the different transactions of Europe. An equally new phenomenon in Russia, this minister not only retains the favor of his sovereign, but also that of the nation. He manages the public opinion of his country, he watches over it, sometimes he even flatters it, and it repays him. It has had some moments of infatuation for Alexander Mikhaïlovitch, even some moments of enthusiasm,—after the affairs of Poland; more than that, it has in a measure brought forward and created him. This elevation of the plenipotentiary of Vienna to the high position left vacant by Count Nesselrode in the month of April, 1856, was not without its results.

In 1815, on his triumphal return from the congress of Vienna, Alexander could select as he wished from the celebrated men who then formed the *état-major* of Russian diplomacy, the least known and the most humble of this illustrious body. Passing over Capo d'Istria, Pozzo di Borgo, Ribeaupierre, Razoumovsky, Stakelberg, d'Anstett, it was lawful for him to confide the direction of the external policy to a German gentleman of Westphalian origin, born at Lisbon, and Russian only by naturalization. In 1856, after the congress of Paris, the choice of Prince Gortchakof for the same position was, we will not say imposed, but certainly indicated to the Emperor Alexander II. by the voice of the people, or, if one likes it better, by that voice of the *salons* which did not delay at this moment in taking more and more a popular tone. And since his *début* at the Hotel of the Place du Palais the former pupil of Zarkoe-Zeloe distinguished himself by liberal ways and advances made in a public spirit, which must have occasionally astonished his predecessor, still living and in possession of the honored title of chancellor. For the first time, a Russian minister had *mots*, not only for the *salons*, but also for the lecture halls and the bureaux of journalists, words which went straight to the heart of the great lady and country gentleman, the humble student and proud officer of the *gardes*. His aphorism on Austria[26] went the rounds of all the Russias. Another aphorism, taken from a circular, soon transported the nation: the celebrated phrase, "Russia does not sulk, but meditates," seemed to be dictated by the very soul of the people, and drew from it a cry of enthusiasm. It was then that one remembered the awakening of the Russian spirit after a long period of compression; the journals, the thoughtful periodicals, inaugurated their joyful *ébats*, the authors, the literary men, began to have an importance hitherto unknown; Alexander Mikhaïlovitch, who always displayed a liking and sympathy for Russian literature, the former fellow scholar of Pouchkine, passed for a patriotic statesman in the eyes of Pogodine, Axakof, Katkof, etc. One perceived that he had a great hatred for Austria, a pronounced desire for the French alliance, and the nation, which also shared equally and even in an exaggerated manner, these two sentiments, saluted in him the national minister *par excellence*. A strange comparison, well made to demonstrate the inanity of words and the instability of things on earth, is the manner in which the most decided partisan of the empire of the Hapsburg, M. de Bismarck, the future conqueror of Sadowa, entered into the *cænaculum* of diplomats; and at the same time it was the implacable enemy of the Germans and the warm friend of the French whom, in 1856, the Russians exalted above all in the person of their vice-chancellor, the statesman who, later, by a policy of omission and commission, was to favor as no one else did, the dismemberment of France and the constitution of a Germany greater, more powerful, and more formidable than the history of past centuries has ever known! It is true that by the "Germans" the Russia of 1856 meant principally the Austrians,[27] and that in the France of that day it admired above all a certain absolutism in the democratic instincts which showed itself touched with the misfortunes of Italy, which professed to sympathize with Roumania, Servia, Montenegro, and which had not yet pronounced the fatal name of Poland.

"Calm yourself," the emperor of the French said to M. de Cavour, in the month of April, 1856, after the closing of the congress of Paris,—"Calm yourself; I have a presentiment that the present peace will not last long."[28] Prince Gortchakof had without doubt the same presentiment, and perhaps others more positive in this respect. The thought of "making war for an idea," the thought of freeing Italy, had long been fixed in the mind of Napoleon III.; at the moment of signing the treaty of Paris "with an eagle's feather," he let his hidden and dreaming glance fall on the classic plains of Lombardy. Now, for the enterprise which France meditated against Austria, and in which it could scarcely count on an angry neutrality of England, it was thought useful to secure in good season the friendship of Russia and Prussia. Prussia had emerged from the Oriental crisis very much weakened with its policy "of the free hand;" England, Austria, and Turkey had even had little desire to admit it to the honors of the congress. The president of the council at Berlin, M. de Manteuffel, was obliged to wait long in the antechamber, while the plenipotentiaries of Europe were in full deliberation, and it was only at the instance of the emperor of the French that the Prussian envoy was at last admitted. Napoleon III. insisted absolutely, in 1856, on allowing *that* Prussia to retake its position in Europe which fourteen years later was to dethrone him! As for Russia, we have already spoken of the politenesses and cordialities of which Count Orlof was the recipient from France during all the time of the congress. Since then, in the successive arrangements of the various difficulties which the execution of some of the clauses of the treaty of Paris caused to arise (Belgrade, Isle of Sérpents, navigation of the Danube, etc.), one saw the arguments or interpretations of the Russian plenipotentiary sustained almost constantly by the plenipotentiary of France. In the different and numerous conferences and commissions which followed in these years, 1856-1859, for regulating the pending questions, the distribution of the votes was almost invariably thus: England and Austria on one side, on the other France, Russia, and Prussia.[29]

Although Prince Gortchakof acknowledged with good grace all these attentions of the cabinet of the Tuileries, he was not sufficiently complaisant to follow it in a campaign of remonstrances against the government of Naples, a campaign undertaken in concert with the cabinet of Saint James, in consequence of the famous letters addressed to Lord Aberdeen by M. Gladstone on the *régime* of King Ferdinand II. A similar intermeddling in the internal affairs of an independent state did not seem very correct in the eyes of the successor of Count Nesselrode; but he was the more forward in seconding the Emperor Napoleon III. in his generous designs every time that there was a question of ameliorating the lot of the Christian populations in the Ottoman empire, of augmenting their autonomy, and, as was said then, of *reforming the Turk*. "To reform the Turk," maliciously thought M. Thouvenel, ambassador of France at Constantinople, "it is necessary to begin by first impaling him;" one commenced, however, by applying to him the question of *hatt-houmayoum*, by interrogating him concerning his intentions in favor of the rajahs of Bosnia, Bulgaria, and Herzegovina, and by thus annoying in a certain degree the cabinets of Vienna and London. Much greater was naturally the solicitude for the vassal States of the good padishah, for Moldavia, Wallachia, Servia, and Montenegro; these States already had a demi-independence, they made it possible to render it entire.

The little Prince of Montenegro, former *protégé* and servitor of the Emperor Nicholas, had come to visit the sovereign of France after the peace of Paris, and since his return had quarrelled with the sultan, in consequence of which the *Algésiras* and *L'Impétueuse* appeared before Ragusa. French vessels in the waters of the Orient to menace Turkey, to the great mortification of England and Austria, to the great rejoicings of Russia, all this scarcely two years after the war in the Crimea! The sight was surely not wanting in originality, and prepared the world for a series of surprises. At about the same time, Servia expelled Prince Alexander Kara Géorgevitch, and recalled to the throne the old Miloch Obrenovitch. The Porte protested, England and Austria joined in this protest; but, thanks to the combined efforts of Russia and France, they ended by acknowledging the right of the national Servian assembly, whose principal grievance against the dethroned prince was his having shown too much sympathy for the allies in the war of 1853! The question of the Danubian Principalities presented an aspect serious, and also *piquant*. France and Russia had begged at the congress of Paris for the complete union of Moldavia and Wallachia; the other Powers were opposed to it, and, weary of war, they had agreed to accept a combination which completely assimilated the administration in the two countries, while maintaining their separation. It was, as later in Italy, the project of confederation opposed to that of unity; but then there was also given on the banks of the Danube the first example of that national strategy, which was soon to show itself on a larger scale in Tuscany and Emelia. The twofold election of Prince Couza was in truth the first trial of that popular diplomacy, which later, in Italian affairs, took pleasure in so often confounding the combinations of high plenipotentiaries and high contracting parties, and proclaimed in the face of the world a deed accomplished by the suffrage of the nation. The popular votes annulling the arrangements of diplomacy, and the understanding of France and Russia to respect these votes, these are the two salient traits of the policy in the years 1856-1859, a policy which the liberal opinion of Europe received with favor without being too much astonished at such a concordance of views between the cabinets of the Tuileries and St. Petersburg on this very ground of the Orient, still warm with the bullets of the war; on this ground, from which Russia should have been, in the opinion of the allies of 1853, completely shut out, and where she now regained influence and a footing, modestly it is true, and under the protecting shadow of France.

At last the Italian complications came, and the government of the czar increased the testimonials of his good relations with the cabinet of the Tuileries. "Our relations with France are *cordial*," replied Prince Gortchakof to Lord Napier, charged by his government with sounding the disposition of Russia in such grave matters. England then made earnest efforts to prevent the war in Italy from breaking out. Lord Cowley, sent with a certain flourish on a mission to Vienna, exerted himself to discover the possible bases of an accommodation, and the cabinet of St. James already flattered itself with the hope of having quelled the tempest, when Prince Gortchakof suddenly proposed a *congress*, and pronounced that fatal word which then, as so often since, was only the signal for a rupture. A congress! A treaty of peace before any hostility, the glory of the triumph without the peril of victory,—that was the eternal *hystéron-protéron* of the Napoleonic ideology, that was the chimera pursued by the dreamer of Ham in the question of the Papacy, in the question of Poland, and of Denmark; and up to the catastrophe of 1870, after the declaration of war, it is curious to see Prince Gortchakof first suggest a remedy which imperial France was yet to recommend so often for all the chronic evils of Europe.[30] The chief of the English government, the old Earl of Derby, complained bitterly of the horrible trick which the proposition emanating from St. Petersburg had played him, and there has never been any doubt in England but that it was brought about by a telegram sent from Paris. Not less serviceable for France did the Russian vice-chancellor show himself in his circular of the 27th May, 1859, when he endeavored to calm the warlike ardor of the secondary States of Germany, and it was in this celebrated dispatch that he made the judicious demonstration as well as the merited praise of the "combination purely and exclusively defensive" of the *Bund*, a salutary combination which permitted the localization of a war become inevitable, "in place of generalizing it and giving to the struggle a character and proportions which escape all human foresight."

Napoleon III. descended to the plains of Lombardy; Austria was vanquished at Magenta and Solferino, and Russia could enjoy its first revenge on the ungrateful Hapsburg, who had "betrayed" it before Sebastopol. The year after, in consequence of the annexation of Savoy, Lord Russell made the solemn declaration to the parliament that his country "should not separate itself from the rest of the nations of Europe; that it should always be ready to act with the different states, if it did not wish to dread to-day such an annexation, and to-morrow to hear another spoken of." That was the funeral oration of the Anglo-French alliance: four years after the war of the Crimea, France had lost one and then the other of its two great allies in the crisis of the Orient, and Russia did not care to complain. It did not protest against the annexation of Savoy; it even declared that it only saw in it a "regular transaction;" but it profited by the moment to make its reëntry into European politics, and bring back on the tapis the question ... of the Ottoman empire! The 4th May, 1860, Prince Gortchakof convoked in his cabinet the ambassadors of the great Powers in order to examine with them the "dolorous and precarious" position of the Christians in Bosnia, Herzegovina and Bulgaria, and soon a circular of the vice-chancellor (20th May) insisted on the reunion of a conference in order to alter the stipulations established by the treaty of Paris. "The time of illusions is passed," Alexander Mikhaïlovitch wrote in this circular; "all hesitation every adjournment will bring grave inconvenience," and he even seized upon the recent liberation of Italy as an argument for the future independence of the populations who awakened all his solicitude: "the events accomplished in the east of Europe have resounded in all the Orient *like an encouragement and like a hope!*" Thus, scarcely four years after the treaty of Paris, Russia began anew to speak to the world of the "sick man," and to do it, it did not shelter itself, as in the conferences and commissions of 1856-1859, under the protection and language of France; it went all alone, and took the initiative in the debate!

This was not enough: in that year alone, 1860, the cabinet of St. Petersburg regained almost all the ground lost since the war of the Crimea; that was a year of peculiar fortune for Russia, for it was a year of universal distrust of France. The acquisition of Savoy, the strange and profoundly immoral spectacle which the negotiations of this treaty of Zurich offered, torn up even before being signed, the Piedmontese annexations in Italy, the expedition of Garibaldi to Sicily, the "new right" of which the official journals in France spoke, and the famous pamphlet on the "Pope and Congress," had caused the alarm and awakened in the highest degree the uneasiness of Europe. Lord Palmerston declared "that he would only be willing to give his hand to a former ally in holding the other on the buckler of defense," and he armed his *volunteers*. Switzerland was violently agitated; the *National-Verein* swore to die for the defense of the Rhine, and even those honest and peaceful Belgians affirmed in an address to the king that "if their independence was menaced, they would submit to the most severe trials." Above these popular frights the cabals of the sovereigns were agitated; the German princes united at Baden, and the emperor of the French thought it opportune to surprise them in a measure in the midst of their deliberations by making that "rapid voyage" from which the "Moniteur" promised "very happy results." "Nothing was wanting but the spontaneity of a proceeding so significant," added the official journal, "to put an end to this unanimous concert of malicious rumors and false estimations. In truth, the emperor, in explaining frankly to the sovereigns united at Baden how his policy never conflicted with right and justice, carried to minds equally distinguished and equally exempt from prejudices, the conviction which does not fail to be inspired by a true sentiment expressed with loyalty." It appeared, however, that the conviction had not worked completely on the prejudices, for, at the close of the reunion of Baden, there was another at Toeplitz, between the Emperor of Austria and the Prince Regent of Prussia, where they agreed on a third which was to be held at Warsaw with the Emperor of Russia,—and the czar accepted the *rendezvous*.

"It is not a coalition, it is a reconciliation which I am going to make at Warsaw," declared the Emperor Alexander II. to the French ambassador, the Duke of Montebello, whose government was naturally much agitated by the turn affairs were taking. In truth, conciliating expressions were not wanting in the dispatch by which Prince Gortchakof "invited the French government to let him know in what measure it thought that it would be able to second the efforts which Russia was making to prevent *the crisis with which Europe was menaced;*" but, however polite these forms were, they did not hide a necessity for explanation. The cabinet of the Tuileries replied by a memorandum in which it gave, above all, "the categoric engagement not to give any support to Piedmont in case that Austria should be attacked in Venetia." The cabinets of Vienna and Berlin made their remarks on several points of the French memorandum, and addressed them ... to the Russian vice-chancellor, who transmitted them to Paris, with the request for new explanations more explicit and more reassuring. Sum total, no positive result came from this meeting of the three sovereigns of the North, who had for a moment caused very grave apprehensions in France. This was because the Emperor Alexander had gone to Warsaw only in a particular interest; he did not wish to make a coalition nor a reconciliation there; he simply wished to show his influence: to give a demonstration of his power. He was flattered at seeing these sovereigns, these German princes, coming to the former capital of Poland to deliberate there on the general situation, and to receive the word of command: that recalled the good days of the Emperor Nicholas. On the other side, Russia was very much pleased at making France feel the whole price of its friendship, at making it understand that its services had now a much greater value, perhaps even their tariff. The clever productions which emanated successively in these years 1856-1860 from the chancellor's office at St. Petersburg, indicated in a very plastic manner the continually ascending advance of Russia since the peace of Paris. In the first of these celebrated circulars, it declared "that it did not sulk, but meditated;" in the second, on the occasion of the Italian complications, it already emerged "from the reserve which it had imposed on itself since the war of the Crimea." After the annexation of Savoy "its conscience warned it of being any longer silent on the unhappy state of the Christians in the Orient, etc." At last, in the month of October, 1860, it was the mouth-piece of the general interests of Europe, the intermediary which demanded explanations from the cabinets of the Tuileries. A modest *protégé* of France, and full of "reserves" until the war in Italy, it ascends in 1859 to the rank of a "precious friend," to become after the interview of Warsaw the important and almost indispensable ally,— an ally very resolute in not accepting a secondary *rôle*, in guarding its position of marked influence, in taking for itself a large part in the great combinations of the future.

Assuredly the desultory, undecisive, and eternally contradictory policy of the Emperor Napoleon III. played into the hands of Russia. But it is just to acknowledge that Prince Gortchakof allowed no chance of fortune to escape, and that without creating the events, he understood admirably how to profit by them. The superiority of the statesman always reveals itself by the measure which he preserves in his "cordiality" and even in his vengeance, by the foreseeing mind which he does not cease to preserve even in the midst of the allurements of success. It is not doubtful for instance that the warnings of Russia after the battle of Solferino, the fears which it then suddenly expressed of not being able longer to restrain Germany in its ardor to go to the rescue of Austria, contributed greatly to the hasty peace of Villafranca, and, however fatal this event was as regards the interests of France and even of Austria, one cannot deny that Russia accomplished its purpose perfectly. In fact, the complete execution of the programme "of the Alps to the Adriatic" would have probably given an entirely different turn to the Italian affairs, would certainly have rendered possible in the future a sincere reconciliation between France and Austria, while the half drawn solution by the peace of Villafranca, leaving all the questions in suspense, could only embitter the relations of the two belligerents, and render the friendship of Russia more precious to France. On the other side, this campaign of Lombardy, while giving satisfaction to the Muscovite hatred sprung from the war of the Orient, was still far from destroying one of the fundamental elements of the traditional policy of the czars as regards Germany. In spite of the loss of Milan, Austria preserved its position intact in the centre of Europe, was a balance for Prussia, and the interview of Warsaw proved that the Russian influence among the Germanic States had certainly not decreased.

Not less circumspect and skillful did the Russian vice-chancellor show himself in not compromising too far in his connivances with the Emperor Napoleon III. during these years 1856-1860, certain general principles of preservation which had made the greatness and strength of the reign of Nicholas. Without doubt, in Servia, in the Danubian Principalities, Alexander Mikhaïlovitch was not of a vigorous orthodoxy, and allowed popular votes to annul there the arrangements stipulated by the treaties; but in comparison with those countries of the Orient Russia has always allowed itself many political licenses. In the affairs of the Occident, on the contrary, Prince Gortchakof took care to remain as far as possible in the traditions and not to overturn too much in the "new right." He let the journals and periodicals of Moscow and St. Petersburg plume themselves at their ease on what Russia boldly contributed to the deliverance of the peoples and to the triumph of nationalities; for himself, in the documents dated at his office, he refrained carefully from all these neologisms and persevered in the terminology consecrated by the old diplomatic language. In these documents he had not spoken at all of the national aspirations nor of the popular votes, when Milan and Savoy changed masters; in the eyes of the Russian vice-chancellor, all these were simply facts of war, "regular transactions." Still less did he care to make the revolutionary propaganda abroad and to associate himself in the commerce of exportation which, according to a malicious remark of those days, Napoleon III. had undertaken with liberal ideas. He declined categorically all participation in the remonstrances addressed to the King of Naples, and declared in his circular of the 22d September, 1856, "that to wish to obtain from a sovereign concessions as to the internal government of his states in a comminatory manner or by menacing demonstrations, was to substitute one's self violently on one's own authority, to govern in his place, and to proclaim without disguise the right of the strong over the weak." Lastly, in his famous note to Prince Gagarine of the 10th October, 1860, he took up the Sardinian government roundly for its conduct in Emilia, Tuscany, the Duchies of Parma and Modena, and strongly opposed the deposal of these princes and the annexations of those provinces, which six years later he was to tolerate, even favor in Germany. "It is no longer," he said in the dispatch to Prince Gagarine, "a question of Italian interests, but of general interests, common to all governments, it is a question which is directly connected with those eternal laws without which, neither order, peace, nor security can exist in Europe." Finally, he sneered at those Jenners of politics who recommend the vaccination of anarchy to remove from it its pernicious character, and who pretend to remove the arms from the demagogy in appropriating to themselves its baggage; "the necessity in which the Sardinian government pretends to be situated in combating anarchy does not justify it, since *it only moves with the revolution to recover by it its heritage.*" In a word, the Russian vice-chancellor profited with prodigious dexterity by the good disposition of France and still more by its errors, without ever sacrificing the will, the decorum, and the principles of his own government to it. He made use of the Emperor Napoleon III. without using him too much, and above all without ever subjecting himself to an order of ideas in which Russia could find any deception. For the good of Russia, for the happiness of Europe, it would have been desirable for Prince Gortchakof to have observed later, in his intimacy with Prussia, a little of that care and that intelligent egotism which he gave proof of in such a superior manner in his intimacy with France. "To love, there must be two," said the great theologian of the Middle Ages on the subject that those centuries of faith called divine love, the relations of the human soul with its heavenly Creator. The precept is assuredly much more to be recommended in the much less mystical relations between the powers of the earth, and the Russian vice-chancellor did not forget it during that first period of his ministry, during those years of "cordiality" with the cabinet of the Tuileries. It was only during the second period that the heart of Alexander Mikhaïlovitch began to control the right of the state, and that the love for M. de Bismarck proved to be stronger than the world, stronger even than Russia and its interests.

II.

While Prince Gortchakof thus reaped the fruits of his "French" policy, among which that of vengeance on Austria was surely not the least sweet or pleasant, his former colleague of Frankfort, having become representative of Prussia at the court of Russia, was consumed at his side by the languishing fever of a man of action trammeled by foolish probity. He had arrived at St. Petersburg in the spring of the year 1859, three months after the famous birthday reception given to M. de Hübner by the Emperor Napoleon III.; the Italian complications were about to break out, and the Russian vice-chancellor lent himself to all those diplomatic tricks which, according to the desire of the cabinet of the Tuileries, would drive the Emperor Francis Joseph to a declaration of war. The new plenipotentiary of Prussia at the court of St. Petersburg had not a moment of doubt concerning the bearing which his government should observe in circumstances so propitious. It was from this time (12th May, 1859) that his confidential dispatch to M. de Schleinitz dates, in which he recommends the rupture with the *Bund*, the radical proceeding by sword and fire, *ferro et igne*. In the preceding year, during a journey to Paris, he had occasion to have an interview with the Emperor of the French, and to recognize his good will toward Prussia, and the unqualified wishes which were expressed in the Tuileries for the greatness and the prosperity of the country of Frederick II. and of Blücher. In the month of November of that same year 1858, Napoleon III. had charged the Marquis Pepoli, then *en route* for Berlin, to represent to the Hohenzollern all the advantages which he would find in a rupture with Austria: "In Germany," the Emperor of the French had said, "Austria represents the past, Prussia represents the future; in linking itself to Austria, Prussia condemns itself to immobility; it cannot be thus contented; it is called to a higher fortune; it should accomplish in Germany the great destinies which await it, and which Germany awaits from it."[31] Thus thought the future prisoner of Wilhelmshoehe on the eve of Magenta and Solferino, and "his excellency the lieutenant" certainly found no objections in such a magnificent programme. But those good ministers of the *new era* at Berlin unfortunately had not the slightest notion of the "new right," and up to the prince regent himself, they did not cease to speak of conquests purely *moral*. They even asked one another at Potsdam if they should not assist Austria, and whether they did not have federal obligations towards the Emperor Francis Joseph! The Samson of the Mark strove in vain against the ties which the "Philistines of the Spree" imposed on him, and the war in Italy became his Dalila: in fact, it was from this epoch that the renowned boldness of the present chancellor of Germany dates.

It is interesting to study, in the confidential letters to Malvina, the state of mind of M. de Bismarck during these years 1859-1860. At the commencement of hostilities, and evidently despairing of seeing his government adopt the line of conduct which he had not ceased to recommend, he left his post, went to Moscow to visit the Kremlin, passed an agreeable day in a villa, so much more agreeable "when one has the feeling of being sheltered from the telegraph." The news of a great battle fought in Lombardy (Magenta) caused him, nevertheless, to return to St. Petersburg. "Perhaps there will be something for the diplomats to do." At St. Petersburg, he learns of the strange desire at Berlin of interceding for Austria, of mobilizing the federal armies, and from it he conceived the greatest apprehensions for his country. He became ill. A very grave case of hepatitis endangered his life seriously. "They covered my body with innumerable cupping glasses large as saucers, with mustard poultices and quantities of blisters, and I was already half way to a better world when I began to convince my doctors that my nerves were disordered by eight years of griefs and excitement without intermission (the eight years of Frankfort!), and that by continuing to weaken me, they would lead me into typhoid fever or imbecility. My good constitution ended by conquering, thanks, above all, to several dozen bottles of good wine."

His good disposition did not the less remain dull and morose, and two months later he avowed that he would not have been sorry to have ended his life then. Austria was vanquished, it is true; she had lost two great battles and one of the richest provinces; but Prussia had not drawn any material, palpable advantage from this disaster of the Hapsburg, and the cavalier of the Mark was not the man to cherish, like his friend Alexander Mikhaïlovitch, a purely Platonic hatred. He consoled himself, however, by the thought that the peace of Villafranca was only a truce: "to wish in the present state of affairs to seriously reconcile Austria with France, is to labor at the squaring of the circle." "I shall endeavor," he wrote at the approach of autumn, 1859, "to cower in my bear-skin, and to bury myself in the snow; in the thaw of next May, I will see what remains of me and our affairs; if too little I shall definitely settle with politics." The following month of May brought grave events; the annexation of Savoy became the signal for the greatest distrust in Europe, of which we have spoken above: but the cabinet of Berlin persisted in its ancient course, and the prince regent had, in July, an interview with the Emperor Francis Joseph at Toeplitz. "I learn," wrote the representative of Prussia at the court of St. Petersburg with undisguised spite, "that we have been shaved at Toeplitz, splendidly shaved; we have let ourselves be taken in by the Viennese good nature. And all that for nothing, not even the smallest plate of lentils." At last, in the month of October, after Castelfidardo and the conquest of the kingdom of Naples, the cabinet of Berlin addressed an energetic note to M. de Cavour, on the bearing of the House of Savoy on the Italian peninsula. The note established that "it is solely in the legal manner of reforms, and in respecting the existing rights, that a regular government is allowed to realize the legitimate wishes of nations," and closes by the following passage: "Called to express ourselves on the acts and principles of the Sardinian government, we can only deplore them profoundly, and we believe that we are fulfilling a rigorous duty by expressing in the most explicit and formal manner our disapprobation, both of those principles and of the application which has been thought could be made of them." One can imagine what bad humor such *naïvetés* would cause to the future destroyer of the *Bund*, to the future spoliator of Denmark, of Hanover, and so many other states. He again thought of leaving the career; he resolved in any case to "cling to the situation of an observer," as regards the monstrous policy which was pursued at Berlin. He is perfectly astonished at the scandal which is caused on the banks of the Spree by the publication of the posthumous journal of M. de Varnhagen, a journal full of piquant revelations concerning the court of Prussia. "Why be so indignant. Is it not taken from life? Varnhagen is vain and *méchant*, but who is not? Does it not all depend on the manner in which nature has ripened our lives? According to what we have suffered from the bites of worms, from dampness, or from the sun, behold us sweet, sour, or rotten."

That did not hinder him, however, from carefully cultivating, during these years 1859-1860, his relations with the political world of St. Petersburg from taking root there, and from attaching by a thousand ties the fortune of his country to this friendship of Russia, of which he understood all the value. The position of the representatives of Prussia has always been exceptional at St. Petersburg; thanks to the near relationship of the two courts, they enjoyed in the winter palace a confidence and intimacy which the envoys of other states scarcely ever obtained there. M. de Bismarck was able to add to these favorable conditions the influence of his personal merit, and the good reputation which he had acquired, in a Russian point of view, during his long sojourn at Frankfort. His former journeys in Courland had made him known and liked by the German nobility of the Baltic Provinces, by the Keyserlingk, the Uxküll, the Nolde, the Bruvern, etc., always so influential at court, in the chancellor's office, and in Russian diplomacy. "The first prophets of the future greatness of M. de Bismarck," says an author very *au fait* in the society of St. Petersburg, "the first who predicted the providential mission which was reserved for him in Germany, were perhaps those barons of Courland and Livonia with whom the present chancellor of Germany had so often passed the hunting season, shared their amusements, their banquets, and their political conversations."[32] The representative of Prussia at the court of St. Petersburg took care, however, not to give himself up too much to this liking for the Courlanders and Livonians; he was careful to place in his affections, or at least in his demonstrations, the greatest part in Russian Russia, autochthonal Muscovy (*nastaïastchaïa*). This enthusiasm for the customs and genius of the "Scythians," this love for the "bear-skin and caviare," was it very sincere? We may perhaps doubt it; it is allowable to suppose that the man who, in the name of his Germanic superiority, has so often and boldly expressed his disdain for the *Welches* and Latins, feels at bottom a still greater contempt for that Sclavic race which every good German makes rhyme with slave (*slave-esclave*).[33] However that may be, never did foreign ambassador on the banks of the Neva have so much devotion as the cavalier of the Mark for the polar stars, or pushed as far as he did the passion of local color. He pushed it so far as to introduce into his house several little bears which (as formerly the foxes at Kniephof) came, at the dinner hour, bounding into the dining hall, agreeably deranging the *convives*, licking the hand of their master, and "biting the calves of the servants' legs."[34] A worthy Nimrod, he never missed an expedition against the black king of the boreal forests; he did not fail to don on these occasions the Muscovite hunting costume, and the team of horses *à la Russe* has remained dear to him up to the present, and even in the streets of Berlin. He also affected to interest himself greatly in the literary movement of the country; he had a Russian professor in his house, and he learned enough of it to be able to give his orders to those people in their native idiom, even to delightfully surprise one day the Emperor Alexander with some phrases pronounced in the language of Pouchkine.

The Russians could not help giving a most cordial reception to a diplomat who showed himself so taken with their usages and customs, with their pleasures and their "peculiarities," and who, moreover, had the advantage of succeeding to that good M. de Werther, whose reputation, neither there nor anywhere else, was exactly that of a too hilarious character. On the contrary, they had never known on the banks of the Neva a Prussian as gay as this excellent M. de Bismarck, as good a fellow, as good a liver, having a loud laugh, coarse jests, and a witty speech. He indulged in all sorts of pleasantries at the expense of the "Philistines of the Spree," the "old fogies of Potsdam," which gave him no small success: a minister plenipotentiary slandering his own government, a grumbling, fault-finding diplomat in the very political sphere which he had the mission to represent and to second, that was an originality which could be appreciated by a world always on the watch for the *piquant* and pleasing. He knew how to please the empress-mother Helen, whose influence at court was considerable, and whose warm support never failed him in consequence, in the most grave moments of his career as minister. The emperor had conceived a great affection for him, invited him regularly to his bear hunts, and did him the honor of admitting him in his *cortége* during his journeys to Warsaw and Breslau to meet the Prince Regent of Prussia. As for Prince Gortchakof, he enjoyed more than ever the society of his former colleague of Frankfort, and the *salons* often repeated a malicious *mot, a méchant* insinuation of which Austria generally had to bear the brunt, and the paternity of which they indifferently attributed first to one then to the other of these two friends, grown inseparable, and whom spiteful intrigues nevertheless wished to separate! At the end of 1859, M. de Bismarck wrote in a confidential letter: "Austria and its dear confederates are intriguing at Berlin to have me recalled from here: I am, however, very amiable. God's will be done!"

At Berlin, in the mean time, they began little by little to glide down a declivity, which would have caused Prussian politics to descend rapidly from the cloudy regions of the *new era* upon that ground of realities and of action to which the tried friend of Alexander Mikhaïlovitch had so long invited them, and, curiously enough, it was precisely the mobilization of the Prussian army in 1859, the mobilization so condemned by M. de Bismarck, which was the immediate cause of this sudden revival fraught with incalculable consequences. It is fashionable now in France to represent the Prussian government as having meditated for half a century a war of revenge and conquest, slowly brightening their arms, and training a succession of generations for the decisive hour of combat. There is nothing more false, however. Neither the government of Frederick William III., nor that of Frederick William IV. ever cherished warlike projects, and even the humiliation of Olmütz was not an incentive to the minister of war at Berlin. The two predecessors of William I. only sacrificed to the military spirit just that which was necessary to insure them a stand among the great Powers, to hold reviews, and to be able to speak of their faithful troops, and of their always valiant swords; at bottom, they were not far from thinking like the Grand Duke Constantine, the brother of the Emperor Nicholas, who one day said naïvely: "I detest war, it spoils the armies!" The swords of Blücher and Scharnhorst were sheathed since 1815; even the adoption of the needle gun in 1847 was only an accident, rather a scientific experiment; in 1848 and 1849, the Prussian troops did not shine with marvelous *éclat* in the war of the Duchies, and were even miserably held in check by the undisciplined bands of the insurrection of Posen and Baden. The brother of the king, who had commanded the troops in Baden, was grievously moved at the sight which his soldiers then presented, and, having become regent of the kingdom (October, 1858), he immediately turned his attention to military reform. Nevertheless it was only the mobilization attempted during the Italian complications (in the summer of 1859) which opened their eyes to all the grave inconveniences and incoherencies of the organization till then in force. Two superior men, MM. de Moltke and de Roon, joined with the prince regent in remodeling the system from the very bottom. They displayed in it an intelligence, an energy, and a rapidity without equal in history; they knew how to profit by all the discoveries of science, and above all did not let the great lesson escape them which a formidable civil war in North America soon taught, a war so rich in experiments and inventions of every kind. In spite of the obstacles which were thrown in their way without cessation from all sides, these two men, at the end of six years, produced an armed force, entirely new, powerful, invincible; and "the instrument," still rough and rudimentary in 1860, proved its ill omened "perfection" on the calamitous day of Sadowa! Not less erroneous is the opinion, very generally spread, however, that the Prussian people had demanded of its government victories and aggrandizement; to refute these perfectly gratuitous suppositions, it suffices to remember that the different parliaments of Berlin did not cease to oppose military reform, and that they had on their side the almost unanimous voice of the people. The ideas of German greatness, of German power, of the German mission, haunt the imagination of professors and authors much more than that of the people; they were academic themes, choice morsels of rhetoric and opposition, still they are much more in vogue south of the Main than north of this river,—and precisely there appears the astounding art of M. de Bismarck in having known how, to speak with Münchausen, "to condense mists into stones of size for a gigantic edifice," and to make of a dream of *savans* a popular passion. The force of will, the force of character, and in one word the genius, can still, even in a century of democratic leveling and uniform mediocrity play a *rôle*, of which our poor philosophy of history scarcely had a suspicion, which drowns so skillfully all responsibility and initiative in the blind fatality of the "masses," and, as a Teutonic proverb says, cannot distinguish the trees on account of looking at the forest. Take from the most recent history of Prussia three or four men who answer to the names of William I., Moltke, Roon, and Bismarck, and the old Barbarossa would very probably up to the present time have continued his secular sleep in the cave of the Kyffhäuser.

Nature delights as well in analogies as in contrasts, and it is thus that the antecedents of this prince regent, who to-day bears the name of William I., Emperor of Germany, does not fail to present some similarity with the past of the extraordinary man, who, at the destined hour, was to forge for him, *ferro et igne*, the imperial crown of Barbarossa. In order to be enlightened concerning these antecedents, it is necessary to turn to the posthumous "Journal" of M. Varnhagen von Ense,—the liberal, crabbed Dangeau, compromising in the highest degree, amiable as a whole, of the court of Berlin,—the same "Journal" whose defense we have seen M. de Bismarck undertake in a confidential letter, against the clamors which this publication had awakened in the capital of Prussia. There is no doubt that Prince William made an energetic opposition to the liberal desires which had signaled the *débuts* of the reign of his brother, King Frederick William IV. He had begun to work out at this epoch *memoirs for consulting* which established his right of *veto* in every amendment of the fundamental laws of the state. The rumor of a formal protest in his name and in that of his descendants against every project of constitution, found credit for a moment even in the heart of the ministry; and under no conditions would he give his consent to the feudal "charter" granted by his brother the 3d of February, 1847, except on the express reservation that the States should not decide on the budget, and should never occupy themselves with foreign affairs. And the unpopularity of the heir presumptive was great before the revolution of 1848; during the fatal month of March of that year, it was against him especially that the fury of the inhabitants of Berlin was let loose, who attributed to him (and wrongly) the order given to the troops to fire on the people. He was then forced to leave the country on a "mission" to London, and the multitude did not forego the satisfaction of inscribing on the palace of the fugitive the words of *national property*. Returned from England after the appeasement of the revolutionary effervescence, he placed himself, in 1849, at the head of the troops to stifle in Baden a ridiculous insurrection, and feigned "important military operations," which kept him in the south of Germany, so as not to be present at the solemn session of the 6th February, 1850, when King Frederick William IV. took his oath to the definite statute.

Afterwards, however, especially towards the last years of the disenchanted and morose reign of his brother, the Prince of Prussia commenced to relax in his "reactionary" vigor, and especially made a sufficiently marked opposition to the "pietist" influences at the court of Potsdam. Affections and family considerations contributed also in creating for the prince a peculiar situation. The esteem and tenderness with which Frederick William IV. surrounded his wife did not always console her for the sterility with which she was afflicted, and the sight of a sister-in-law a happy mother of children destined for the throne, probably to be called some day to occupy the throne, produced coolness and irritation which the wife of the heir presumptive sharply resented. The Princess Augusta was not of a disposition to bear certain thrusts. Sprung from that House of Weimar which was always distinguished by its taste for arts and pleasure, she early had her own acquaintances, friendships, and a bearing sufficiently different from the ordinary way of the court to resemble occasionally a divergence sought after with intention. The wishes of the Princess Augusta did not fail to finally exercise their influence on her husband, and the project, long nursed by the august couple, realized at last in 1857, of uniting their eldest son with the daughter of Queen Victoria, was regarded as the first concession made to popular opinion. In fact, courtiers were not wanting at Potsdam, the terrible M. de Varnhagen tells us, who asked in their soul and conscience if it were quite worthy of the House of Hohenzollern to ally itself by blood with a dynasty which was only half sovereign, and held in dependence by a house of commons! How the times and customs have changed at this court of Potsdam which last year saw the heiress presumptive of the throne of Prussia and Germany, this same daughter of Queen Victoria, send affectionate telegrams to Doctor Strauss when dying, and render to the author of the

"Life of Jesus" an homage *in extremis* which transported with enthusiasm all the valiant cavaliers of the *combat of civilization*!

Habituated in a manner, and for several years already, to consider the brother of the king as reconciled to modern ideas and favorable to the cause of progress, the nation was much less astonished than charmed to hear him, on his accepting the regency, use liberal and constitutional language. A "new era" was to commence for Prussia; that word was almost officially adopted to designate the change of system, and in a memorable address, delivered on the 8th November, 1858, to the cabinet which he had formed, the prince regent sketched the programme of a reparative policy. He besought his councilors to bring about ameliorations in that which was arbitrary or contrary to the wants of the epoch. While defending himself against a dangerous *laisser aller* towards liberal ideas, and expressing the will "to courageously hinder that which has not been promised," he did not the less proclaim the duty of keeping with loyalty the contracted engagements, and of not hindering useful reforms. The address ended with the phrase become celebrated, and since then so frequently cited, "that Prussia should make '*moral conquests in Germany*.'"

The harmony between the regent and the nation was not, however, of long duration; the relations were not slow in cooling and proceeding towards a complete rupture, thanks especially to the projected reform of the army. The prince had this reform at heart: the wants of 1859 had only convinced him of the absolute urgency of a measure with which his mind had been occupied for many years; but the deputies of the nation refused to follow him in this road, and opposed him tenaciously and firmly. They did not understand the obstinacy which the prince displayed in a project which answered neither to the wants nor to the aspirations of the country, and they laughed at those who pretended that once in possession of his new "instrument," the Hohenzollern, would *do great things*! They had resisted judiciously, says a German author, the temptation of the parliament of Frankfort in 1849, and the provocation of Olmütz in 1850; they had let pass the opportunities which the wars of 1854 and 1859 presented. The love of peace was absolute, there was a complete absence of ambition, they were perfectly resigned to the political situation which they occupied, and on the other side no one wished to admit that a kingdom so peaceable could be menaced by neighbors. In such a state of affairs, every aggrandizement of the army drawing after it an increase of military and financial charges, already heavy enough for the citizens, only seemed to the country an inconceivable caprice of its rulers.[35] The chambers refused the demanded credit; the government went its way and continued its expenditures. The military question thus became a question of budget, and soon transformed itself into an irremediable constitutional conflict. Towards the end of 1861, no other remedy could be seen for the situation but a *coup d'état*.

Not less profound and irresistible was soon the change in the ideas of the court of Potsdam, as regarded the external policy. In proportion as the "instrument" perfected itself (and it perfected itself rapidly), one began to ask one's self about the most practical and fruitful employment for it. One did not yet distinctly know what one wished, but one wished it with strength, with the strength which one drew from the battalions increasing without cessation. Assuredly one always saw nothing but moral conquests in Germany, but one thought that a moral in action, aided somewhat by needle guns, would give excellent results. The atmosphere was charged with electricity and with the principles of nationality, and it was not only the professors and orators of the *National Verein* who recommended a "united Germany with a Prussian point (*mit preussischer Spitze*)." When, in the month of October, 1860, the envoy of Prussia, Count Brassier de Saint-Simon, read to Count Cavour the famous note of M. de Schleinitz against the Italian annexations, the president of the Sardinian council listened in silence to the harangue, then expressed his great regret at having displeased the government of Berlin on this point, but declared that he consoled himself with the thought that "Prussia would one day, thanks to Piedmont, profit by the example which he had given it." In France, the journals of the democratic authority, the devoted organs of the "new right," did not cease to praise the "Piedmontese mission" of the House of Hohenzollern, and we have recalled above the encouragements which Napoleon III. sent to Berlin after 1858. The visit made by King William I.[36] to the Emperor of the French at Compiègne in the month of October, 1861, was in this respect a symptom more significant, since none of the sovereigns of the North had till then given this mark of courtesy to the choice of universal suffrage. Strange rumors began to spread concerning the alliance of the three courts of the Tuileries, of St. Petersburg, and of Berlin, and they continued up to the month of March, 1863. Publications of mysterious origin, but which denoted a very specious knowledge of political affairs, spoke of the "*great combination of states* summing up in three races,—the Roman, Germanic, and Sclavic,—to which corresponded three centres of gravity, France, Prussia, and Russia, and of the definite establishment of the peace of the world by means of a *triple alliance of universal monarchies*, in which their full expression (*Abschluss*) would not only find the three principal races of the European system, but also the three great Christian churches!"[37] Lord Palmerston declared at this very epoch in parliament, with his Britannic *désinvolture*, "that the situation seemed pregnant with at least half a dozen respectable wars;" and in spite of the obscurity which still covers the transactions of the years 1861-1862, it is not doubtful that Napoleon III. had then occasionally brought up in his scheming mind a combination embracing at once the Orient and the Occident, a combination as vague as gigantic, and of which Prince Gortchakof prepared to profit with his tried dexterity. Whatever these shadowy projects were, the Hohenzollern had only to be satisfied with his sojourn at Compiègne, which he was to recall with a certain tenderness two years later in his polite reply to the invitation of the Congress. In October, 1861, Napoleon III., at Compiègne, probably made use of no other language than that which he had used in 1858 at Berlin by the mediation of the Marquis Pepoli, the fatidical language, "on the great destinies which awaited Prussia in Germany, and which Germany expected from it."

It was thus that the difficulties from within and the facilities from without, the parliamentary conflicts in the interior and the political constellations in the exterior united, towards the end of 1861, in equally urging the King of Prussia to energetic resolutions. A man of vigor was wanted for the vigorous actions which were projected, and the glances naturally fell on that grumbling diplomat at St. Petersburg, who, for so many years already, had not ceased to criticise the ministers of the *new era*, and to blame their conduct from without as well as from within. In spite of the promise which he had given "to confine himself to his situation as an observer," M. de Bismarck had not failed from time to time to give a thrust during those years 1860 and 1861, and to repeat without cessation the precept of Strafford, the precept of thorough (*à outrance!*). We see him during these years making very frequent journeys to Germany, seeking opportunities of meeting the head of the state, of conversing with him on his ideas and presenting him various memoirs. In October, 1861, on the very eve of the journey to Compiègne, he submitted to him a little project, from which he expected some success, and of which it is not so difficult in fact to imagine the tenor, when, above all, one takes care to study a confidential letter written by him a few days before (18th September, 1861), and directed entirely against a political programme which the conservative party in Prussia had published. In this curious letter he rises with violence against the *Bund*, "the hot-bed of particularism," demands "a (*straffer*) firmer concentration of the armed forces of Germany, and a more natural configuration of the frontiers of the States;" but, above all, he puts his party on guard against *the dangerous fiction of a solidarity which would exist between all the conservative interests*. To triumph over this "dangerous fiction" strongly rooted in certain minds, there was in truth the great difficulty for the future minister of William I., his *omne tulit punctum*, for it is not so easy in this order of things to well distinguish between reality and fiction; it is perhaps even perilous to discuss them, and a Retz would certainly have said of the conservative interests what he so finely remarked of the right of peoples and of that of kings, "that they never agree so well together as in silence." M. de Bismarck was once more obliged to combat this "fiction" at Berlin as at St. Petersburg, and if the mind as open as subtle of his friend Alexander Mikhaïlovitch allowed itself most often to be convinced without too much assistance, it was not the same with the Hohenzollern, who, afterwards, on many an occasion, and in decisive moments, was to feel the scruples, the shudders, and what Falstaff calls the "tertian fevers of conscience."

On the return of William I. from Compiègne, the nomination of the cavalier of the Mark to the direction of affairs was already a well-arranged and fixed matter. M. de Bismarck soon afterwards came to assist at the coronation of the king at Koenigsberg, and he only returned to St. Petersburg to take leave definitely. At the beginning of the month of May, 1862, he was again at Berlin; at the great military parade which was held in the capital on the occasion of the unveiling of the statue of Count de Brandenburg (17th May), the political men, the deputies, and the high functionaries of state looked upon him already as the future "Polignac" of Prussia. The fears and the hopes which such a provision excited were not, however, so soon to be realized, and the world was somewhat perplexed in suddenly learning that M. de Bismarck was to be appointed to the post in Paris. Did he still hesitate to take charge of the burden of power, and did he in any case prefer to await the result of the new elections which were to be held in Prussia? It is more probable that before inaugurating his government of combat he wished to add some new conversations to those which were held at Compiègne, to take once again the measure of the man on whom a then universal belief made the destinies of Europe depend, and to prepare in general the minds in France for the new policy which he was to inaugurate.

He only remained at Paris two months, during the two delightful months of May and June, but this short stay sufficed for him both to complete his studies and to throw light on his religion. He had more than one conversation with the sovereign of France, whose profound ideas every one exalted at this time, commented *ad infinitum* on the smallest words, admired even his silence, and whom he, however, the future conqueror of Sedan, did not hesitate in his confidential effusions to define even then as "a great unrecognized incapacity." He saw also the influential men in the government, and in society, and strove to rally them to his ideas and his projects. He did not conceal that his sovereign would not delay to appeal to him, and he exposed without a *détour* the line of conduct which he would adopt on such an occurrence. What history will perhaps most admire in the present chancellor of Germany, will be the supreme art with which he sometimes handled the truth: this man of genius has understood how to give to frankness itself all the political virtues of knavishness. Very artful and very cunning as to the means, he has nevertheless always been, as regards the goal which he pursued, of a *désinvolture*, of an indiscretion without equal, and it was thus that he had at Paris in 1862 those astonishing and confidential conferences which only amused and which should have made them reflect.[38]

France,—said M. de Bismarck then and since, in 1862 as in 1864 and 1865, every time that he conversed with any of the political men from the banks of the Seine,—France would be wrong in taking umbrage at the increase in Prussian influence, and, the case occurring, at its territorial aggrandizement at the cost of the small States. Of what utility, of what help are then those small States, without a will, without strength, without an army? However far the designs and wants of Prussia could reach, they would necessarily stop at the Main; the line of the Main is its natural frontier; beyond that river, Austria will guard it, even its preponderance will increase, and there will thus always be in Germany two powers balancing one another. Good order will gain, and certainly France will lose nothing there, it will even draw immense advantages for its politics, for its movement in the world. In fact Prussia has an unfortunate, impossible configuration; *it wants a stomach* on the side of Cassel and Nassau, *it has a dislocated shoulder* on the side of Hanover, it is in the air, and this painful situation necessarily condemns it to follow entirely the policy of Vienna and St. Petersburg, to turn without rest in the orbit of the holy alliance. Better outlined, planted more solidly, having its members complete, it would be itself again, would have freedom of movements, the *freedom of alliances*, and what alliance more desirable for it than that with the French Empire? More than one question pending to-day, and almost unsolvable could have been settled then with perfect security: that of Venice, that of the Orient,—who knows? perhaps even that of Poland! Finally, if the possible aggrandizements of Prussia seem to be excessive, and to break the balance of strength what would prevent France from growing, from increasing itself in turn? Why should it not take Belgium, and *destroy there a nest of demagogy*? The cabinet of Berlin would not oppose it; *suum cuique*, that is the antique and venerable device of the Prussian monarchy.

All that said with liveliness, with spirit, with intelligence, accompanied by many an ingenious malicious remark, happy *mots* on men and things, on that chamber of lords at Berlin, for instance, composed of respectable *old fogies*, and the chamber of deputies, equally composed of old fogies, but not respectable, and on an august personage, the most respectable, but the greatest old fogy of all. M. de Bismarck had at Paris during these two months almost the same success which had accompanied his three years' sojourn on the banks of the Neva. The important men, however, were careful not to overdo it; they readily recognized in him all the qualities of a man of intellect, but they could not make up their minds to consider him a *serious man*.

In the last days of the month of June, the new representative of Prussia at the court of the Tuileries undertook a pleasure trip in the south of France. He visited in turn Chambord, Bordeaux, Avignon, Luchon, Toulouse, and made an excursion in the Pyrenees. "The chateau of Chambord," he wrote in a letter dated the 27th July, 1862, "answers, by its isolation, to the destinies of its possessor. In the great porticoes, in the splendid halls, in which formerly the kings with their mistresses held their court and their hunts, the playthings of the child of the Duke of Bordeaux now form the only furniture. The *concierge*, who served as my guide, took me for a legitimist, and *crushed* a tear in showing me a little cannon of his prince. I paid him a franc more than the tariff for this tear, although I feel but little desire to subsidize Carlism." At Bordeaux he rejoiced in having been able to "study *in the original*, and in the cellar of those great masters called Lafitte, Mouton, Pichon, Larose, Margaux, Branne, Armillac, etc.," who are generally known in Germany only through bad translations. He is delighted with his tour in the Pyrenees, but above all the Baths of Biarritz and St. Sébastian made him happy. He "devotes himself there entirely to the sun and to the salt water," he forgets politics, and knows neither journals nor dispatches. It was at this moment (the end of September, 1862) that he received from his sovereign the pressing call to go to Berlin. The elections had given a deplorable result, the immense majority of the new chamber belonged to the *progressionists*. They had not been able to decide at Berlin on the choice of the president of the future ministry,—"a cover for the government pot," as M. de Bismarck said; he was to fill those functions in the interim by taking the portfolio of foreign affairs. Burned by the sun of the South and fortified by the waters of the Gulf, "tanned and salted," the former aspirant for the inspectorship of dikes in a district of the Mark, started for his country to fill there the first position in the state. He only, so to speak, crossed Paris this time, but he remained there long enough to leave a characteristic *mot*, which summed up his entire programme. "Liberalism," said the designated chief of the Prussian government, in taking leave in the bureaux of the Quai d'Orsay, "liberalism is only nonsense which it is easy to bring to reason; but revolution is a force, which it is necessary to know how to use."

III.

UNITED ACTION.

I.

However great one wishes to make the share of genius in the work of M. de Bismarck, one cannot deny that a great part also comes from the unforeseen, from an extraordinary combination of circumstances, in one word, from that goddess Fortune whom the *minnesinger* of the Middle Ages did not cease to praise in song, whom Dante himself did not fail to extol in the immortal verses, "The course always luminous like a star in heaven, and the decree always hidden like a serpent in the grass." Without doubt, one can admire the extreme audacity with which the present chancellor of Germany has so often let fall from his hand the *iron dice of destiny*; one can even, to speak with the witty Abbé Galiani, suspect more than one cogged one in such a persistent "*pair royal of six*." It is not less true that in his long career as player, the president of the council at Berlin has occasionally met, in the most decisive moments, such marvelous luck as no human wisdom could foresee, that no political subtlety could prepare, and in which the hardy *punter* only had the merit, very considerable it is true, of not letting the vein exhaust itself or of using up the series. One of these magnificent strokes of luck, one of these perfectly prodigious events fell to the lot of William I. on his accession to power, in the month of January, 1863. This event laid the first foundations of his future greatness, it became the mainspring of his action in Europe, the Archimedean point from whence afterwards he raised up a world of daring projects, and it is necessary to bear it well in mind.

The ideal which M. de Bismarck had before him in taking into his hands the reins of state, was the aggrandizement, "the rounding off" of the monarchy of Frederick II. He had made the premature avowal of it at the time of his mission to Paris; he also declared it very frankly in the first sitting of the commission of the chamber at Berlin, scarcely a week after having been made minister (29th September, 1862). He certainly did not foresee in what measure he should realize this ideal, to what limits he could extend in Germany conquests which should cease to be "moral;" but he clearly foresaw that in this attempt he would find a resolute adversary in Austria, and he made up his mind to it.[39] The only question which engrossed him was the attitude which the other great Powers of Europe would maintain in view of certain events. Among them, he did not count England; with his rare political sagacity, he had early appreciated to what state of domestication and mildness that excellent school of Manchester had reduced the leopard formerly so fierce, and his conviction that proud Albion would not think of evil, and would even allow itself to be disgraced a little, was soon to be fully justified in the piteous campaign of Denmark. "England is far from entering into my calculations," he said in 1862, in a familiar conversation, "and do you know when I ceased to count her? From the day when she renounced of her free will the Ionian Islands; a Power which ceases to take and begins to surrender is a used-up Power." France and Russia remained, and it was not forbidden to think that, skillfully managed, these two states would favor to a certain degree the Prussian designs, or at least would not oppose them too strongly. On the banks of the Neva old grudges existed, sprung from the war of the Orient, imperfectly gratified by the war of Lombardy; the old relations between the Gottorp and the Hohenzollern, always cordial, had become more intimate than ever, thanks to the recent efforts of M. de Bismarck during his sojourn at St. Petersburg; finally, there was his friend Alexander Mikhaïlovitch, former colleague of Frankfort, so prepossessed in favor of the new minister of King William I., so well united with him in the hatred against Austria, and also so well warned against the "dangerous fiction" of a solidarity which should exist between all the conservative interests. On the banks of the Seine, in the Tuileries, still so much dreaded, there reigned a sovereign who, by dint of studying the general good of humanity, lost more and more the consideration of the French state, and whose vague vacillating regard it was not very difficult to dazzle, especially when one mirrored before him the "new right" and the affranchisement of Venice. Moreover, since the congress of Paris, there was established between the two cabinets of the Tuileries and St. Petersburg a "cordiality" which increased from day to day, and in which Prussia began to have a very large share: was there not ground to hope for the latter, in the enterprise which it meditated, a generous coöperation or at least a cordial neutrality of the two Powers so friendly to one another, and so unsympathetic towards the House of Hapsburg?

And yet such an enterprise was so profoundly contrary to the well understood interests and to the firmly rooted traditions of Russia as well as of France, the substitution in the centre of Europe of a great military and conquering monarchy in the place of a pacific confederation, and one "purely defensive," presented such manifest inconveniences, even such evident dangers for the security and equilibrium of the world, that the president of the council at Berlin could scarcely entertain as regards this matter too flattering hopes. The bitter resentments at the winter palace, and the sweet dreams at the palace of the Tuileries, could not long prevail against the reality of geography and the brutality of facts. Unless at Paris and St. Petersburg there was a complete want of statesmen with a little political discernment in their minds, a little national history in their souls, one might wager that the two governments, Russian and French, would not remain indifferent spectators to such a formidable overturning in the balance of the Continent. From well-wishing, their neutrality would not delay in becoming by degrees watchful and alarmed, would even change to declared hostility, as the

Prussian successes became marked, and it was this cordiality between the two empires, apparently so favorable to Prussia, which would then form another peril, facilitating prompt and decisive action against the Hohenzollern. Such being the situation of Europe at the beginning of the year 1863, what the new minister of William I. could wish for in his boldest combinations, invoke in his most golden dreams, was some unforeseen incident, some extraordinary event which should embroil in an irremediable manner the two emperors Alexander II. and Napoleon III., which should revive at St. Petersburg all the ancient rancor towards Vienna, which should permit Prussia to attach Russia to itself by ties stronger, more indissoluble, while preserving its necessary good relations with the cabinet of the Tuileries. A chimera! the boldest constructor of hypotheses would have certainly cried, before such demands; a problem of algebra and political alchemy unworthy of occupying a mind however frivolous! Well! chance, that providence of the fortunate of earth, did not delay to cause an event which realized to the profit of M. de Bismarck all the conditions of the indicated problem, which filled all the points of such a fantastic programme. "If Italy did not exist, it would be necessary to invent it," the president of the council at Berlin said later in 1865; in the month of January, 1863, he certainly did not think otherwise concerning the Polish questions.

History offers few examples of a fall so rapid, so humiliating, from the sublime to the odious and to the perverse, than was presented on the banks of the Vistula by that lamentable drama which, after two years of bitter revolutions, reached its final catastrophe in this month of January, 1863, as if to celebrate the joyful accession of M. de Bismarck to power. Certainly there was something very poetic and very exalted in those first manifestations from Warsaw, when a people so long, so cruelly tried, knelt one day before the castle of the lieutenant of the king in mute complaint, holding only the image of Christ, and demanding only "its God and its country!" The lieutenant of the king, who was no other than the old hero of Sebastopol, Prince Michael Gortchakof, had a horror of a conflict so unequal, so strange; he appealed to St. Petersburg, and,—miracle of divine pity,—from that place, whence for thirty years only orders of blood and punishment had gone forth, there came this time a word of clemency and reparation. A generous spirit then animated the governing and intelligent classes in Russia, they were under the influence of ideas of reform and emancipation, they desired the esteem of Europe, the friendship of France, and they had the very sincere desire to be reconciled with Poland. The Emperor Alexander II. sent his brother to Warsaw; a patriot of rare vigor of mind and of character took in hand the civil government; the instruction, the justice, the administration received a national impress; a modest but certain autonomy was assured for the country. The precepts of the most common wisdom, the instinct of preservation, the terrible lessons of the past, should have all counseled the Poles to profit by this good disposition of their sovereign, to put to proof the granted institutions, to accept with *empressement* the hand stretched out to them. In fact everything counseled them thus, but they bent to the anathema which the Holy Scriptures had long before pronounced against every kingdom which allows itself to be guided by women and children. The women and the youth of the schools resolved to continue to multiply the manifestations which had succeeded so well, and which, in ceasing to be spontaneous, became theatrical and sacrilegious. The European demagogy hastened to transport to a ground so overturned its emblems, its words of disorder, its secret societies, and its *instrumenta regni*; from afar, from the midst of the Palais Royal came recommendations "to leave the Catholic mummeries and to make barricades." The great conservative party showed itself cowardly there as elsewhere, as everywhere, as always; and, in wishing to save its popularity, it lost a whole population. One made a void around the brother of the emperor, around the patriotic minister, and this void was not slow in being filled by horror, by terror and crime. The government struggled in vain against a shadowy organization which enveloped it on all sides; it took contradictory and violent measures. The demagogy gained its cause; it succeeded in throwing into a powerless, foolish revolt an unhappy people which for a century seemed to have imposed on itself the task of astonishing the world by periodical resurrections, and of disheartening it at the same time by suicides, alas, not less periodical!

This criminal folly of a nation could only be equaled by the heedlessness not less culpable with which Europe encouraged and fanned it. Europe, which had not dared to touch the Polish question during the war of the Crimea, thought it opportune to sympathize, to trifle with it in this moment, the most ill-timed and the most desperate! Lord John Russell was the first to enter the lists. In 1861 he wrote the famous despatch to Sir J. Hudson, and persuaded himself and England that by it he had delivered Italy. The year afterwards, in the celebrated dispatch of Gotha, he conceived for Denmark a most original constitution in four parts, with four parliaments, and thus gave the signal for the dismemberment of the Scandinavian monarchy. This time he believed that he ought to recommend parliamentary institutions for Poland; and to the observation of the Russian ambassador that it would be difficult for the czar to favor on this point his Polish subjects over his own national ones, he naïvely asked why he would not extend the same benefit to all the Russias?[40] Count Rechberg, the fatal minister who then directed the external affairs at Vienna, experienced on his part the desire of showing himself compassionate; he accorded himself the malicious and very costly pleasure of paying the cabinet of St. Petersburg, in Polish coin, for the sympathies which this latter had shown for the Italian cause. As if Austria had not already suffered enough from the imaginary grievances of the Muscovites as regards the pretended "treason" during the war of the Crimea, it desired to give it very legitimate grievances by a very real "connivance"[41] in Gallicia; Gallicia became, in fact, the refuge, the depot of arms, and the place of revictualing for the insurgents of the kingdom.

It is just to acknowledge that the French government had long hesitated before starting on a way so perilous. From the first period of the Polish agitation, a note published in the "Moniteur" of the 23d April, 1861, had put the press and public opinion on guard against "the supposition that the government of the emperor encouraged hopes which it could not satisfy."

"The generous ideas of the czar," continued the note of the "Moniteur," "are a certain gauge of his desire of realizing the ameliorations of which the state of Poland admits, and we should wish that it be not hindered by irritating manifestations." The French government persevered in this sensible and perfectly amicable attitude towards the czar during the years 1861 and 1862, in spite of the interest which the Parisian press did not cease to take in the "dramatic" events of Warsaw, in spite of several animated debates which were held in the English parliament, and which were rather addressed to France than to Russia. The Britannic statesmen in fact had not thought it useless during those two years 1861 and 1862 to slightly embarrass the cabinet of the Tuileries in its very pronounced liking for the Russian alliance by the frequent and sympathetic evocation of the name of Poland. Lord Palmerston especially, in a very *witty* speech on the 4th April 1862, exalted the Poles, praised their "indomitable, inextinguishable, inexhaustible" patriotism, while not neglecting to recall to them the cruel deceptions which a French emperor had already caused them "at another epoch." Napoleon III. always resisted the unguarded emotions at home, as well as the selfish excitements from abroad. Even on the 5th February, after the breaking out of the fatal revolt, M. Billault, the minister-orator in the midst of the legislative body, harshly qualified the Polish insurrection as the work of "revolutionary passions," and insisted with force on the danger of "useless words and vain protestations;" but the noisy language of the English ministers, the enigmatical attitude of Austria, and lastly the military convention which M. de Bismarck concluded with Russia (8th February, 1863), and which he made public, ended by involving him. After having done so much for seven years to gain the Russian "cordiality," after having sacrificed to it almost all the fruits of the war of the Orient, Napoleon III. overturned brusquely a scaffolding so laboriously constructed, and prepared to organize against the government of the czar a *great European remonstrance* of which the first and terrible effect was naturally to increase in Poland the torrent of blood and tears. The general cry at Warsaw was then that the insurrection must last to justify the intervention of Europe,[42] that it was necessary to let as much Polish blood flow as sympathetic ink flowed from the chancellors' offices. One knows the deplorable issue of this great diplomatic campaign, which lasted nine months, and only served to demonstrate the profound disagreement between the Powers of the East. The foreign intermeddling wounded the pride of Russia, and impelled it to undertake against the Polish nationality a work of general, methodical, implacable extermination, and one from which it has never since desisted. However frivolous the diplomatic tourney of the Occidental Powers in favor of Poland was, the Russians did not the less think that they had been menaced with a moment of extreme peril, and that they had only escaped, thanks to the firmness of their "national" minister, to his patriotic courage, to his acute, dignified, and vigorous dispatches. Certainly the minister is, humanly speaking, very excusable for not having protested against a belief so flattering: he let it go, he let it be said that he had repulsed a new invasion and had "overcome Europe:" *scripsit et salvavit!* He was made chancellor, he received enthusiastic ovations from his compatriots, he became the idol of the nation by the side of M. Katkof and the sanguinary Mouravief. During a whole year he did not attend a single banquet in the most obscure corner of Russia without these three names "saviors and blessed" being celebrated by speeches, fêted in toasts, congratulated by telegrams, and, whatever repugnance the descendant of the Rourik and the foster child of the classical humanities must have felt in his spiritual tribunal at being thus constantly coupled with a fierce journalist and with a frightful executioner, he made the sacrifice to his love for his country and for popularity. In his well meaning ardor to receive the homage which came to him from all sides, he even so far forgot himself one day as to thank with a stereotyped smile the German nobility of the Baltic provinces for a diploma as honorary citizen which had been sent him, and the national party reproached him with a certain bitterness for the "culpable delight" to which he gave way on this occasion. Alexander Mikhaïlovitch had all the honors of the sad campaign of 1863; the profits of it went to another, to the former colleague of Frankfort, to the president of the council at Berlin, who was to find in it a solid and assured basis for all the great strategy in the future. We will show how the balance sheet of the situation, which created, towards the end of 1863, the *great European remonstrance* in the affairs of Poland, presented itself to the interests and the hopes of Prussia: the happy quiet of England was duly established; France and Russia were from this time forward embroiled, and in an irreparable manner; the resentment against Austria had grown stronger than ever at St. Petersburg, and also the Prussian minister had more than ever the right of counting on the grateful friendship, on the devotion to any extent, of Prince Gortchakof; lastly, it was not so difficult to foresee that after his signal check of Warsaw the Cæsar of the new right would hasten to cast his glances on Venice, to wish to "do something for Italy," and would therefore favor more benevolently "a young power of the North" in its enterprises against the Hapsburg, to whom the Napoleonic ideology had long since assigned "a great destiny in Germany."

It would, however, do too much honor to human genius to credit M. de Bismarck with a clear and precise view at first sight of all the favorable, even prodigious consequences, which the fatal insurrection in Poland was to bring him. Many circumstances seemed rather to indicate that, especially in the beginning, the Prussian minister only groped and sought his way in unfrequented paths. A curious matter, and which perhaps might give cause for reflection even to-day, M. de Bismarck, who had certainly studied Russia well, who had lived there for several years, and had just left it, seems to have very seriously doubted the strength of this empire in 1863, and doubted it so far that he did not even think it capable of conquering in that miserable affray with the unhappy Polish youth! He expressed his fears on this point before the plenipotentiaries of England and Austria,[43] and went so far one day as to become very confidential on this subject to the vice-president of the Prussian chamber, M. Behrend. "This question," said the minister of William I., towards the middle of the month of February, "can be solved in two ways: it is either necessary to stifle the insurrection promptly in concert with Russia, and to come before the Eastern Powers with an accomplished fact, or one can let the situation develop and aggravate itself; wait till the Russians are driven from the kingdom, or reduced to invoke aid, and then *proceed boldly and occupy the kingdom for Prussia*; at the end of three years all of it will be Germanized.... But that is a ball-room plan which you propose to me, cried out the stupefied vice-president (the conversation took place at a court ball). No, was the answer: I am speaking seriously of serious things. The Russians are tired of the kingdom, the Emperor Alexander himself told me at St. Petersburg."[44] This thought of recovering the line of the Vistula, lost since Jena, haunted more than once the mind of M. de Bismarck during the year 1863: let it be well understood, he did not wish to obtain the "rectification of the frontier" except with the consent of the Emperor Alexander II., but he did not neglect the means which could force to a slight extent such a solution. One of the most intimate confidants of the minister, and now the representative of Germany to the court of King Victor Emmanuel, M. de Keudell, proprietor of vast domains in the kingdom of Poland, profited by his relations with the prominent men of the unhappy country to advise them on several occasions to look to Berlin for help, to demand there, for instance, a *temporary* Prussian occupation which would render them not liable to Russian duty! In looking carefully into the history of this fatal insurrection, one will perhaps find there other Prussian agents, much more obscure, but also much more compromising than M. de Keudell. Did the president of the council at Berlin seriously hope to obtain so much from the "lassitude" of the Emperor Alexander and the friendship of the Prince Gortchakof?

Whatever these hopes or *arrière-pensées* were, M. de Bismarck used a restless ardor in making evident from the time of his *début* his absolute solidarity with the Russian vice-chancellor as opposed to the East. He offered him a military convention in the most spontaneous, even impetuous manner; he undertook his defense on every occasion, and did not cease to aid him faithfully, ardently, in passages of diplomatic arms with the cabinets of England, France, and Austria, experiencing with pleasure the first fire of the notes of M. Drouyn de Lhuys, supporting with joy the universal clamors of the press, responding with haughtiness to the interpellations of his parliament. The great men of the progressionist party understood nothing, on this occasion as on so many others, of the policy of their "Polignac;" they thought it inopportune, perilous, and demanded where the German interest was in all that? To which the Polignac replied one day in the chamber with this veiled and yet very significant image, that, "Placed before the chess-board of diplomacy, *the profane spectator* believes the game ended at every new piece that he sees advanced, and can even fall into the illusion that the player is changing his objective point."

Certainly M. de Bismarck did not change his objective point at all, and always had in mind the aggrandizement of Prussia; but it is evident that up to the autumn of that year, 1863, he had no well-fixed plan; he "moved his pieces" in different directions, and awaited the inspiration of chance to know from what side he should strike "the blow,"—from the Main, from the Vistula, or from the Elbe? He had aimed at Cassel for a moment, and had thrown himself with some bluster into the constitutional conflict of this country with the elector; he had even given on this occasion the pleasing spectacle of a minister intervening in a neighboring state to force the prince there to the most strict observation of parliamentary rule, while himself governing without regard for the constitution, and by means of taxes levied contrary to the vote of the chamber. Without speaking of the adventurous projects which were cherished at Berlin touching a possible rectification of frontier from the side of the Vistula, on the banks of the Elbe there was the old, everlasting question of the Duchies, a question hushed up since the treaty of London, but reawakened anew in 1859 in consequence of the events in Italy, and become even more dangerous since a famous dispatch, mortal for Denmark, which Lord John Russell, in a moment of inconceivable thoughtlessness, had issued from Gotha, the 24th September, 1862,— precisely the day of M. de Bismarck's accession to the ministry! The secondary States, the Diet of Frankfort, and M. de Rechberg himself, had become very ardent, and vied with each other in German patriotism in this cause of Schleswig-Holstein, a cause which at bottom they thought to be chimerical, and by which they only wished to embarrass Prussia, to convince it of "national lukewarmness." The temptation became great to take at their word the secondary States, the Diet of Frankfort, even Austria, to unite them against Denmark in a war which would give Prussia the magnificent port of Kiel, and would permit it, moreover, to try the "instrument" which King William I. "had been perfecting" for four years, ... provided that the war could be *localized*, and that the European Powers would not put themselves in the way as in 1848! The president of the council at Berlin did not entirely despair of succeeding by patient and wise manœuvres. He counted on the friendship of Prince Gortchakof, on different political constellations, finally on the strange confusion, and, to speak with Montaigne, on "the great hubbub of brains" which certain principles of the new right and of nationality had introduced into each chancellor's office of the Continent. He said to himself occasionally, that in this grave enterprise he would certainly have for a determined adversary only that good Lord Russell, who, after his fatal dispatch of Gotha, had again altered his mind, had even constituted himself the advocate, the protector, and the *mentor* of the unfortunate government of Copenhagen: such a partner did not greatly frighten the bold cavalier of the Mark.

At first, however, and as long as the negotiations on Poland lasted, the cavalier of the Mark thought that he ought to use prudence and simulate to the cabinet of Saint James extreme indifference on the subject of this "vexatious" affair of the Duchies. Nothing is more instructive than to follow in the state papers, as well as in the documents communicated to the *Rigsraad*, the intimate and almost daily effusions by which M. de Bismarck had been able to persuade, up to the last hour, not only Lord Russell and his envoy Sir A. Buchanan, but also M. de Quade, the Danish minister at the court of Berlin, that this question of Schleswig-Holstein was a *hobby* of the secondary States and of Austria, that Prussia was far from sharing those Teutonic effervescences and concupiscences, and that it would do all that lay in its power to calm, to allay them. The 14th October, 1863, two weeks after the Diet of Frankfort had decreed the federal execution in Holstein, M. de Bismarck stipulated in a conversation with the envoy of Great Britain, Sir A. Buchanan, to *prevent this execution*, if Denmark accepted the English mediation.[45] Denmark accepted it, and Lord Russell could at last breathe. Moreover, on the 6th November, 1863, M. Quade wrote from Berlin to his government: "The first minister of Prussia, be it on account of his personal views, or on account of the attitude taken by England, has put the affair in a position that *exceeds greatly all that one could have hoped*. I am not certain whether the question is regarded at Vienna with the same clearness and the same warmth (warmth for the interests of Denmark!) as it is here." Thus Sir A. Buchanan and M. Quade still judged the situation on the 6th November. But they were not slow in being brusquely awakened from their illusions by a despairing dispatch from the principal secretary of state, dated the 9th November, and couched in these terms: "If the information which reaches me is exact, M. de Bismarck no longer offers any objection (*n'oppose plus aucune objection*) to the federal execution in Holstein; the government of her majesty can only leave to Germany the responsibility of exposing Europe to a general war." The information was unfortunately only too correct, and the vexations of the good Johnny commenced.

Two important facts had taken place in the interval of three weeks which had passed since the conversation of the 14th October; in this interval, the cabinet of Saint James had abandoned to the Russian government the affairs of Poland, and the Emperor Napoleon III. had launched into the world a fantastic project of a congress *for the arrangement of all the pending questions*! Charmed in the highest degree with the aid which M. de Bismarck lent him in this month of October in the Danish difficulties, the principal secretary of state had at last decided to make him the sacrifice so often demanded, of the Polish question, even to recall by telegraph a courier, bearer of a very comminatory note addressed to the government at St. Petersburg, and to replace this missive by a most humble dispatch, which renounced all ulterior controversy on this subject (20th October).[46] On his part, the Emperor of the French, kept informed of these intrigues, profoundly vexed at this abandonment by England, and not being able to resolve to accept his check, nor, above all, to make the avowal of it without ceremony before the legislative body, had thought (5th November) of that call for a general congress which only increased the uneasiness of Europe, and especially inspired the chief of the foreign office with unspeakable fears. Not content with replying to the invitation of the cabinet of the Tuileries by a most bitter and offensive note, Lord John Russell bestirred himself to preserve the foreign courts from the contagion of the French idea; he almost entirely lost from view the dangers of Denmark, and only cared to combat the project of Napoleon III., a project assuredly without vitality, and which, in order to die its natural death, had no need of such a display of British forces. The president of the Prussian council thought that the moment had come to begin his game. The last shadow of an Eastern understanding disappeared; only the alliance of Russia and Prussia remained intact, unshaken, in the midst of the general disorder of the cabinets. No European concerted action for the protection of Denmark was to be feared. M. de Bismarck could now "no longer have any objection" to the federal execution in Holstein; and soon an unhoped-for event, one of those magnificent strokes of fortune, such as the minister of William I. has so often met with in his marvelous career, proved that he was decidedly in luck. The sudden death of King Frederick VII. (15th November, 1863) has something so tragical, so fatal to the destinies of Denmark, that it makes one think of one of the most disconsolate sayings that antiquity has bequeathed to us, that mournful cry of the historian: "*Non esse curæ deis securitatem nostram, esse ultionem.*"

This death gave in truth an entirely new turn to the Teutonic demands towards the unfortunate Scandinavian monarchy. Germany did not content itself with a federal execution in Holstein; it pretended not to recognize the sovereignty of the new king, Christian IX., in the Duchies, and wished to enthrone there that intriguing and treacherous family of Augustenburg from whom M. de Bismarck himself had lately obtained the retraxit for one million and a half *rixdalers* paid by the government of Copenhagen. And it was only from this moment that the plans of the minister of William I. seemed to be finally settled; decidedly it was from the side of the Elbe that Prussia was to begin to "round itself" and complete its unity! The resolution once made, M. de Bismarck carried it out with ardor, with audacity, with incomparable acuteness. This trial stroke was a master stroke; and the great Machiavelli would certainly have found a "divine" pleasure in contemplating the address, or, as he would have said, the *virtu* with which the cavalier of the Mark knew how, in the space of some weeks, to engross the attention of this poor Lord Russell; to encircle the Emperor Napoleon; to involve Austria in a distant expedition equally unjust and foolish; to make use of and at the same time oust the *Bund*; to strike the secondary States with terror and throw off their *protégé*; lastly, to take into his own hands the holy cause of the German country, and, according to the word of the Apostle, make himself all things to all men!

The spectacle which Europe presented at the beginning of the year 1864, was certainly one of the strangest and most painful that history has known. Two great Powers, jealous of one another, and even destined to soon fight in mortal combat for the spoils torn from their victim,—two great Powers, at once incited and cried down by a whole league of princes and peoples of Germany, attacked a feeble state, but nevertheless an old and glorious monarchy, and one whose existence was proclaimed by all the cabinets to be necessary to the balance of nations; they attacked it under the most futile pretext, in the name of a cause which the very chief of the coalition had formerly qualified as "eminently iniquitous, frivolous, disastrous, and revolutionary." It was, moreover, to punish King Christian IX. for his disobedience to the *Bund* that Prussia and Austria had charged themselves with this work of "justice;" and this work they inaugurated with a formal declaration of their own disobedience to the same *Bund*; they acted "as proxies for Germany," and entire Germany protested against the usurpation of the mandate! All these monstrous things Europe saw and let pass, this same Europe which, in 1848 at the time of the first German aggression against the Scandinavian monarchy, had not failed in its duty, and had fulfilled it nobly in spite of the great revolutionary tempest which might have served it as an excuse. The Powers were then unanimous in defending the weak against the oppressor; the Emperor Nicholas was in accord on this point with the Republic of General Cavaignac, and it was only the diplomats improvised by the "surprise" of February who had not shown at this time a sufficient knowledge of the conditions necessary for the equilibrium of the world. It has been reserved for the most tried statesmen, for chancellors grown old in the tradition and respect for treaties, for the representatives of regular and strong monarchies, to allow the consummation of a revolutionary work which the Bastide and Petetin would have thought their duty not to admit![47] Without doubt it is, above all, England who will bear before posterity the shame of the ruin of Denmark, for she it was who had taken in hand the cause of the Scandinavian kingdom, who had counseled, guided, reprimanded up to the last day, and who had solemnly declared *that in the moment of danger it (Denmark) should not fight alone*; it would, however, be unjust to pretend to completely exonerate the rest of the European Powers. More than one thoughtful and honest mind assigned at that time to this dismemberment of a monarchy in the nineteenth century all the import that another dismemberment had had in the preceding century, and foresaw from it with anxiety great overturnings and formidable catastrophes in the future. The *naïfs*, or, to speak with M. de Bismarck, the *profane*, could alone believe the game finished after this first stroke dealt to the right of nations, after this first exploit also of the marvelous "instrument" which the Prussian government had employed so many years and so much time to "perfect."

The cannon of Missunde was for the cavalier of the Mark what the cannon of Toulon had formerly been for a certain officer of Corsica, and this short campaign of the Duchies revealed many things to the future conqueror of Europe. He learned there that legitimate rights, sacred treaties, stipulated minutes, the sworn faith and many other old-fashioned things reputed inassailable were much more feeble and decaying than the poor fortresses erected by the Danes in the preceding ages, and, if Moltke and Roon made in this war a perfectly satisfactory trial of their needle gun, he could for his part prove the precious, unalterable qualities of his own instrument. It must be plainly said that during the whole of this expedition against Denmark, Prince Gortchakof did not cease to favor the Prussian minister by all means, to tender him with ardor, and very often privately, a helping hand at each new difficulty. His aid was absolute and the more efficacious since it took the appearance of a busy neutrality in search of a pacific arrangement. It was thus that he aided the president of the council at Berlin in forcing into the stubborn head of Lord Russell the equally specious and pleasing reasoning, that the occupation of Holstein by the federal troops would become a title of validity in the hands of the new King of Denmark. "M. de Bismarck told me," Sir A. Buchanan wrote on the 28th November, "that a federal execution would prevent any revolutionary movement in Holstein, and would be at the same time to a certain degree an *indirect recognition* of King Christian IX. as Duke of Holstein on the part of the Diet of Frankfort. His excellency affirmed that the alarming state of Germany forced him to proceed at once to the execution; but he could not or would not explain to me how such an execution could be a recognition of the sovereignty of King Christian, and could avoid the appearance of an occupation." Three days afterwards, the 1st December, Lord Napier wrote on his part from St. Petersburg: "The language of Prince Gortchakof makes me believe that he is persuaded that M. de Bismarck has *moderate views* in this question. The vice-chancellor is disposed to consider a federal execution, if it is well conducted, as a *preservative measure*. In his opinion, the federal troops, acting according to judicious instructions, will assure order and maintain the necessary distinction between the legislative and the dynastic question." "*I despoil, then I recognize!*" said M. de Bismarck by a logic belonging to him alone,[48] but which Prince Gortchakof shared at this moment, and which the two friends soon tried to apply also to Schleswig, after the chief of the foreign office had resigned himself to it in Holstein. "This morning the Russian vice-chancellor suggested to me," again wrote Lord Napier from St. Petersburg under date of the 11th January, "that one should bind Denmark to *admit* the occupation of Schleswig by the forces of Austria and Prussia under title of a *guarantee* given to these two Powers as regards the German population of the Duchy." Thus the state papers and the documents communicated to the *Rigsraad* continue to instruct and edify us; one does not find there a single insinuation or "suggestion" sent from the banks of the Spree against Denmark which was not at once reverberated on the banks of the Neva. And yet Denmark has always been the friend and the *protégé* of the empire of the czars! More than any other Power in the world, Russia was interested in preserving the liberty of the Baltic, in not letting the port of Kiel fall into the hands of Germany; more than any other Power, also, it was interested in remembering that Courland and Livonia talked German much more purely and harmoniously than Schleswig! Lastly, it was certainly the cause of the revolution against that of legitimate sovereignty which was engaged in this debate on the Eider; the old Nesselrode had declared so in a celebrated circular, and what would the Emperor Nicholas have said of such complacency for revolution on the part of a Russian chancellor? Alexander Mikhaïlovitch will yet cause the astonishment of history by the immensity of his gratitude towards M. de Bismarck.

II.

Thus was inaugurated, concerning Poland and Denmark, that common action of the two ministers of Russia and Prussia, which was to continue for so many years, and have such a considerable, such a disastrous influence on the affairs of the Continent. With this year 1863 the second period of the ministry of Prince Gortchakof commences, his second *term*, which was assuredly much less open to discussion. To the French "cordiality," properly dosed and taken in fact as a tonic, which had prevailed till then, the Prussian friendship, undeniably too passionate and too absorbing, succeeded. In fact, in this second period, Alexander Mikhaïlovitch no longer preserved that calm and reserved mind, and that intelligent egotism which made his fortune at the time of his intimacy with the Emperor Napoleon III.; he embraced all the opinions, every cause of his formidable friend at Berlin, unfortunately without possessing his astonishing flexibility of mind, his marvelous art of turning and twisting. Nothing, for instance, equals the address with which M. de Bismarck can, if necessary, forget a disagreeable past, and, above all, be unable to remember his wrong-doings toward others; in fact, he has a charming euphemism, he calls them *misunderstandings*. More than once, from the height of the tribune, he has adorned with this name his long and outrageous conflict against parliament which he sustained up to the war of 1866 against Austria (a little misunderstanding which cost 40,000 men their lives!). And how can one help admiring the affection, the enthusiasm, which he has inspired in that excellent Lord Russell, certainly the statesman whom he ridiculed and ill-treated the most in 1863, during the Danish contention? As for his Polish quarrels with the Eastern Powers in the same year (1863), he was the more ready to forget them as those very Powers felt that a great act of folly had been committed. He dictated to King William a most polite reply, full of tender souvenirs of Compiègne, in answer to the letter of Napoleon III. concerning the congress, and toward the end of the year he was already in touching accord with the cabinet of the Tuileries concerning the treaty of London, a treaty which guaranteed the entireness of the Danish monarchy, and which a circular of M. Drouyn de Lhuys now qualified as an *impotent work*! As regards Austria, he soon granted it full indulgence for its Polish error in the spring, and even forgave the very reprehensible enterprise which it attempted in the month of August at Frankfort, on *the day of the princes*. In the month of November he had already made it his companion and accomplice in the wars of the Duchies. Prince Gortchakof appeared in a very different light; he was never willing to pardon France and Austria for their intermeddling in the affairs of Poland, and remained immovable to every attempt at reconciliation. He knew no intimacy except with the cabinet of Berlin, and his former colleague of Frankfort became his only confidant and ally. The famous aphorism of 1856 then underwent an important modification; beginning with 1863, the Russian chancellor began to sulk while continuing to *meditate*, and the Achaeans have paid dearly for this spite of Achilles. The "sulks" of Alexander Mikhaïlovitch have been almost as fatal for Europe as the dreams of Napoleon III.

This Napoleonic policy regarding the affairs of Germany, at once reasonable and chimerical, ingenious and ingenuous, which he sincerely thought would work good, and which only accumulated disasters and ruin, seemed like a dream, a real *summer night's dream*. One day they had a sublime vision at the Tuileries: Italy was completed in its unity, Austria reëxalted, Prussia rendered more homogeneous, Germany more satisfied, Europe regenerated, and

France consolidated and glorious. All this only depended on a single hypothesis, but a hypothesis which did not exist, on a battle fought and won by the brave *Kaiserliks* always inured against this Prussian *Landwehr* which for half a century had not smelt powder, and it was on this frail skiff, on this "nut-shell," as the Puck of Midsummer Night's Dream had said, that the fortune of Cæsar and that of France was embarked! In fact, at this moment, all the world believed in the incomparable military superiority of Austria over its bold rival in Germany; no one admitted the possibility of a Prussian victory, still less a victory as decisive, as startling as that at Sadowa. "That was," M. Rouher said later, in a memorable session of the legislative body,— "that was an event which Austria, which France, which the military man, which the simple citizen had all considered as unlikely; for there was an universal presumption that Austria would be victorious and that Prussia would pay, and pay dearly, the price of its imprudence." This presumption, very real and universal at that time, remained the sole excuse of Napoleon III. before history, for that lamentable phantasmagoria which was announced to the world by the speech of Auxerre in the month of May, 1866, but whose origin goes back as far as the convention of September and the first journey of M. de Bismarck to France after his campaign in Denmark in the autumn of 1864.[49]

"I have at least one superiority over my conqueror," the Emperor of Austria, Francis I., said to M. de Talleyrand, the negotiator of the peace of Presburg, with a dignity not without keenness; "I can reënter my capital after such a disaster, while it would be difficult for your master, in spite of all his genius, to do the same thing in a similar situation." This curious *mot* displayed in a striking manner the profound, incurable vice of all Cæsarism. No more than the conqueror of Austerlitz, could Napoleon III. accept a check; he was obliged *to do great things*, condemned to success and prestige. Soon after the misadventures and the miscalculations in the affairs of Poland, of Denmark, and of the congress, he was forced to look out for a revenge, he cast his glances from north to south, "struck an attitude" by means of the convention of September, which seemed to be the preface of a new and great work. He was isolated in Europe, incensed against England, very much embarrassed in regard to Russia, more than cool with Austria, and it was with a certain inward trepidation that one saw M. de Bismarck hasten to France (October, 1864) at the first news of the convention concluded with the cabinet of Turin. Evidently "something was to be done for Italy;" without rancor, as without prejudices, the president of the Prussian council came to renew the conversations broken off two years before at the time of his short mission to Paris.

He added nothing to the truth; he only affirmed that his alliance with the Hapsburg in the war against Denmark had been a simple incident, and he allowed to be clearly seen his desire to keep for Prussia the countries recently conquered on the Elbe in the name of the Germanic Confederation. For the rest, he only varied the ancient theme on the inevitable imminent duel between Berlin and Vienna, on the advantages which Italy might gather from it, on the advantage that would accrue to France, having Prussia, with a better defined and firmer outline, as its natural, unfailing ally in all the questions of *civilization* and *progress*. Such expressions, coming from a minister who had shown his character in the campaign of the Duchies, now met an auditory much more attentive than that of 1862. Without yet taking him for a perfectly *serious* man, they began to recognize in him the qualities of a useful man, of a man of the future, whom Italy should cultivate with care, whom France, for its part, should watch carefully, encourage, and manage. The leaders of the imperial democracy, Prince Napoleon first of all, showed themselves especially taken with the prospectives which were opened to them. A distinguished member of this group, a diplomat reputed to be acute above all, and whose name even allied him to the Italian cause, was sought out in his retreat and placed at the head of the mission at Berlin, elevated now to an embassy. Another member of the "party of action," equally unattached for some time, a former ambassador at Rome, was not long in being recalled into the councils of the empire: by the side of M. Rouher, he was destined to form there a useful counterpoise to the slightly "antiquated" ideas of M. Drouyn de Lhuys. Finally, on the other side of the Alps, at Turin, a general, well known for his "Prussomania," had taken in hand the direction of political affairs on the 23d September. Each of these personages,—M. Benedetti, M. de La Valette, General La Marmora,—will have his *rôle* and his day in the great drama of 1866.

At this time, however, in the autumn of 1864, no plan was fixed or even discussed: one had only come as yet to simple confidences, to vague and fleeting conversations, to that which, in diplomatic language, one had not even dared to call an exchange of ideas; but the impression which the Prussian minister obtained from this rapid journey to France was sufficiently encouraging for him soon to launch that circular of the 24th December, 1864, which became the point of departure for his action against Austria. It was in this circular, in fact, that M. de Bismarck broached for the first time the question of the countries of the Elbe, which he well knew to be a question of war. Six months before, in the peremptory declaration made the 28th May, 1864, in the midst of the conference of London, Austria and Prussia had demanded the "reunion of the Duchies of Schleswig and of Holstein in a single state under the sovereignty of the hereditary Prince of Augustenburg," and the cabinet of Berlin took care to add then that this prince had, "in the eyes of Germany, *the greatest right* to the succession; that his recognition by the *Bund* was consequently assured, and that, moreover, he would reunite the *indubitable suffrages* of the great majority of the population of this country."

Quite different were the sentiments of the Prussian minister towards the end of the same year, some time after his return from Paris. In a circular dispatch addressed to the German courts, the president of the council of Berlin declared now (24th December, 1864) that grave doubts assailed his mind touching the titles of the Duke of Augustenburg, that several serious competitors, such as the Princes of Oldenburg and Hesse, had arisen in the interval;[50] that in the midst of such multiplied and such confused claims he was perplexed; that his conscience was not sufficiently enlightened on this point of right; that he felt the need of meditating and of "consulting the legists!"

The world knows the magnificent decree which the "legists"—the syndics of the crown—did not delay in pronouncing, as well as the conclusions which the scrupulous minister conscientiously drew from them. There were judges at Berlin, and they proved it in overruling all parties, in declaring them all badly grounded in their pretensions: Hesse, Oldenburg, Brandenburg, Sonderburg, Augustenburg, none of them had the right of succession to Schleswig-Holstein. The King of Denmark alone had the titles! But as the King of Denmark had been forced by the war to abandon the provinces of the Elbe to the sovereigns of Prussia and Austria, M. de Bismarck concluded therefrom that the two monarchs could dispose of their "property" as they wished, without any intervention of the *Bund*, and he demanded of the Emperor Francis Joseph the cession of his part of the conquest for ready cash. The Prussian minister made this impudent demand in an arrogant dispatch, full of menaces, dated the 11th July, 1865, from Carlsbad, from the very place where the old King William had come to enjoy the Austrian hospitality during the season. The alarm was great for some weeks. M. de Bismarck made no mystery of the negotiations which he entered upon with Italy; he said to M. de Gramont "that far from dreading the war, he desired it by all means;" some days after, he even declared to M. de Pfordten, president of the council of Bavaria, "that Austria could not sustain a campaign, that it would suffice to strike a single blow, to fight a single and great battle from the side of Silesia to obtain satisfaction of the Hapsburg." In reality, he only wished to sound the ground and to make a careful examination. At this moment he was not yet sufficiently sure of the disposition of the Emperor Napoleon to dare to risk the great cast; he also wanted time to persuade the pious Hohenzollern to pronounce the "God wills it!" of a fratricidal war. He had to content himself with that convention of Gastein (14th August, 1865) which was only a provisional arrangement, yet the first breach made in the rights of the *Bund*, and like an indirect consecration of the conclusions which he had pretended, to draw from the decree pronounced by the famous syndics of the crown.

The very day on which he signed this equivocal transaction at Gastein, M. de Bismarck wrote his wife a short note as follows: "For several days I have not found a moment of leisure to write you. Count Blome is again here, and we are doing our best to preserve peace and stop up the crevices of the building. Day before yesterday I devoted an entire day to hunting. I think that I wrote you that I returned disgusted from my first expedition; this time I at least killed a roe, but I saw nothing else during the three hours that I devoted without cessation to experiments on all sorts of insects, and the noisy activity of the cascade below me drew from my heart the cry: '*Little brook, leave there thy murmur.*'[51] After all, it was a very good shot made across the precipice. The animal, killed instantly, fell with its four feet in the air from a height of several church steeples into the torrent at my feet." After all, he no more missed the shot than when he slew, in order that he might no longer be the cherished candidate of the *Bund*, the poor Augustenburg, and made the little Duchy of Lauenberg fall into the Prussian game-bag! This fact of the chase and of diplomacy even had an extraordinary reëcho in Germany, in France, and even as far as Lord Russell, who experienced the shock. The principal secretary of state insisted on the honor of associating himself with M. Drouyn de Lhuys in a very eloquent protest against the arrangements made at Gastein, and the iron-clad squadron of England, which had not appeared in the Baltic since the war of Denmark, came this time at least to pay a courteous visit to the French fleet at Cherbourg. There, however, the demonstration of the two Powers of the East limited itself; M. de Bismarck could enjoy in peace his triumph and the title of count which the fortunate campaign of 1865 brought him.

Is it admissible to depart from the gravity of history to describe still another incident of Gastein, a little *genre* picture of manners which was much talked of at this epoch, and even became the object of confidential explanations between the president of the Prussian council and a devoted friend, all extremely devout? And why not, since the letter of M. de Bismarck to M. André (de Roman) concerning Mlle. Pauline Lucca is one of the most curious pages of his familiar correspondence, if it throws light in a very picturesque manner on that vast and bald forehead on which the hand of King William had just placed the coronet of a count. Well, in the midst of those political negotiations and the deer hunts, M. de Bismarck found time at Gastein to be photographed in a romantic attitude with Mlle. Lucca, first *cantatrice* of the royal opera at Berlin. The photographs caused a certain scandal on the banks of the Spree; the leaders of *the party of the cross* were especially moved at the thermal license which the former Levite of the tabernacle, the fervent disciple of MM. Stahl and de Gerlach, took. M. André (de Roman) was perfectly willing to accept the *rôle* of Nathan in the Bible, and, in a sermon written in entire confidence, he did not limit himself to talking of the Bethsabea of the opera; he also spoke some well-chosen words touching the reparation by arms which the first minister of Prussia had but lately wished to impose on the good Doctor Virchow, the very learned and very peaceful discoverer of *trichina*. M. André found that that was not the conduct of a true Christian; he did not conceal that his old friends sighed at not seeing their Eliakim assist at divine service, and even began to be rather uneasy at the state of his soul. It was to such a sermon that M. de Bismarck replied by the confidential letter which follows, and which a lucky indiscretion has since given to the public, a letter assuredly very characteristic, and which makes one think once more of Cromwell, whose memory has been so often called forth in the course of this study:—

> "DEAR ANDRÉ,[52]—Although my time is very much restricted, I cannot, however, refuse to reply to a summons addressed to me by an upright heart, and in the name of Christ. I am profoundly pained at scandalizing Christians who have faith, but I have the certainty that it is an inevitable circumstance in my position. I will not yet speak of the parties who are necessarily opposed to me in politics, and who not the less count in their midst a great number of Christians, who have far preceded me in the way of salvation, and with whom, nevertheless, I am obliged to be in conflict on account of matters which, in my estimation as well as theirs, are terrestrial; I appeal only to what you yourself said: 'That nothing that is omitted or committed in the elevated regions remains hidden.' Where is the man who, in a similar situation, would not cause scandal, rightly or wrongly? I will grant you much more still, for your expression 'does not remain hidden' is not exact. Would to God that apart from the sin the world knows I had not upon my soul others which remain unknown, and for which I can only hope for pardon in my faith in the blood of Christ! As a statesman, I even think that I use far too much consideration; according to my idea I am rather cowardly, and that perhaps because it is not so easy in the questions which come before me to arrive always at that clearness at the bottom of which confidence in God exists. He who reproaches me with being a political man without conscience, wrongs me; he should first commence by himself testing his conscience on the field of battle. As regards the matter of Virchow, I have long since passed the age in which, on similar questions, one seeks counsel from flesh and blood. If I expose my life for a cause, I do it not

only in this faith which I have fortified by a long and painful combat, but also by fervent and humble prayer before God; this faith, the word of man cannot shake, not even the word of a friend in the Lord, and of a servant of the church. It is not true that I have never attended a church. For just seven months, I have been either absent from Berlin or ill; who then can have made the observation on my negligence? I willingly agree that it has often happened, much less for want of time than for considerations of health, especially in the winter; I am always ready to give more detailed explanations to all those who consider it their vocation to be my judges in this matter: as for you, you will believe me without other details of medicine. As to the Lucca photograph, you would probably judge less severely, if you knew to what chance it owes its origin. Besides, Mlle. Lucca, although a *cantatrice*, is a lady whom the world has never, any more than it has me, reproached with illicit relations. Nevertheless, I would have certainly taken care to keep away from the glass pointed at us, if I had in a tranquil moment reflected on the scandal which so many faithful friends would find in this jest. You see by the details into which I enter that I consider your letter as well meant, and that I do not dream in any way of placing myself above the judgment of those who share with me the same faith; but I expect from your friendship and from your Christian knowledge which you commend to others, in future circumstances, more indulgence and charity in their judgments: all of us have need of them. I am of the great number of sinners to whom the glory of God is wanting; I do not hope the less with them that in His mercy, He will not withdraw from me the staff of the humble faith by the aid of which I seek to find my way in the midst of the doubts and dangers of my position; this confidence, however, should not render me deaf to the reproaches of friends, nor impatient at proud and harsh judgments."

Let us lock up the hair shirt with the discipline; let us only think of the diplomat in tunic and helmet, of the "iron count" (*der eiserne Graf*), as his people soon called him, and let us look at the disposition of France towards him at the moment when, after having left the rugged valley of Gastein, he prepared to visit the delightful region of Biarritz, to salute, interrogate, divine, and ... cast down the sphinx!

In the councils of the empire the debates had become from day to day sharper between the ancients and the moderns, between those zealous for the new right and the partisans of a more circumspect and traditional policy, in proportion as the Austro-Prussian conflict had grown more bitter and aggravated. The ardent ones would have willingly concluded an offensive and defensive alliance with Prussia. They showed the irresistible movement which was drawing Germany towards unity, and the advantages which France would reap by favoring this evolution in place of opposing it, by attaching to itself by the ties of an eternal recognition the Piedmont of Germany, as it had already done with that of the peninsula. Passionate friends of Italy, and still more violent adversaries of Austria, this bulwark of the reaction, of legitimacy and of temporal power, they cherished in the kingdom of Frederick the Great the incontestable representative of civilization, and trembled at seeing it going toward certain defeat in an unequal contest with the *Kaiserliks*. To hear them, the united action of France, Italy, and Prussia was not too much to preserve the cause of progress and to place Europe on new and immovable bases. Why, however, should not Belgium be the legitimate recompense of the French efforts in favor of Germany, as Savoy had been in consequence of the constitution of the kingdom of Italy, and how decline a combination in which each of the three nations representing *par excellence* modern ideas on the Continent was called to complete its respective unity?

Very different was in this respect the sentiment of the "ancients," the statesmen of the old school, of a whole political group of which M. Drouyn de Lhuys was in the cabinet the most authorized and clearsighted, if not the firmest. First casting aside all desire for Belgium, as a certain cause of a formidable conflict with England, they asserted the absolute impossibility of finding for France a compensation, however small it might be, in proportion to the injury which the unification of Germany would cause it. Without misunderstanding the Germanic aspirations for a federal reform, for a more homogeneous and united constitution, they asked what obligation France was under to hasten such a work, and if in any case it were not more desirable that such a transformation should be accomplished by the enlightened and pacific classes, by the federal diet, even by Austria,—always respecting acquired rights and particular sovereignties,—rather than by a power peculiarly military, bureaucratic, and centralistic? Was not that also the almost general wish of the other side of the Rhine, of the dynasties as well as of the chambers, of the princes as well as of the peoples, and had not the pretension of Prussia, among others, of confiscating for its own profit the conquest of Denmark aroused the consciences of all of them? Only the press of France and Italy which persisted in speaking of "the Piedmontese mission" of the Hohenzollern; on the banks of the Main and Elbe, every one rejected this pretended mission, and even the *National-Verein*, brought into contempt some time before while demanding "a united Germany with a Prussian point," did not the less repudiate M. de Bismarck, and declared him unworthy of taking in hand so holy a cause. As to the danger of seeing Prussia succumb in the conflict, and thus render the Hapsburg all powerful in Germany, there was a very simple means of preventing such an eventuality, that was to refuse the government of Berlin any aid in the enterprise which it meditated. However bold in truth M. de Bismarck was, it was not doubtful that he would never dare to defy Austria and its allies of the *Bund* in the face of a formal veto of France, which at the same time would take from him all hope of aid from Italy.[53] The plan to follow in such events seemed then as clearly indicated as singularly easy. Without mixing directly in German affairs, without wounding at all the Teutonic susceptibilities, one could oppose an insuperable barrier to Prussian ambition; one had only to maintain the *statu quo*. Such a policy would inevitably have the warm support of England, and would encourage the resistance of Austria and the secondary States. Without doubt, the Venetian question would be thus warded off; but, besides that, the peace of Europe and the greatness of France were well worth "the pearl of the Adriatic;" it was not forbidden to have great hopes for the city of lagoons from the progress of time, and from the good relations preserved and augmented between France and Austria.

Generally silent in the midst of these contradictory debates, loving, moreover, to plan beneath the passions and agitations of his surrounding counselors in the serenity of a calm and meditative intelligence, the Emperor Napoleon III. slowly ripened a project which seemed to him to sufficiently take into consideration the different arguments of the two sides, and which, moreover, well answered the recommendation made by him at about the same time to his minister of foreign affairs, *inertia sapientia*! Italy naturally was of more real interest to him than to M. Drouyn de Lhuys; that was a passion, perhaps indeed a youthful contract, and it was even so with the Empress Eugenie, who had become ardent for the affranchisement of Venice since the entry of M. de La Valette to the ministry, also since the day when M. the Cavalier Nigra had turned some couplets full of graceful allusions to a gondola which she had had made for the lake of Fontainbleau. Not less inveterate, but much more fatal, was Louis Napoleon's liking for the country of Blücher and Scharnhorst; the "great destinies" of the monarchy of Brandenburg in Germany formed one of the articles of his cosmopolitan faith. "*The geographical position of Prussia is badly defined!*" as he cried out the following year, at a solemn moment, and in a document too much forgotten.[54] He certainly did not intend to destroy the empire of Hapsburg, and allow the Hohenzollern to rule from the Sound to the Adriatic, as such a course would have readily recognized the *intransigeans* and the know-nothings of the principle of nationality. A strong appreciator of logic in the affairs of states, and in that (in that alone, perhaps!) truly French spirit, the former prisoner of Ham would have willingly constructed an essentially Protestant Prussia opposed to a traditionally Catholic Austria in the centre of Germany, leaving for the secondary States an intermediary and fluctuating situation in a religious as well as in a political point of view. An augmented and rounded Prussia on the Elbe and the Baltic, and thus rendered "stronger and more homogeneous in the North," seemed to him a useful combination, almost indispensable, counterbalancing Russia, and it was perfectly just that in exchange for new and vast Protestant territories, which it would acquire, the monarchy of Frederick II. should lose Silesia, a Catholic country and former patrimony of Hapsburg, that it should also renounce the Catholic provinces of the Rhine, situated too far outside of its natural orbit. "One would thus maintain for Austria its great position in Germany," above all its position as a great Catholic state, and the return of Silesia would be for the Emperor Francis Joseph an ample compensation for the Venetian province which he would cede to King Victor Emmanuel. For the secondary States of the Confederation, one would mediatize for their profit several of the little unimportant princes; one would add to them, perhaps, as a new member of the *Bund*, a new State composed entirely of Rhenish provinces taken from Prussia; one would assure for them, in any case, "a closer union, a more powerful organization, a more important *rôle*," which the great leaders of the party of Würzburg, the advocates of the *triad*, MM. de Beust, de Pfordten, and de Dalwigk, did not cease to demand. A curious fact, in these vast projects which embraced the world and which tended to determine and to satisfy the "legitimate wants" of Italy, Prussia, Austria, the Germanic Confederation, the only obscure question, and never decided in the mind of the French sovereign, was that of the compensations which, in the presence of this universal alteration, he could claim for his own country. He did not dare to touch the problem of Belgium; it would be, he declared very honestly, "an act of brigandage."[55] Neither did he deceive himself on the impossibility of annexing important Germanic territories; generally he stopped at the idea of a simple rectification of frontiers on the side of the Saar and the Palatinate, and of the neutralization of the German line of fortresses on the Rhine. Even reduced to these modest proportions, the end did not seem to him to be less worthy of being ardently pursued, in view of the very great and moral satisfaction France would find in the achievement of its work in Italy, and in the rational ordering of affairs in Germany.

Moreover, that which, in the situation in which he was engaged, especially flattered his instincts, generous at bottom and vaguely humanitarian, was that he hoped to reap considerable advantages for his own country, for the entire universe, without any necessity of drawing the sword, without spilling a drop of blood, "by moral force only," by the ascendancy of the name of France. He was resolved to "remain in a watchful neutrality," not to leave it except in the extreme case of the too complete victories of one of the belligerents menacing "the overthrow of the equilibrium and the modification of the map of Europe for the benefit of a single Power." He proclaimed it very loudly, on all occasions, and gloried in such "disinterested" policy,—a very strange policy, however, and which, according to the very judicious *mot* of Prince Napoleon, declared itself in advance *hostile to the conqueror.* "You have changed the address of your letter," said with fine raillery the conqueror of Austerlitz to the Prussian envoy who brought him the congratulations of his sovereign; the nephew of Napoleon I. acted in such a manner that he could not change the address, alienating in advance the still unknown conqueror. It is true that he believed he knew him, that, with all the world, he saw him in the Emperor of Austria, and that he counted on making with him preventive arrangements. Moreover, even should the army of William I. show itself much superior to the general opinion one had of it,—and, more perspicacious in that than his followers, he fully admitted such an eventuality,—still he only saw in this case a long and fatiguing conflict which would exhaust the two parties and would allow him more easily to intervene as judge of the combat and as protector of the right. He thus hoped, in any case, at his time and at his convenience, to be able to pronounce a word of peace, of equity, and of equilibrium, and he was convinced that "this word would be heard." It was important for the moment that Prussia should begin the combat, and to decide it in its favor it would be necessary for it to procure the alliance of Italy. It was also necessary to carefully avoid with the court of Berlin an untimely debate on the combinations and compensations to come; the least insistence on this delicate point might wound the patriotic feelings of William I., cool his warlike ardor, destroy in the embryo a world of great things, *novus rerum ordo*! It was better to ask nothing, to promise nothing, to compromise nothing. Moreover, what use in demanding notes of a bankrupt, taking sureties from one whose fate seemed so little assured, and whom, according to all probabilities, one would soon have to protect, to defend against too hard conditions which its Austrian conqueror would wish to impose on it?

So complicated and specious as was the strategy planned by the Emperor of the French, there is no doubt that M. de Bismarck penetrated it from the beginning, that he divined it, foresaw it in some way, even before it was completely fixed in the mind of its author, and we have on this subject a most striking proof. In the month of August, 1865, at the time when the first conferences were held between the two governments of Prussia and Italy against Austria, which were soon to interrupt the brusque conclusion of the armistice of Gastein, M. Nigra wrote to General La Marmora, being evidently inspired by the observations of his Prussian colleague at Paris, Count Goltz: "The cabinet of Berlin would not wish that, war once declared and begun, France should come, like the Neptune of Virgil, to dictate peace, lay down conditions, or convoke a congress at Paris."[56] Thus all is foreseen in those few lines written long before Biarritz, all up to that congress which a Napoleon III. would naturally not fail to extol one day or another, and which he in fact was to advance in the month of May, 1866. "The difficulty consists, then," continues M. Nigra in his dispatch, "in obtaining from France a promise of absolute neutrality. Will, or can, the Emperor Napoleon make this promise? *Will he give it in writing as Prussia wishes it?*" This promise of *absolute* neutrality M. de Bismarck certainly did not obtain at Biarritz (October, 1865), still less was there a question of any engagement *in writing*; but he learned there from august lips that Italy was right in wishing to "complete its unity," that it should not fail to profit by the first favorable occasion,—that France, for its part, was resolved to respect Germany, not to contradict on the other side of the Rhine the "national aspirations." Unless the map of Europe was to be modified to its detriment, France would preserve the neutrality, and this neutrality would not be other than "favorable" to a combination in which the interests of Italy were engaged. It is allowable to recall a reminiscence which is like a fragment of the conversations of Biarritz in this curious declaration, made six months afterwards by the president of the council of Prussia to General Govone,[57] "that apart from the profit which he might find in it, and with no *regard for principles*, the Emperor of the French would sooner approve the great war for the German nationality than the war for the Duchies of the Elbe!"

What, during his sojourn at Biarritz, could hardly have escaped a sagacious observer like M. de Bismarck, was the hold which his profound attachment for the country of Cavour and Manin had on the mind of Louis Napoleon; there was the key to the position, the real word of the Sphinx, and that certainty acquired, compensated in the eyes of the Prussian minister for many still disquieting doubts, made him pass over many a reticence of the august, taciturn man.[58] For certain reasons, he could even congratulate himself on the reserve which he preserved towards him, on the care which he took to avoid a discussion in detail; that released him on his part from any precise engagement, from any premature offer; it allowed him to confine himself to generalities, to make fantastic journeys over spaces and centuries,—and he neglected nothing. He spoke of Belgium and a part of Switzerland as the necessary and legitimate complement of French unity,—of the common action of France and Germany for the cause of progress and humanity,—of a future accord between Paris, Berlin, and Florence, even London and Washington, to conduct the destinies of Europe, to regulate those of the entire world, to lead, for instance, Russia to its real vocation in Asia and Austria to its civilizing mission on the Danube. How many times was seen on this henceforward historical coast of the Gulf of Biscay, the Emperor Napoleon slowly walking and leaning on the arm of Prosper Mérimée, while the president of the Prussian council followed him at a respectful distance, haranguing, gesticulating, and generally receiving for reply only a dull and slightly incredulous look, and how the thought remains to-day sadly fixed on this strange group of the romantic Cæsar, the romancing Cesarean and the terrible realist who, very obsequious at this moment towards his imperial host, four years later was to harshly assign him the prison of Wilhelmshoehe! From time to time Napoleon III. caused the author of "Colomba" to understand by a furtive pressure of the arm how amusing he found this diplomat with the futile imagination, this representative of a more than problematical Power, who so cleverly dismembered Europe and distributed the kingdoms. "He is crazy!" he even whispered one day in the ear of his companion; but, before recriminating a remark so cruelly expiated since, one can well recall the following passage of a dispatch which General Govone wrote the year after: "In speaking to me of Count Bismarck, M. Benedetti told me that he was, so to speak, a *maniacal* diplomat,"[59] and M. Benedetti took care to add that he had long known his man, that he had "followed" him for nearly fifteen years!

Is it not necessary in fact to be a little *maniacal*, to have that "little grain of folly" which Molière attributes to all great men, and which Boerhaave believes he finds in every great genius,[60] to launch the monarchy of Brandenburg into an adventure so eminently perilous as that of 1866? The minister of William I. remarked correctly, however, at Paris, that he would perhaps meet a second Olmütz, and his biographers quote a characteristic speech of his, "that death on the scaffold is under certain circumstances neither the most dishonorable nor the worst of deaths." In a diplomatic point of view, his only assurance was the profound love of Napoleon III. for the Italian cause, and after as before Biarritz the "Neptune of Virgil" arose, always menacing, free to pronounce his *quos ego*: the war once declared and begun, France could always dictate peace, lay down the conditions or convoke a congress. The whole point, then, was not to allow the benevolent neutrality of Napoleon III. the time to work those infallible changes; all that was necessary was to act quickly and well, to strike a blow at the beginning which should dictate peace to Vienna and respect to Paris; victory was only possible at this price! But, however, there has always been luck and misfortune in the affairs of this world,—"the all powerful God is capricious," according to the singular expression of M. de Bismarck at one of the most solemn moments,[61]—how far could one count on an army formed only a few years before, and which, as well as its chiefs, had never gone through a great campaign? An extraordinary circumstance in truth, and one which will never cease to be an astonishing fact in history, of the two eminent men who took upon themselves more especially the terrible responsibility of commencing the combat, neither of them had had a superior command, or had made his name illustrious on a historical field of battle! Before 1864, the only campaign in which General Moltke had ever assisted was that of Syria between the Turks and the Egyptians; in 1864 he had borne arms against his own country in that invasion of Denmark which was certainly not calculated to produce Turennes and Bonapartes. General de Roon had formed a part in 1832 of a "corps of observation" which watched the French besieging Antwerp, and had only distinguished himself since by books of military geography. "After all that we have heard said of these officers," General Govone wrote from Berlin on the 2d April, 1866, "the army is not enthusiastic for the war against Austria; there is rather in its ranks sympathy for the Austrian army. I know well that the war, once declared, the army will be electrified, and will do its duty bravely; but it is neither a spur nor a support for the policy which Count de Bismarck wishes to make prevail."[62]

As to public opinion in Germany, as to the national sentiment of the blond children of Arminius, far from finding there a "spur and support," the Prussian minister only met with repugnance and imprecations. All the Napoleonic ideology was necessary to see in the conflict which was preparing "the great war for German nationality," all the blindness of the authoritative and democratic press in France was necessary to assimilate the enterprise of M. de Bismarck on the other side of the Rhine to the work of Cavour in the peninsula. The German nationality was neither oppressed nor threatened from any quarter; none of the States of the *Bund* groaned under a foreign dominion; the ruling houses in Hanover, Saxony, Württemberg, Bavaria, etc., were indigenous, antique and glorious, popular and liberal dynasties; the larger part of these countries enjoyed a constitutional and parliamentary system unknown at Berlin; the cities of Frankfort, Hamburg, Lubeck, Bremen were even republics! To-day, when success has obscured the conscience and even the memory of contemporary generations, and when a sad philosophy of history is always on the point of justifying the present by falsifying the past, one is prepared to recognize the "providential," irresistible movement which drew Germany towards Prussian unity, and to almost call with M. de Bismarck the campaign of 1866 "a simple misunderstanding." The truth is that this campaign was a civil war, a fratricidal combat, and it was not only the Prussian people which repudiated the thought and even cursed its author on the eve of Sadowa. On the eve of Sadowa, the principal cities of the kingdom, Cologne, Magdeburg, Stittin, Minden, etc., sent addresses to the sovereign in favor of peace and against "a baleful policy of the cabinet," the great corporation of merchants of Koenigsberg, the city of Kant, even decided to no longer celebrate the king's birthday. On his arrival at Berlin, General Govone wrote: "Not only the upper classes, but even the middle classes are against or unfavorable to the war. This aversion shows itself in the popular journals; there is no hatred of Austria. More than that, although the chamber has neither great prestige nor great popularity, the debates still create adversaries for Count de Bismarck." Two months later, and at the approach of hostilities, he wrote: "Unfortunately the public mind in Prussia does not awaken in a perceptible manner, even face to face with a situation so decisive, so vital for the country."[63]

It is true that none of these obstacles were of a nature to disturb the president of the council at Berlin in his resolutions, nor to retard the course which was traced out. On the contrary there were quite other difficulties and falterings against which he stumbled in the court itself, with the old fogies of Potsdam, especially with his sovereign, and in many a circumstance the "iron count" could well say, like a certain cardinal, "that the cabinet of the king and his *petit-coucher* embarrassed him more than all Europe." In spite of the faith of William I. in his "mission from above," in spite of the equally strong resolution to preserve at any price his good port of Kiel, he did not the less look upon an open conflict with the Emperor of Austria, an act of hostility declared against this German sovereign who bore the venerated name of Hapsburg, as the last of extremities, and he did not wish to have recourse to it until after having exhausted all the means of an amiable settlement. For the extreme case, and in opposition to Napoleon III., he also greatly preferred the little war for the Duchies to "the great war for German nationality;" but what he disliked above all things, was the idea of a compact with Italy, a veritable compact, offensive and defensive, in place of a "generic" treaty with a vague declaration of *alliance and friendship*, and only destined, as one had persuaded him from the first, to make Austria reflect and bring it to an adjustment. He, the loyal Hohenzollern, to make war on a Hapsburg on joint and equal terms with a *Welche*,—he, the Lord's anointed, the old combatant of the holy alliance, to become the brother in arms of a Victor Emmanuel, that representative of revolution, that usurper who had overthrown so many legitimate princes, besieged and dethroned his own nephew, and made Garibaldi in a red shirt sit near him, in the coach of the king!

The faltering and compunctions on this point were very sincere. Notwithstanding what has been said, nothing less than the marvelous art of M. de Bismarck was necessary to triumph in the end over these "syncopes" of the mission, to operate on these tumors of the conscience. "There is my doctor!" said the old monarch of Prussia one day to a Russian princess who congratulated him on his good health, pointing to his first minister.[64] The difficulty of *gaining over the king*, of triumphing over his *superstitions*, over the *old ideas*, over his *legitimist scruples*,—these words were continually on the lips of M. de Bismarck in the confidential interviews of the spring of 1866, which the valuable reports of General Govone have so fortunately preserved for posterity. Assuredly, in studying those reports, as well as the other dispatches which M. le Marquis La Marmora wished very much to deliver to the public, one can enjoy the spectacle of a comedy in five different acts, all doing little honor to human nature; one can ask who bears away the palm in duplicity of language, and in *æs triplex* of the forehead, the grandsons of Machiavelli or the heirs of the Teutonic order; one can admire there how, to use an ingenuous expression of the Italian negotiator, the Southern *viper* attempts to *bite the charlatan* of the North, and the charlatan puts his foot on the viper.[65] What, however, is the most curious and the most instructive in these documents is the quantity of matters which the president of the Prussian council succeeded in this short space of some months in teaching his august master, a still greater quantity than he had made him forget. Without doubt, one of the most remarkable of these forgetfulnesses is a certain *word of honor* given in *June*, 1866, by a very august personage to the Emperor Francis Joseph, *that there was no treaty signed with Italy*,[66] when that treaty, a treaty of offensive and defensive alliance in good and due form, already counted at this moment two months of existence, which had been signed at Berlin the 8th April by the respective plenipotentiaries, ratified by the King of Italy at Florence on the 14th, and then ratified on the 20th by the King of Prussia at Berlin.

By the side of official Italy, the minister of William I. had taken care to equally attach discontented Italy, which murmured in the shallows of the young monarchy, and General La Marmora complains on several occasions, in his interesting book, "of the intimate and cordial relations which the minister of Prussia at Florence, Count d'Usedom, entertained with some members of the party of action," and whose untoward advice it followed only too often. On his part, the consul of Prussia at Bucharest held in hand (February, 1866) the thread of a conspiracy which was to bring about the fall of the Prince Couza, and make a considerable difference in the action of the government at Berlin. "Liberalism is childishness which it is easy to bring to reason; but revolution is a force of which it is necessary to know how to avail one's self," the cavalier of the Mark one day said at Paris, and he did not delay to prove the two truths of his aphorism. It is known that his relations with Mazzini were kept up a long time even after Sadowa,[67] and the engagements contracted in 1866 towards Prussia by the Magyar chiefs have since influenced, influence still at the present time, and much more than is generally thought, the external policy of the empire of the Hapsburg. It was also in the conventicles of the men of the European revolution where the fantastic plan of campaign was worked out, which M. d'Usedom wished to force on General La Marmora in his famous dispatch of the 17th June;[68] in it he recommended making war thoroughly, to overturn the quadrilateral, to march along the Adriatic, to penetrate into Hungary, which would at once rise at the name of Garibaldi: "we will thus strike Austria, not at the extremities, but at the heart!" As to the endeavor to form, under the orders of the refugee General Klapka, a legion composed of deserters from the Austrian army, the president of the Prussian council greatly wished to affirm before the chambers of Berlin, in his celebrated speech of the 16th January, 1874, that he had *rejected with energy all those projects at the beginning of the war.* "It was not until after the battle of

Sadowa, at the moment when the Emperor Napoleon III., by a telegraphic dispatch, had caused the possibility of his intervention to be seen,—it was not till then, and as an act of legitimate defense, that I did not order but only tolerated the formation of this Hungarian legion." Unfortunately, the dates are not quite in accord with the declarations of the present chancellor of Germany. The battle of Sadowa was fought the 3d July; but on the 12th June, M. de Bismarck let the Italian government know that it had definitely accepted the aid of the Sclavic and Hungarian defections,[69] and it is established by evidence that, long before Sadowa, even before any beginning of war, the Prussian government had had recourse to a means which, according to the chancellor's own expressions, "would excite to revolt and treason the Magyar and Dalmatian regiments of the Austrian army." Let us not forget, however, that, while treating with Mazzini and M. Klapka, the minister of William I. was not sparing in denouncing to Europe the Jacobin spirit of the House of Hapsburg: "The king, our august master," said a Prussian dispatch of the 26th January, 1866, "is grievously affected at seeing in the Duchies of the Elbe, and under the ægis of the Austrian eagle, revolutionary tendencies, hostile to all thrones. If at Vienna they believe that they can tranquilly assist in this transformation of a race distinguished up to the present time by its conservative sentiments into a hot-bed of revolutionary agitations, we cannot do it for our part, and we are decided not to do it."

It was in the midst of such dark intrigues, and of negotiations more or less regular, of preparations for war and a continual exchange of notes, of parliamentary conflicts and of almost continual daily combats with the "old fogies" of the court, that the first six months of the year 1866 passed for the president of the council at Berlin, and rarely has a statesman lived through a more troubled or disturbed period. The waves of events first cast him ashore, then threw him back again, and seemed to remove him farther than ever from his goal. The revolution in Roumania, and the election of Prince Hohenzollern by the people of Bucharest, was, for instance, a great stroke of fortune, for this incident brusquely shut a door through which, in the opinion of more than one politician at that time, the Venetian question might have resulted in peace,[70] and it was through efforts of the French, who had contributed to the installation of the young Prussian prince on the banks of the Danube! However, immediately after, M. de Bismarck was again aroused from his security by vague rumors of conferences between Austria and France, touching the city of Saint Mark. He, at least, profited by them to persuade the king to sign the secret treaty of the 8th April with the government of Florence; but soon the offer of disarming, made by the cabinet of Vienna, the debates in the midst of the legislative body, and the manifestations of public opinion in France, more and more favorable to the cause of peace, produced a despairing lull, and again gave courage to the numerous partisans of Austria at the court of William I. The Emperor Napoleon III. then rendered to the Prussian minister the signal service of again putting in motion the great political machine which began to slacken. He made the speech of Auxerre (6th May), and defied, with scorn, the treaties of 1815. That did not, however, prevent him from immediately baffling all the plans of M. de Bismarck, by the sudden proposition of a congress, and, at this new occurrence, which seemed to compromise everything, the president of the council at Berlin spoke *for the first time* of compensations for France. "I am much less German than Prussian," he said to General Govone; "I would not have any difficulty in ceding to France the whole country comprised between the Rhine and Mosel, but the king would have very grave scruples."[71] Let it be well understood, he would in return demand of the French government an active coöperation in the war. But what did not enter at all into the views of Napoleon III. was, that the state of opinion in France did not even permit it to be thought of. In the interim, he learned that new negotiations had just been entered on between Austria and France concerning Venice, and that on the other side the king was making, without his knowledge, propositions to the Emperor Francis Joseph for an amicable arrangement: William I. always preferred the little question of the Duchies to the great war for the German nationality! One can surmise what must have been at this moment the state of mind of the minister who, for so many months, complained before the Count de Barral, Italian plenipotentiary at Berlin, of being betrayed by his agents at London, at Florence, and at Paris. Moreover, he considered his life in danger since an attack made on his person the 7th May; he was not without uneasiness about his sojourn at Paris during the congress in which he was going to take part, and which he dreaded for so many other reasons. "He does not go out unaccompanied," wrote the Count de Barral, the 1st June, "and agents of French police will come as far as the frontier to follow him during the whole journey."[72]

The journey did not take place, as is known; Prussia, in the words of M. d'Usedom, was "rescued from the congress," and Prince Gortchakof contributed largely to this work of salvation. Always a ready friend, he was the first to think that the projected conference had no "practical aim" with the reservations which Austria wished to bring to it,[73] and thus gave the signal for the general overthrow. From that time M. de Bismarck set himself to "work on the mind of his royal master," and he ended by freeing him from all *scruples*. "His majesty," Count de Barral telegraphed even on the 23d May from Berlin, "was very much *moved* at the situation, of which he spoke with great tears in his eyes." Two weeks later, the 8th June, the king wept no longer, but "he still had in his voice something sad, indicating clearly the decision of a resigned man, who believed that he could not act differently. His majesty told me that he had full confidence in the justice of his cause. I have a clear conscience," he added, with a moved air, and placing his hand on his heart; "for a long time I have been accused of wishing war for ambitious views, but now the whole world knows who is the aggressor."[74]

"I will return *via* Vienna or Munich, or I will charge with the last squadron, which will never return," M. de Bismarck said to a foreign ambassador, at the moment of leaving Berlin for the head-quarters, the 30th June, 1866. Two days later he was already at Jitschin, on the field still smoking from a great battle which had just been fought there. "I have just arrived," he wrote to his wife from Jitschin; "the ground is still heaped up with corpses, horses, and arms. Our victories are much greater than we thought.... Send me some French romances to read, but not more than one at a time. May God keep you!" This was written the 2d July, 1866; the next day the battle of Sadowa was fought; the next day Germany was at the feet of this singular lover of *French romances*; and the Emperor Napoleon III. was sadly awakened from his own romance, from his long humanitarian dream. Like the Titania of the "Midsummer Night's Dream," imperial France saw all at once that, in a state of inconceivable hallucination, she had caressed a monster.

And while so many events were taking place on the world's stage, great, marvelous, and terrible events, Russia continued to sulk and meditate; it meditated in the perpetual adoration of Prussia. One seeks in vain for a trace of its action in the events which, nevertheless, concerned in so high a degree its interests, its family alliances, its secular traditions. "Since I have been in Russia," wrote M. Benedetti to his chief in the spring of the year 1866, "let me mention that I have always remarked, not without surprise, the indifference with which the cabinet of St. Petersburg seems to me, from the beginning, to watch the pretensions of Prussia and the eventuality of a conflict between the two great Germanic Powers; and what I have not been less struck with is the *constant security* in which I have found M. de Bismarck as to the attitude and the intentions of the Empire of the North." Russia was silent in 1865 during the crisis of Gastein; in the month of May, 1866, it only accepted the invitation to the congress to make them despair and to discourage the other Powers from it; it was absent from the deliberations of Nikolsburg and of Prague; it left to France the care of making efforts for the South of Germany, for Saxony; it even left it the honor of stipulating a clause in favor of unhappy Denmark, the country of the future empress! One moment, it is true, M. d'Oubril, the Russian ambassador at Berlin, a diplomat of the old school, had shown himself very much alarmed at the victories and conquests of the Hohenzollern; he was ordered in all haste to St. Petersburg, and "returned from there in a few weeks entirely reassured, and affecting a satisfaction which was not disturbed a single instant either by the reverses of the German princes allied with the House of Russia, or by the developments which Prussia made in its military power."[75] Prince Gortchakof did not sacrifice to the old idols of the right of nations and of the balance of power;

he did not share certain prejudices touching the "solidarity which should exist among all the conservative interests;" and he had too lofty a soul to be jealous of a good neighbor. Moreover, had he not too "vanquished Europe," three years previously, in the memorable campaign of Poland? Some august personages, some princesses and grand duchesses, had said in vain, with the women of the Bible, that Saul killed his thousands, but David tens of thousands; they had in vain showed their despoiled relations and their confiscated patrimonies; Alexander Mikhaïlovitch did not envy the young laurels of his former colleague of Frankfort, become Chancellor of the Confederation of the North. He rejoiced in seeing Austria severely punished and France well mortified; for the rest, he thought that nothing was changed, and that there was only one more great chancellor in this century.

IV.

THE ECLIPSE OF EUROPE.

I.

In the little *salon* of the house Jessé, situated on the Rue de Provence at Versailles, in the first of the sad month of November, 1870, sat by the side of the fire two illustrious speakers, whose movements Europe in suspense watched with the most intense anxiety. Leaning his elbow on a writing table, on which "two bottles with candles in their necks did service as lights,"[76] M. de Bismarck had asked M. Thiers for permission to smoke a cigar, while he rested from the negotiations pursued during the whole day concerning the armistice and the peace, and entered into a conversation full of *abandon* and gossip on the events of the war. Among other things he related that the Emperor Napoleon III., having retired to a little garden after the capitulation of Sedan, grew pale at seeing him arrive armed with two pistols in his belt: "He thought me capable of an action in bad taste." One would scarcely be deceived in supposing that the man who since the attack of Blind had not ceased to show a very nervous solicitude for his person,[77] attributed here in this circumstance, and surely very ungenerously, to the unhappy monarch sentiments which were far from his mind. However that may be, the Prussian minister took pleasure during whole hours in the reminiscences and stories in which he showed all his brilliancy of mind; and on his part M. Thiers, scarcely returned from that journey of forty days, during which he had twice crossed Europe and negotiated with so many sovereigns and ministers, was not behind hand with *piquant* anecdotes and ingenious ideas. He thought, however, that it was necessary to recall, after some time, the serious matters which brought him to the head-quarters; but M. de Bismarck,—this "savage full of genius," as the French statesman soon called him in his effusions at the bishop's palace at Orleans,—seemed to wish to prolong as much as possible a delightful chat, and, taking the hand of M. Thiers, he cried out, "Allow me, I beg of you; allow me, it is so pleasant to be a little while with civilization!" The *civilization*, allowed at last to plead his cause anew, did not the less find the old "iron count" in the affable and fluent talker of a few moments before: the arts had decidedly in no respect softened the political manners of the *savage*. Then M. Thiers remembered the favorable disposition which he had found in Russia, and he thought it useful to make the most of it in a moment so critical. During his sojourn at St. Petersburg, he had addressed to the delegation of Tours a telegraphic dispatch singularly hopeful. "He had every cause," he said, "to be very much satisfied with his reception by the emperor, the imperial family, Prince Gortchakof, and the other dignitaries as well as with that of Russian society in general. The emperor and his chancellor had expressed themselves warmly against the exorbitant conditions of peace laid down by Prussia; they had declared that Russia would never give its consent to conditions which were not equitable; that, in consequence, the consent of the other Powers would likewise be wanting; the exactions of Prussia would only be from the effect of force, and would not rest on any sanction."[78] Without entering into such developments, M. Thiers spoke this time in general terms of the marks of solicitude which "his friend Prince Gortchakof" had given him, and ended by stating that Russia had become alarmed and irritated. At these words, M. de Bismarck got up and rang: "Bring the portfolio that contains the papers of Russia." The portfolio having been brought, "Read," said he; "here are thirty letters from St. Petersburg." M. Thiers did not fail to profit by the permission: he read, he understood, and he was disabused.

Yet, it would not have been difficult for the illustrious historian of the Consulate and the Empire to have spared himself this cruel deception, to have avoided, also, more than one false step in his rapid course across Europe, if he had only wished to consult competent men or even paid them the least attention. M. de Beust, for instance, was perfectly able to enlighten him on the real relations between Russia and Prussia; but it was especially M. Benedetti who could have told him the precise and already old date of the understanding agreed upon by the two courts of Berlin and St. Petersburg in view of a war with France, as well as the very extraordinary circumstances which had accompanied this understanding. Let us briefly recall here those circumstances, endeavoring to free them as much as possible from certain obscurities with which the interested parties continue to surround them, and let us return once more to the day after Sadowa, to the public or secret transactions which followed this dreadful day. The greater part of the political combinations which were to be so fatal to France in the war of 1870, were contrived and consolidated during that equally gloomy and turbulent period, during the two months of July and August of the year 1866.

"None of the questions which touch us can be solved without the consent of France," the Emperor Napoleon III. had declared the 11th June, 1866, in a solemn document produced before the legislative body; and among those questions any "modification of the map of Europe to the exclusive profit of a great Power" was naturally placed in the first rank. But, using that equally immense as unhoped-for victory of the 3d July, 1866, Prussia intended changing the map to its exclusive profit. In place of "maintaining for Austria its great position in Germany," as the imperial letter of the 11th June had demanded, Prussia demanded that the empire of the Hapsburg should be totally excluded from the Germanic Confederation; in place of according to the secondary States "a more important *rôle*, a more powerful organization," it aspired to the complete hegemony over all Germany, and furthermore wished to complete large annexations in the countries occupied by its troops.

In fomenting this war which was to end in such unforeseen results, the imperial policy had above all pursued two ends,—the affranchisement of Venice, and the equitable settlement of affairs in Germany. Venice was ceded, ceded even before the commencement of hostilities, and in accepting this cession, in announcing in the "Moniteur" this "important event" after the great disaster of General Benedeck, the Emperor Napoleon, in the judgment of his minister of foreign affairs, was the more bound not to allow Austria and its allies to be overwhelmed as it concerned the vital interests of France itself. The minister demanded, in consequence, his august master to convoke the legislative body, to send to the frontier of the East an army of observation of 80,000 men whom Marshal Randon would bring together very quickly, and to declare to Prussia that they would occupy the left bank of the Rhine, if it was not moderate in its demands towards the vanquished, and if it realized territorial acquisitions of a nature to destroy the equilibrium of Europe.

Assuredly, after the terrible experiences of the year 1870, these very legitimate doubts as to the efficaciousness of the measures proposed by M. Drouyn de Lhuys in the month of July, 1866, can be raised; it is nevertheless well to remember that the prestige of France was still great and almost intact; that in a week Austria could bring back from Italy 120,000 or 130,000 soldiers still fresh from the victory of Custozza, and that the troops of General Moltke already began to experience the natural consequences of the whole war, although fortunate. "Prussia is victorious," wrote the ambassador of France at the court of Vienna, "but it is exhausted. From the Rhine to Berlin there are not 15,000 men to be met with. You can be master of the situation by means of a simple military demonstration, and you can do it in all security, for Prussia is incapable at this moment of accepting a war with France. Let the emperor make a simple military demonstration, and he will be astonished at the facility with which he will become, without striking a blow, arbiter and master of the situation." In the confidential letters addressed by M. de Bismarck to his wife during this campaign, there are some traces of anxiety which at this moment assailed his mind, especially of his efforts to talk sense to the overexcited, "to the good people who do not see farther than their noses, *and swim at their ease on the foaming wave of the phrase.*" Six days after Sadowa, on the way to Vienna, he wrote from Hohenmauth: "Do you still remember, my heart, that we passed by here nineteen years ago, in going from Prague to Vienna? No mirror then showed us the future, neither did it in 1852, when I crossed this iron line with the good Lynar!... As for us, all is well, and we will have a peace which is worth something, if we do not exaggerate our demands and do not think that we have conquered the world. Unfortunately we are as quick to get drunk as to despair, and I have the unthankful task of pouring water in the foaming wine, and to show that *we are not alone in Europe* and that we have three neighbors." Lastly, in his celebrated speech of the 16th January, 1874, in the Reichstag, the chancellor of Germany, in speaking of those decisive days, made the important avowal, that, "if France had then had only a few available troops, a small body of French troops would have sufficed to make quite a respectable army by joining the numerous corps of South Germany, which on their part could furnish excellent materials whose organization alone was defective. Such an army *would have first placed us in the prime necessity of covering Berlin, and of abandoning all our successes in Austria.*" Let us add to that that Germany was still effervescent against the "fratricidal" policy of Prussia, that the proceedings and the exactions of Generals Vogel de Falkenstein and Manteuffel had exasperated the minds of all on the banks of the Main: there was a single instant, very fleeting also, it is true, when the appearance of the French on the Rhine would not have wounded the Teutonic susceptibilities, would have even been saluted with joy! "Sire," said to the Emperor Napoleon III. one of the most eminent ministers of the Germanic Confederation,—"sire, a simple military demonstration on your part can save Europe, and Germany will also preserve an eternal recollection of it. If you let this moment pass, *in four years from now* you will be forced to make war against Prussia, and then you will have all Germany against you."

But the fright caused by the prodigious victories of Prussia was too great in the Tuileries to allow the preservation of the *sang froid* which the circumstances so imperiously demanded. The needle gun was also a revelation which, by turns, exalted or depreciated beyond measure by authorities reputed competent, contributed not a little to increase the perplexities springing up on all sides; lastly, doubts arose even as to the possibility of getting together the 80,000 men of whom the minister of war spoke. The fatal expedition to Mexico had swallowed up almost all the arms, and almost all the troops of France! They were forced to make the strange avowal that they had desired with ardor, favored, provoked the greatest European complications without even asking if, at the critical and foreseen moment of the rupture of the equilibrium of the world, they would be in a condition to make even a simple military demonstration. The *party of action* in the councils of the empire would then have had a good chance to praise Prussia as the powerful agent of civilization and progress, to rise against the tendencies, always Austrian, of the bureaux of the Quai d'Orsay, and to recommend more than ever an alliance with M. de Bismarck: it was necessary to give him *carte blanche* in Germany, and to complete French unity in acquiring Belgium. M. Drouyn de Lhuys did not take the trouble to demonstrate the inanity, the temerity of such suggestions, and he asked, not without bitterness, how France, which they declared incapable of placing on foot even a corps of observation on the Rhine, would be strong enough to attack Antwerp, provoke England, and end by probably arraying against itself all the Powers of Europe, among whom Prussia would not be the last? He was not behind hand in recriminations; he showed the officious and culpable zeal which had been used in order to incite war, the consequences of which he, for his part, had never ceased to dread, as they had taken care to place no limit to the *license* allowed to one of the parties, the most redoubtable, the most skillful, and from which it was most essential to take sureties in advance. On the side from which it was never threatened, it had neglected no precaution; in case of the victory of Austria, Venetia would have nevertheless been acquired by Italy. "In my opinion," ingenuously added the minister, "in a French point of view it is a bad result; but the emperor insisted on it, above all, and I have procured it for him." It was certainly the least that could be asked, he thought, that they should allow him to obtain, on the other hand, compensations, *French this time*, which alone could justify before the nation the kindnesses shown to Prussia.

The debates were long and very violent for several days, and different influences worked in the most opposite directions. The party of the *Palais Royal* was not the only one, however, to preach the abandonment of the conqueror of Sadowa; in a certain measure it found its adherents among statesmen the most moderate in their opinions, and ordinarily the most calm in their judgments. M. Rouher was one of the first to oppose any armed demonstration on the Eastern frontier, and soon we even hear him speak of a *necessary and fruitful* alliance between France and Prussia! "Austria," thought another important member of the privy council, "only inspires to-day that interest, so near to indifference, which one feels for the strong become weak through their fault, not having foreseen or prepared themselves. *Up to the present time, all is for the best!*"[79] While M. Magne thus pronounced the *væ victis* on the empire of the Hapsburg,—without thinking that four years later, alas! Europe would use almost the same expressions in regard to France itself,— an august woman, a sister of the King of Würtemberg, and a near relative of the imperial family of France, used different language. "You cherish strange illusions," said she; "your prestige has diminished more in these last two weeks than during the whole duration of your reign. You allow the weak to be destroyed, you let the insolence and brutality of your nearest neighbor grow beyond measure; you accept a gift, and you do not even know how to address a kind word to him who gives it. I regret that you do not believe me disinterested in the question, and that you do not see the fatal danger of *a powerful Germany and a powerful Italy*. The *dynasty* is menaced, and it will suffer the consequences. Do not believe that the misfortune which overwhelms me in the disaster of my country makes me unjust or distrustful. Venice ceded, it would be necessary to succor Austria, to march to the Rhine, impose your conditions! To let Austria be slaughtered is more than a crime, it is an error!" Error or crime, the decision on this point had been already reached, before this warm appeal from the Queen of Holland reached the Tuileries.[80] Napoleon III. was very ill at this epoch, struggling against the first advances of a cruel disease which never forsook him,—in consequence less than ever inclined to vigorous resolutions; and, on the 10th July, after a grand council of ministers held at Paris in presence of the emperor, the Prince de Metternich was obliged to telegraph to Vienna that France would only interfere in the conflict through its diplomats.

Yet there was something more efficacious, more loyal in any case, in trying only a vain isolated mediation, full of perilous reticence and selfish calculations: that was simply to agree on a harmony of action among the Powers on a question certainly eminently "European," and which interested the equilibrium of the world in so high a degree. A word from France in the sense indicated "would certainly have been listened to," to borrow an expression from the imperial letter of the 11th June, for it was Prince Gortchakof himself who spoke at this moment of the necessity of a general congress.[81] Threatened with the first and violent commotion caused by the sudden undermining of Austria at the sight of so many relations and cousins of his august master menaced with spoliation and ruin, the Russian chancellor had in truth given this true description of the situation. So devoted as he was to his former colleague of Frankfort, so fascinated by his genius, Alexander Mikhaïlovitch had not yet sufficiently cast aside the old Adam, the *attaché* of the suite of Count Nesselrode at the reunions of Laybach and Verona, to admit in a trice that such a considerable transformation of the public right could be effected without the knowledge of Europe and without its consent. Why did the cabinet of the Tuileries not appreciate the solution offered by the Russian chancellor? Why did it not try to provoke a concerted action of the Powers in view of an overturning so menacing for the balance of the states? Why did it not see that in treating separately with M. de Bismarck it only made the game for the conqueror? In spite of all his triumphs, even in spite of all his audacity, the Prussian minister would have been slightly embarrassed in asking before the areopagus of the Powers for the almost complete abolition of the treaties of 1815, the dethronement of the old House of the Guelphs, or the expulsion of the empire of the Hapsburg from the bosom of Germany; and one will see in the sequel the cleverness which he used in escaping from such a necessity and in making France an accomplice in the eclipse of Europe. Strange fatality of the Napoleonic ideology! The dreamer of Ham had passed all his reign in proposing congresses, in invoking them at the most inopportune moments, under the least propitious circumstances, and he neglected to apply this panacea, so celebrated and recommended, on the only occasion where it was demanded by good sense and good right, in the only crisis in which it could become useful and salutary! The not less surprising good luck of the minister of William I., who was "saved from the congress," according to the *mot* of Count d'Usedom, and saved on two occasions in the space of some weeks: in the month of June, thanks to the kindness of Prince Gortchakof, and in the month of July, thanks to the infatuation of France! They were not ignorant at the Tuileries of the desire manifested in a moment of happy inspiration by Alexander Mikhaïlovitch; but the treaties of 1815 had been so eloquently "cursed" in the speech of Auxerre, they had announced with so much noise the "important event" of Venice and had illuminated Paris! As always, they clung to the *prestige*, to the glory of appearing as the "Neptune of Virgil," in the eyes of the profane, and they hoped more than ever to obtain some good God-send by again obliging the "Piedmont of Germany." Consequently M. Benedetti received the order to present himself at the head-quarters in Moravia, to offer to M. de Bismarck French mediation, and to "sound" him on the advantages that in justice he could scarcely fail to accord to the ardent mediator.

II.

There is nothing more curious than the language used by the minister of Prussia to the ambassador of France at those first conversations in Moravia! M. de Bismarck began by renewing the fantasies of Biarritz, and it was the very opposite of a Tilsit who appeared to form plans at the head-quarters at Brünn: the son of Frederick William III., conquered at Jena, seemed to wish to offer to the nephew of Napoleon I. to share the world with him, to share it to the detriment of Russia and England! "He endeavored to prove to me," wrote M. Benedetti on the 15th July, "that the reverses of Austria allowed France and Prussia to modify their territorial situation, and to solve at the present time the greater part of the difficulties which will continue to menace the peace of Europe. I reminded him that treaties existed, and that the war which he desired to prevent would be the first result of such a policy. M. de Bismarck answered me, that I misunderstood, that France and Prussia, united and resolved to remodel their respective frontiers by binding one another by solemn engagements, were henceforward in a position to regulate together these questions, without fear of meeting an armed resistance *either on the part of England or on the part of Russia*." In other words,—and these words were likewise employed in the report of M. Benedetti,—the Prussian minister believed that "he could free himself from the obligation to submit to the control of Europe," thanks to a separate agreement with France. As to the means to bring about this precious agreement, it was perfectly simple: France had only to seek its fortune along the Meuse and the Escaut. "I do not tell your excellency anything new," wrote M. Benedetti to his chief, some days after, from Nikolsburg, in announcing to him that M. de Bismarck was of the opinion "that we should seek compensation in Belgium, and that he offered to act in concert with us." He did not, however, utterly repel the idea of giving France its share on the Rhine, not, for instance, in the Prussian territories, where it would be difficult to persuade King William to renounce any portion of his possession; "but something could perhaps be found in the Palatinate," that is, in Bavaria. He was always "much more Prussian than German," and reasonable terms could be made with the Walhalla.

The French government fell into the trap which was thus set, and it then aided Prussia in *freeing itself from all control of Europe*, in working at these preliminaries of Nikolsburg, signed the 26th July, and which sealed the exclusion of Austria from Germany, and constituted a confederation of the North, under the hegemony of the Hohenzollern. This grave attack on public right and the equilibrium of the world once conceded, and the war virtually ended, one began to talk of compensations. In a letter addressed to M. de Goltz, and dated from Vichy the 3d August, M. Drouyn de Lhuys declared that the emperor, his august master, "had not wished to complicate the difficulties of a work of *European interest* in treating *prematurely* with Prussia" on territorial questions; but the moment seemed finally come to consider these questions, all the more as they were preparing to obtain large annexations north of the Main. "The king," M. de Bismarck had written to M. de Goltz the 10th July,—"the king cares less for the constitution of a political northern confederation, and *above all desires annexations*; he would rather abdicate than return without an important territorial acquisition."[82] In fact, besides the Duchies of the Elbe, the abandonment of which had been stipulated at Nikolsburg, Prussia still wished to absorb the free cities, Cassel, Hanover, even Saxony, and at the Tuileries they hoped to measure the French demands according to the number of souls and of square leagues that William the Conqueror should demand for himself. "The great war for German nationality," which the popular Cæsar had recommended at Biarritz, turned in a measure into "this human cattle market," so blamed at the congress of Vienna, at the "execrated" treaties of 1815,—and how is it possible not to acknowledge that France played a *rôle* there unworthy of itself? It was for it to deny at once the new and the old right, the principle of national will as well as that of the legitimacy of princes; it wished, moreover, to realize an illicit gain and a paltry sum on the occasion of a great universal calamity, and, to speak with the English humorist, to profit by the eruption of Vesuvius to boil an egg! M. de Bismarck uttered at this moment a cruel *mot*, but which was not entirely unmerited. "France," said he to a former minister of the Germanic Confederation,—"France *follows a Trinkgeld policy* (*la France fait une politique de pour-boire*)."

A letter written by M. Rouher on the 6th August, 1866, and since found among the papers of the Tuileries,[83] makes us see the strange illusions which the French government then cherished, and the ambassador of Prussia at Paris did his best to sustain. "M. de Goltz finds our pretension legitimate in principle," wrote the minister of state; "he considers that satisfaction ought to be given to the only wish of our country to constitute between France and Prussia *a necessary and fruitful alliance*." The embarrassment is solely to determine the sum of the demands that should be put forward. "The empress would demand much or nothing, in order not to compromise our final pretensions." As for M. Rouher, he thinks that "public opinion would have *food* and *direction*, if to-morrow we could say officially, Prussia consents that we retake the frontiers of 1814, and thus efface the consequences of Waterloo." Let it be well understood, the minister of state does not admit "that this rectification would serve as a receipt for the future!" "Without doubt, new facts must develop in order that new pretensions arise, but these facts will certainly be developed. Germany is only in the first of those numerous oscillations which it will undergo before finding its new position. Let us be more ready, in the future, to better profit by events; opportunities will not be wanting. The States south of the Main, especially, will be, in a few years from now, an apple of discord or a matter for a compromise. M. de Goltz does not dissimulate at present the covetousness as regards this group of confederates." Thus, at the very moment that they boasted of "saving" the States of the South, of establishing on the other side of the Rhine a new political combination which the minister of state was soon to adorn with the famous name of *three fragments*, and to declare, marvelously reassuring for France, they already waited for an opportunity to abandon this combination, and to traffic for it "at a reasonable price!"

How naïve to think that after Sadowa and Nikolsburg, the ruin of Austria consummated, Germany completely subjected, all intervention of Europe checked, and the military weakness of France proclaimed to all the winds,[84] that one would find Prussia accessible to those arrangements which it had not wished to make before its immense victories, at the moment of its greatest perplexities, and in the midst of the anguish of a crisis which all the world agreed in proclaiming perilous in the extreme! Even on the 8th June, on the eve of the war, M. Benedetti thus summed up the state of public opinion in Prussia in regard to France: "The apprehensions which we inspire everywhere in Germany still exist, and they will awaken unanimously and violently at the least sign which would allow our intention of enlarging our boundaries towards the East to be guessed. The king, like the most humble of his subjects, would not bear at this moment the suggestion of the probability of a sacrifice on the Rhine. The crown prince, so profoundly convinced of the dangers of the policy of which he is the witness, declared, not long ago, to one of my colleagues, with extreme vivacity, that he preferred war to cession, if it was only the little county of Glatz."[85] And it was the same diplomat who had so appreciated the situation before the campaign of Bohemia, it was this same ambassador who now took upon himself to present to M. de Bismarck the demands of the cabinet of the Tuileries, who even submitted to him on the 5th August a project for a secret treaty, implying the abandonment to France of all the left bank of the Rhine, without excepting the great fortress of Mayence! "In view of the important acquisitions which the peace assures to the Prussian government," said M. Benedetti, "I was of the opinion that a territorial remodeling would hereafter be necessary for our security; I have instigated nothing, I have still less guaranteed the success; I have only allowed myself to hope for it, provided that our language were firm and our attitude resolute." Was firmness wanting, or was too much of it shown? In any case, M. de Bismarck asserts that he replied in a tone which certainly showed no irresolution. "Very well," he replied to the pressing entreaties of the ambassador, "then we will have war. But let his majesty well observe, that such a war could become in certain eventualities *a* war with a revolution, and that in presence of revolutionary dangers, the German dynasties would prove to be much more firmly established than that of Napoleon."[86]

That was not, however, the last remark of the Prussian minister. Perfectly decided not to admit the discussion on the subject of the Rhine, he took care, nevertheless, not to completely discourage the French ambassador, and to continue a game with him which later, in his circular of the 29th July, 1870, he called by the name, unknown until then in the diplomatic dictionary, of *dilatory negotiations*. He spoke of his liking for Napoleon III., of his great ambition to solve in concert with him the important problems of the future. "Prussia needs an alliance with a great Power;" that was his inmost conviction; he did not cease to preach it to the king his august master,—and what alliance more desirable, in a point of view of progress and of civilization, than that with the French empire? He thus returned to his recent effusions of Brünn and Nikolsburg; he insinuated "that *other arrangements* could be made which would satisfy the respective interests of the two countries,"[87] and he strengthened M. Benedetti in his design to return to Paris and to expose the situation.

At Paris the conflict of Powers was carried on with vigor between the minister of foreign affairs and the ambassador of Prussia, M. de Goltz, ably seconded by the *party of action*, to which the arrival of M. Benedetti (11th August) brought considerable support. M. Drouyn de Lhuys was not at all surprised at the *Prussian ingratitude*, as M. Benedetti had expressed it in one of his last dispatches,[88] but, by a logic which escapes us, he did not the less rejoice at seeing the French demands at last stated, "They can be taken up again in good time." He had no doubt of the use that they would soon make on the banks of the Spree of the project of the treaty of the 5th August! He hoped, besides, that the final refusal given at Berlin would cause the ardent promoters of dangerous intrigues to reflect that it would prevent certain engagements for the future which he apprehended above all. M. de Goltz suddenly told him that he had come to an agreement with the emperor concerning the annexations to be effected by William I. in Northern Germany, and a letter addressed the 12th August by the chief of state to the Marquis de La Valette cut short all controversy with Prussia. "It results from my conversation with Benedetti," wrote Napoleon III. to the minister of the interior, "that we will have all Germany against us for a small profit; it is important not to let public opinion be mistaken on this point." The misfortune was only that the imperial government allowed itself at this moment to be misled on a very dangerous point, and that Belgium became for it, from that time, the object of a negotiation as deceptive as fatal, and from which later, at the beginning of the war of 1870, it in vain endeavored to elude the crushing responsibility.

That M. de Bismarck was, from the beginning, the great tempter of the imperial government, and the tempter repulsed even for a long time, in these shadowy projects concerning the country of the Meuse and the Escaut, is a truth which to-day cannot be doubted, the authentic documents published lately suffice to convince the most incredulous mind. It was not only in his conversations with General Govone that the president of the Prussian council indicated on several occasions, and very clearly, Belgium and certain parts of Switzerland as the most proper territories to "indemnify France:" long before the spring of the year 1866, even long before the interview of Biarritz, M. de Bismarck had tried to *sell the bear-skin*, as Napoleon III. said to him one day. General La Marmora, who understood it a long time, adds that "the bear was neither in the Alps nor in the Carpathians; he was very well (*stava benone*) and he neither wished to die nor to be caged up."[89] Such suggestions were, without doubt, of a nature to startle the *party of action* in the councils of the empire, they were, however, eagerly received by it; but scornfully checked, up to that point, by M. Drouyn de Lhuys, treated as "projects of brigandage" by the chief of the state, they had to await that hour of *patriotic anguish* which marked the arrival of Benedetti, to be at last taken into serious consideration.

Certainly the ambassador of France at the court of Berlin had, in this year 1866, a very difficult and painful situation, we had almost said a pathetic one. He had worked with ardor, with passion, to bring about this *connubio* of Italy and Prussia, which seemed to him to be an immense good fortune for the imperial policy, a brilliant victory gained over the old order of things to the profit of the "new right" and Napoleonic ideas. In the fear, very well founded besides, of seeing this work miscarry and Prussia draw back, if one spoke to it of eventual compensations and preventive engagements, he had not ceased to dissuade his government from any attempt of this kind, and to lay stress upon the fierce, intractable, and suspicious patriotism of the House of

Hohenzollern, even to the point of being sometimes suspected at the Hotel of the Quai d'Orsay of somewhat exaggerating the colors, and of making a certain devil blacker and more German than he really was. The work had at last succeeded; succeeded beyond all expectations; succeeded in inspiring fear, in suddenly convincing M. Benedetti "that a territorial remodeling was henceforth necessary to the security of France." This remodeling he had flattered himself for a moment with having obtained on the Rhine: "He had not guaranteed the success, but he had allowed himself to *hope* for it." Refused with firmness, if not with pride, "and having taken the measure of Prussian ingratitude," he was nevertheless soon given to hope what the minister of William I. had insinuated to him, "that other proper arrangements could be made to satisfy the respective interests of the two countries," and he had grasped at the expedient which was thus pictured before his eyes, with so much the more feverish energy as he saw in it a new triumph for the modern right and the principles dear to his party. Anxious to repair the consequences of a policy to which for his part he had contributed more than any other to make it successful; recognizing, however, the difficulties, if not the impossibility, for the court of Berlin to cede any portion of the German soil, and always convinced of the sincere desire of M. de Bismarck "to indemnify France,"[90] at this decisive hour he made himself, at the side of Napoleon III., the interpreter of the ideas which he had gathered from the head-quarters at Brünn, and pleaded with warmth for this necessary and fruitful alliance with Prussia, which, extolled for a long time by the Palais Royal, had recently deluded even the well balanced mind of M. Rouher.

Let it be well understood, there was no question of immediate action, of which, indeed, the military situation of the country allowed no thought; the question was simply of an agreement and a solidarity to be established for future eventualities, for the time more or less distant, but inevitable, when Prussia should think of crowning its work, of freeing the Main, of extending its rule from the Baltic to the Alps,—this question was of *boldly taking stand on the ground of nationalities*! "If France boldly takes its stand on the ground of nationalities," said a curious note found among the papers of the Tuileries, and which incontestably sums up the ideas of the party of action at this epoch,[91] "it is necessary to establish now that there exists no Belgian nationality, and to fix this essential point with Prussia. As the cabinet of Berlin seemed to be, on the other hand, disposed to enter with France into arrangements which would suit France, there would be time to negotiate a secret act which should bind the two parties. Without pretending that this act was a perfectly sure guarantee, it would have the double advantage of compromising Prussia, and would be for it a gage of the sincerity of the policy or of the intentions of the Emperor.... To be certain of finding at Berlin a confidence which is necessary for the maintenance of an intimate understanding, we must try to dissipate the apprehensions which have always been entertained, which have been reawakened, and even overexcited by our last communications. This result cannot be obtained by words; an act is necessary, and one which will regulate the ulterior lot of Belgium in concert with Prussia, in proving at Berlin that the emperor seeks elsewhere than on the Rhine the extension necessary for France since the events of which Germany was the theatre. We must at least have a relative certainty that the Prussian government will not oppose our aggrandizement in the North."

III.

It was with the mission of negotiating a *secret act*, binding the two parties in the sense indicated by the note which we have just given, that M. Benedetti left Paris towards the end of the month of August. The act was to provide for an offensive and defensive alliance between the two states, and, in exchange for the recognition of the changes already accomplished or still to be accomplished in Germany, to assure to Napoleon III. the diplomatic aid of Prussia for the acquisition of Luxemburg, and its *armed* aid at the moment when France should judge it opportune to annex Belgium. Immediately on his arrival at his post the French ambassador went resolutely to work: he carried on the negotiation *without the knowledge of his immediate chief*, and only referred to the emperor and the minister of state.[92] He begged the president of the council of Prussia to regard the propositions of the 5th August, those relative to the left bank of the Rhine, as null and void, as a joke of M. Drouyn de Lhuys during the sickness of his august master, and submitted to him a new project in five articles concerning Belgium. It matters little that the ambassador of France had with him the minute of it which he had written in the cabinet of the Prussian minister, at his request, and, "in some measure at his dictation;" it is certain that Benedetti acted according to the instructions from Paris,[93] and that M. de Bismarck on his part did not decline such overtures. He had even made observations on some of the terms employed in the draft, and insisted on introducing several changes in the text. The project thus amended was sent to Paris, and returned anew to Berlin with rectifications made by the emperor and M. Rouher. On the banks of the Seine, in the councils of the small number initiated in the secret, they were full of expectation and cheerfulness; they debated the question of the successor of M. Drouyn de Lhuys, and the opinions were divided between M. La Valette and M. Benedetti; they exchanged ideas which were soon expressed in a sadly celebrated document, and they rejoiced at seeing "the treaties of 1815 destroyed, the coalition of the three Powers of the North broken, and Prussia made sufficiently independent and sufficiently compact to ignore its former traditions."[94] All of a sudden a discouraging dispatch from the ambassador of France at the court of Berlin (29th August) troubled their minds, and they had again some apprehensions on the subject of the "necessary and fruitful alliance" which they flattered themselves with having established.

The conferences had continued up to the last days of the month of August, and M. de Bismarck had lent himself with good grace to the *dilatory negotiations*. In the mean time, the peace of Prague, the definite peace with Austria, was signed (26th August); the States of the South had adhered one after the other to the stipulations of Nikolsburg, and solemnly recognized the confederation of the North, as well as the territorial acquisitions of Prussia. The secret act concerning Belgium was in the hands of the minister of William I., and only needed to be fairly copied and signed, but at this moment M. Benedetti suddenly met with strange inconceivable distrusts which did not fail to wound him deeply. M. de Bismarck hesitated, spoke to him of his fears "that the Emperor Napoleon would wish to make use of such a negotiation to create suspicion between Prussia and England." The stupefaction of the French ambassador was extreme. "What degree of confidence can we on our side accord to those open to such suspicions?" he asked in his dispatch of the 29th August.[95] The proceeding seemed to him unjustifiable, and, in order not to be tempted to qualify it, he judged it opportune "to go for a fortnight to Carlsbad where he would hold himself ready to return to Berlin on receipt of the first telegram which M. de Bismarck should address to him." Slightly moved at this circumstance, the court of the Tuileries was not the less obstinate in believing in the *secret act* which was preparing at Berlin; it dismissed M. Drouyn de Lhuys, and long before the arrival of his successor from Constantinople, M. de Moustier, they hastened to publish that famous circular of the 16th September, which bore the signature of the minister of the interior, M. de La Valette, and was one more pledge given to the conqueror of Sadowa. The manifest praised the theory of combinations and affirmed that "Prussia, enlarged, free henceforth from any solidarity, would assure the independence of Germany;" as to the most secret hopes, scarcely an allusion was made to them: "France can only desire territorial aggrandizements which do not alter its powerful cohesion." Nothing happened, however, and M. Benedetti waited in vain under the elms and the beautiful firs of Carlsbad: M. de Bismarck gave no sign of life. He had gone to Varzin, from whence he did not return until the month of December. The *dilatory negotiations* had borne all their fruit in the month of August, and the French government would have been too happy if all those shadowy intrigues had remained for it only a simple deception: they became its chastisement.

M. de Benedetti had, however, pretended to know his man, to have *followed* him for fifteen years! He had followed him in any case during the negotiations of the spring which brought about the treaty between Prussia and Italy; he had then contemplated the magnificent tilt between the *viper* and the *charlatan*, and himself very judiciously judged a situation in which the plenipotentiaries of the two countries had surpassed one another in miracles of the true Punic faith. "M. de Bismarck and General Govone distrusted and still distrust one another," M. Benedetti wrote in his dispatch of the 27th of March, 1866. "It is feared at Florence that, finding itself in possession of *an act which places Italy in a certain degree at its discretion*, Prussia will make known the stipulations of it at Vienna and will persuade the Austrian cabinet, by intimidation, to peacefully make the coveted concessions. At Berlin, they fear that Italy, if they promised to negotiate on these bases, will directly inform Austria before concluding any treaty, and will thus try to obtain from it the abandonment of Venice." After a similar experience *in anima vili*, how could M. Benedetti have left on the table of the president of the council of Berlin his compromising autograph on the subject of Belgium, *an act which in a certain degree placed France at the mercy of Prussia*? How could he be astonished at seeing his interlocutor "open to certain suspicion," and did he not on the contrary make the same calculations for his own account and profit? It was, however, very foolish to suppose that M. de Bismarck had the will to do unto others that which he declared he did not wish others to do unto him! And the ambassador of France would have scarcely been wrong in crediting this charitable thought to his interlocutor, however unevangelical, for the amusing or rather the sad part of the affair,—the true humor of all this imbroglio, as the Bardolph of Shakspere would say,—is that the cavalier of the Mark had already executed precisely the manœuvre, indifferently chivalric surely, of which he pretended to suspect Napoleon III., and that the thing was done at the moment when he demanded if they had nothing in their hands and pockets. They had left in his hands two very secret and dangerous documents, the two plans of the treaties on the Rhine and Belgium,[96] and he took care not to avail himself of them immediately at the expense of the interested parties, whom he had every interest to attach to himself.

The preliminaries of Nikolsburg, the reader will remember, had stipulated that the States of the South should remain outside of the new confederation directed by Prussia, and that they should form among themselves a restricted union. That was the great success obtained by the French mediation, the salutary combination of the *three fragments*, much more favorable to the interests of France, according to its opinion, than that of the former *Bund*, the ill-omened creation of 1815. It is true that among the persons initiated in the secret of Benedetti's mission, "this group of confederates" was only regarded as "a matter of business for a reasonable profit;" in waiting, however, they "saved" the South, and M. Drouyn de Lhuys honestly exerted himself, in this month of August, 1866, to aid the unhappy plenipotentiaries of Bavaria, of Würtemberg, of Hesse, etc., who had gone to seek a definite peace at Berlin. M. de Bismarck had first frightened them by his fiscal and territorial demands; they had invoked and obtained the support of the emperor, and in the Tuileries they flattered themselves with having in truth persuaded the minister of William I. to more equitable sentiments. Still, on the 24th August, M. Drouyn de Lhuys wrote to his agent in Bavaria: "I am happy to think that our last step has not been without influence on the result of a negotiation which is ending in a more satisfactory manner than the cabinet of Munich had at first thought possible;" and it was not only M. Benedetti who took to himself in this matter the credit of playing the fine *rôle* of moderator.[97] The truth is, that if M. de Bismarck ended by becoming more moderate and even amicable towards the Southern States, he had very different motives than the desire of being agreeable to the cabinet of the Tuileries. He had simply shown to "the group of confederates" the project of the treaty of the 5th August; he had made them see that the French government, at the same time when it seemed to protect, sought to extend itself together with Prussia at their expense, and demanded portions of the Palatinate and of Hesse. In place of demanding from them the sacrifices which they feared, the minister of William I. offered to defend them against the "hereditary enemy." There was no hesitation: the States of the South surrendered, and Prussia concluded with them (from the 17th to the 23d August) *secret* treaties of offensive and defensive alliance. The contracting parties guaranteed reciprocally the integrity of their respective territories, and the States of the South engaged to place, in case of war, all their military forces at the disposal of the King of Prussia. The "matter of business," on which M. Rouher had counted, was henceforward out of the market; the line of the Main found itself free before it had been traced on the official map of Europe, and from the month of August, 1866, M. de Bismarck could count on the armed coöperation of all Germany.[98]

The military conventions with the States of the South were kept rigorously secret for a long time, and it was not till the spring of the following year that M. de Bismarck found it convenient to give them a crafty publicity in reply to the speech of the minister of state on the *three fragments*. Up to that time M. Benedetti had been ignorant of them, like other mortals, but he had shown himself more clear-sighted as regards another very grave event, contemporary with these conventions concluded with the South, and he recognized from the beginning the ominous bearing of the mission of General Manteuffel to St. Petersburg in the month of August, 1866. It must not be forgotten that at the bottom of the "new policy" which during this month they were flattering themselves with having inaugurated at the Tuileries by a cordial understanding with the court of Berlin, a Russian problem was agitating. Would the monarchy of Brandenburg, "rendered sufficiently independent and sufficiently compact to loosen itself from its traditions, free henceforward from all solidarity," decide to break its secular and hitherto unrelaxed ties with the empire of the czars? That was the true and vital question of the future. "Prussia must have an alliance with a great Power," the minister of William I. did not cease to reiterate at this epoch; but, as Austria was destroyed, and England had long since condemned itself to widowhood, only France and Russia remained, between whom the lucky conqueror of Sadowa had then the position of the Don Juan of Mozart, between Doña Anna and Doña Elvira. Surprised in the darkness, imposed upon in a moment of deplorable misunderstanding, the proud and passionate Doña Anna occasionally cast glances of defiance and *venganza*, oftener, alas! looks still ardent from the last embrace, and betraying the secret flame, which even said very plainly, that she would go still farther, provided there was reparation, provided that a marriage followed, if it was only a clandestine marriage. Russia was Doña Elvira, the former, the *legitimate* ally a little vexed at recent neglect, even very gravely injured in family interests, but always loving, always fascinated, and only waiting for a kind word to forget all and to throw herself into the arms of the fickle one. We only speak briefly of Zerline, of Italy, a cunning and lively soubrette, intruding herself everywhere, in love, she also, the poor little thing, with the irresistible seducer, and often treated very cavalierly, happy, nevertheless, to be pinched privately, and to say that she also was "protected by a great lord."

Such being the situation in this decisive month, the ambassador of France to the court of Berlin experienced a violent shock in learning one day of the sudden departure for St. Petersburg of General Manteuffel, the general-diplomat, more diplomat than general, the confidant, *par excellence*, of King William, and always the man for private missions. "I have asked M. de Bismarck," M. Benedetti hastened to write to Paris, "what I should think of this mission, confided to a general commanding troops in the campaign. After having pretended that he thought he had informed me of it, M. de Bismarck assured me that he had told M. de Goltz, in order that he might instruct you." Strictly speaking, one finds it natural that the king wished to plead before his imperial nephew the extenuating circumstances of a painful situation, which forced him to take the goods and the crowns of several very near relations of the House of Romanoff; but the French ambassador was above all struck by the circumstance that the journey of M. de Manteuffel had been decided the day after he had delivered his project of the treaty. "I asked the president of the council," he continues in the same dispatch, "if this general officer had been informed of our overture; he answered that he had had no occasion to make him a party to it, but that he could not guarantee to me that the king had not told him the substance. I should add, as I have told you by telegraph, that I gave a copy of our project to M. de Bismarck on Sunday morning, and that General Manteuffel, who had scarcely removed his head-quarters to Frankfort, was called to Berlin in the following night." Towards the end of the month of August, when M. de Bismarck for the first time showed his hesitation in signing the secret act concerning Belgium, M. Benedetti wrote, in a letter to M. Rouher, concerning the mission that M. de Manteuffel continued to fill at St. Petersburg. "They have elsewhere obtained assurances which dispense with our aid," said he; "if they decline our alliance, it is because they are already provided, or on the eve of being."[99]

General Manteuffel remained several weeks at St. Petersburg; he stayed there long enough to dissipate a certain sadness caused by the recent misfortunes of the Houses of Hanover, Cassel, Nassau, etc., all allied by blood to the imperial family of Russia, also long enough to communicate such projects and show autographs by which they had treacherously endeavored to turn the Hohenzollern from his loyal, unalterable affection for his relative of the North. Thanks to all these proceedings, and all these attentions, the good harmony between the two courts became greater than ever; they easily explained the past, and arranged for the future, and the ambassador of France at the court of Berlin was not deceived in designating, from this moment, the "bear," whose skin the general-diplomat had gone to sell on the banks of the Neva. To speak in the words of the Marquis La Marmora, it was a bear of the Balkans, which had not been well for a long time, and which the Emperor Nicholas had declared *sick* twenty years before. One will see in the sequel that Alexander Mikhaïlovitch did not the less miss the deer at the general hunt in 1870, that he scarcely succeeded in getting for himself a handful of hair well fitted to adorn his helmet; that takes nothing from the merit of the perspicacity which the unfortunate negotiator of the *secret* act concerning Belgium had given proof of on this occasion. M. Benedetti early foresaw the desolating truth, which, for M. Thiers, was not visible until very late, at the bottom of this *Russian box* which M. de Bismarck allowed him one evening, at Versailles, to rummage with a liberality which was certainly not free from malice.

In endeavoring, after the great disaster of the campaign of Bohemia, to obtain from Prussia compensations first on the Rhine, then on the Meuse, the Emperor Napoleon III., in those months of July and August, 1866, had only facilitated for M. de Bismarck the two great political combinations which were since, in 1870, of such prodigious use: the armed coöperation of the Southern States, and the moral aid of Russia in case of a war with France. The chief fault, however, of the Napoleonic policy the day after Sadowa, was to have so well served Prussia in its desire to escape from all control on the part of Europe, and to have given its sanction from the very first to such an immense derangement of the equilibrium of the world, without the cause being brought before the areopagus of nations. This forgetfulness of the duties towards the great Christian family of states was only too quickly and too cruelly avenged, alas! and Prince Gortchakof, in 1870, only followed a recent and lamentable example in allowing France and Germany to decide their quarrel in the lists, in hindering all common action of the Powers, all European concert. "I see no Europe!" cried M. de Beust, in 1870, in a celebrated dispatch, and no one thought of disputing this dolorous affirmation. A few only observed with sadness that the eclipse had already lasted several years, that it dated from the preliminaries of Nikolsburg and from the treaty of Prague.

V.

ORIENT AND OCCIDENT.

I.

"They have provided themselves elsewhere," the French ambassador at the court of William I. sadly wrote, in the last days of the month of August, 1866, on seeing Prussia so brusquely break off the *dilatory negotiations* concerning Belgium; and it is just to add that he has never since ceased to clearly appreciate the situation, and to keep his country constantly on its guard as regards the confidential harmony and absolute agreement between the two courts of Berlin and St. Petersburg after the mission of General Manteuffel. If he nevertheless endeavored for some time to obtain a compensation for his country,—a very modest one, it is true, and consonant with the new fortune of France,—if, during the first months of the year 1867, he particularly flattered himself with obtaining from the kindness of M. de Bismarck the permission to buy Luxemburg from the King of Holland, if he even once went so far, during a hasty journey to Paris, as to affirm, in a confidential conversation, that he already had the fortress of Alzette "in his pocket," it was not that he thought it possible to return to the beautiful dream of the head-quarters of Brünn, and to effect that "necessary and fruitful alliance with Prussia" with which at a certain moment some sanguine minds on the banks of the Seine had been deluded. He was only persuaded that the conqueror of Sadowa would not envy France this paltry atonement of Luxemburg, that he would even find it worth while to "indemnify" the Emperor Napoleon III. so cheaply, so that, in the words of the poet, "the lion would only gape before such a little morsel." The lion roared, however, shook his mane with fury, and signified harshly that it had done forever with any *politique de pour-boire*. But even this only confirmed M. Benedetti in the opinion that they had provided themselves elsewhere, and that henceforward they were on the verge of great trouble. He thought rightly that M. de Bismarck must be very sure of the support, in any case, of his former colleague of Frankfort, to refuse to France even this moderate prize (*aubaine*), and to give it on this occasion "the measure of its ingratitude."

At the same time with the affair of Luxemburg, the events in Crete showed in their turn to the cabinets of Vienna and the Tuileries how far Prince Gortchakof was already pledged to M. de Bismarck, and how resolved to sacrifice to his friendship with Prussia the most brilliant prospects. Whoever reads attentively the curious exchange of notes which the troubles of Crete had caused, will see that, during the entire epoch from the month of November, 1866, to the month of March, 1867, the two governments of Austria and France had sought to sound the designs of the court of St.

Petersburg, and to make very significant advances to it. The insurrection of the Candiots, one will remember, in the autumn of 1866, surprised and moved Europe, scarcely recovered from the violent shock of Sadowa. Immoderately exaggerated by the journalists, who were more or less interested, after having excited lively sympathy in Russia, the insurrection ended by seriously occupying the attention of the chancellors, and seemed for a moment destined to bring before the cabinets the whole question of the Orient in its appalling *ensemble.* Certain cabinets did not even seem greatly dismayed at the contingency: instead of conforming with the constant traditions of diplomacy in the Ottoman affairs, instead of quelling the disturbance and lessening as much as possible its proportions and bearings, M. de Moustier thought that he ought "to find means to pacify the Orient," and busied himself "in convoking a sort of *consultation of doctors* to learn the opinion of each one concerning the remedy to be applied to the evil."[100] Still more astonishing was the language used by the government of Vienna, by the Power which up to that time and always had contented itself with sustaining Turkey *per fas et nefas*, without demanding anything from it, no more for the immediate subjects of the sultan than for the tributary provinces. Resolutely breaking with these habits of the past, M. de Beust, who had at this time just undertaken the direction of affairs in Austria, wrote on the 10th November, 1866, to his ambassador at Paris that, while desiring to preserve the throne of the sultan, "Austria could not refuse its sympathies and its support in a certain degree to the Christian peoples of Turkey who have at times just demands to make, and who are connected with some of the peoples of the Austrian empire by close ties of blood and religion." Questioned some days later (28th November) by the envoy of Russia at the court of Vienna, the Austrian minister did not hesitate to reply that he was disposed to favor amongst the Christians of the Orient "the development of their autonomy and the establishment of a limited self-government by a bond of vassalage." Lastly, in a remarkable dispatch addressed to Prince Metternich and dated the 1st January, 1867, M. de Beust proposed "a revision of the treaty of Paris of the 30th March, 1856, and subsequent acts," announcing in advance his desire to make over, in the arrangement to intervene, the greater part to Russia. He had no trouble in showing that "the remedies through which they had sought, in the course of the last few years, to maintain the *statu quo* in the Orient, had shown themselves insufficient to subdue the difficulties which grew with each day." "The physiognomy of the Orient taken as a whole," continued the dispatch, "shows itself to-day under an essentially different aspect from that which it had in 1856, and the stipulations of that epoch, exceeded as they are on more than one important point by after events, no longer answer to the necessities of the actual situation." In a word, M. de Beust looked to nothing less than to a joint intervention of the European Powers in the affairs of Turkey, without concealing that in such a situation, "there would be an opportunity to take into consideration, in a fitting degree, the natural *rôle* which the commonalty of religious institutions would secure for Russia in the Orient," and clearly showing the necessity of relieving the empire of the czars of the onerous conditions which were imposed upon it in the Black Sea, "in order to secure for himself by a conciliating attitude the sincere coöperation of this Power in the questions of the Levant."

It was truly a bold plan; it did not even fail to violently shock the French feelings. Was it not in truth to erase with a single stroke a past of ten years, to lose all the fruit of the Crimean war? They had some repugnance in avowing to themselves that the treaty of 1856 had not existed for a long time, alas! since the day when the French government had broken by its gratuitous kindness towards Russia this cluster of the three great Occidental Powers which alone could assure its efficacious execution. Since then the act had gradually become void, had been violated in the majority of the stipulations; and the conference of Paris, charged nominally with watching over the observance of the treaty, was always restricted, as the Austrian dispatch observed, "in giving its sanction to facts accomplished outside of its sphere of action, and which were not in harmony with the agreements placed under its protection." However, on the day after Sadowa, Prince Gortchakof did not fail to seize the first opportunity to begin to prepare the epitaph of the treaty of Paris. "Our august master," said the Russian chancellor in a document dated the 20th August, 1866, and marked by fine irony,—"our august master does not intend to insist on the general engagements of the treaties *which have no value except by reason of the accord existing between the great Powers in order to make them respected*, and which to-day have received, by *the want of this joint will*, too frequent and too severe blows not to be rendered *invalid.*" It was exactly this *collective will* which M. de Beust expected to revive and strengthen in projecting the revision of the act of 1856. According to his opinion, the treaty of Paris had not attained its purpose, which was to insure the entireness and the vitality of the Ottoman empire. On one side the Occidental Powers have imposed on Russia on the banks of the Euxine a restriction of its rights of sovereignty which a great empire could not definitely accept, and from which sooner or later it would seek to free itself. On the other side, and as regards the Christian population of the Levant, they contented themselves with promulgating a firman promising reforms, and leaving Turkey to itself, instead of reserving for Europe the right to watch over the Ottoman government with a gentle but continued vigilance, so that it should fulfill its duties toward the rajahs, and by a wise and honest administration become independent and strong. The treaty of Paris had only, thought the Austrian minister, given to Russia what the Crimean war ought to have refused it above all,—the monopoly of influence over the rajahs; this monopoly it continued to exercise as in the past, in a hidden manner, it is true, but so much the more dangerously as it recognized no competition. M. de Beust wished to reëstablish the competition, or rather he wished to establish a general agreement "to make the Christian populations of the sultan *the debtors of all Europe*, in giving them, by the care of all the guaranteeing courts, autonomous institutions according to the diversity of religions and races,"[101] and he hesitated the less to make to this vast conception the sacrifice of the article of the treaty of Paris touching the neutralization of the Black Sea which Austria had combated from the beginning, and to which it had only given its adherence at the last moment to humor the Occidental Powers and put an end to the Crimean war, the events of which had since demonstrated its complete inefficacy. It was under the influence of the disaster of Sinopa that France and England had hoped to restrain the naval forces of the czar in the Euxine. They had thus thought to shelter Constantinople from a blow from the Russian hand; but on this point, as on so many others, the physiognomy of the Orient had essentially changed. Russia no longer meditated a *coup de main*: it advanced more slowly, but much more surely, towards its goal. The pacification of the Caucasus[102] the irremediable weakness of the Porte and the daily increasing discontent of the rajahs, as impatient of the Turkish yoke as they were devoted to their sole protector, the czar, were worth to it all the vessels of the Black Sea. "However, have they really freed Constantinople from all danger on that side?" asked the Austrian minister. "Supposing that Russia decides to construct vessels in the Sea of Asoph, will war be declared to hinder it?" And the cabinet of Vienna concluded by these characteristic words: "The question of *amour-propre* should not be decisive in view of the immense interests which are at stake to-day." In fact, they could not insist too much on this truth: the clause on the subject of the Euxine had been for a long time only a "question of *amour-propre*" between the Occidental Powers and Russia; nor could one deny that M. de Beust saw far and justly in his dispatch of the 1st January, 1867. On the day after Sadowa, he sought to reconstitute Europe, to regain it, if we are allowed to express ourselves thus, and he knew how to fix the price of it.

In a different direction, France exerted itself on its part to accede to the views of the cabinet of St. Petersburg in concentrating its efforts principally on the question of the hour, on this Candian insurrection, of which public opinion in Russia had so ardently espoused the cause. M. de Moustier proposed to Prince Gortchakof "an understanding on the eventualities which might arise in the Orient," and, after having already spoken of a "consultation of doctors," in a dispatch addressed to the ambassador of France at Constantinople (7th December, 1866) he even pronounced the words "heroic remedies." By this always medical euphemism, one understood, at Paris, the annexation of the isle of Crete to Greece, "the only possible issue," Prince Gortchakof had affirmed, the 16th November, 1866, "if the Powers will leave expedients and palliatives, which up to the present time have only increased for the future the present difficulties." The marriage of the young King of the Greeks, George I., with the Grand Duchess Olga Constantinovna, was then a decided matter, and at the Tuileries one demanded nothing better than to make the isle of Crete the "dowry" of the Russian princess. In fact they would not have felt any inconvenience, it seems, in increasing this dowry with Epirus and Thessaly: that was going very far, much farther even than could be desired by Russia, which had no interest in "allowing such an extension of Greece that it might become a powerful state."[103] It was the reconciliation between France and Russia that gave birth to the plan of a common proceeding to demand of the Turkish government the realization of the internal reforms, and the cession of Crete, disguised under the proposition of a plebiscite, a proceeding which was effectively realized in the month of March, 1867, and to which Austria, Prussia, and Italy rallied. Without doubt there was still a great deal of vagueness, and above all of desultoriness in the situation which began to take a form at this moment, and it was to be regretted that France and Austria had not previously agreed to be of one mind on the nature of the offers which they intended to make to Russia; but the offers were very real and very great, we cannot deny that; and it only depended on the successor of Count Nesselrode to arrange, to adjust, and to turn them to the profit and the glory of his august master. England could not oppose serious obstacles to the joint will of France, Russia, and Austria, in the affairs of the Levant; it was already resigned, and certainly the fruit which Prince Gortchakof saw ripening in the spring of 1867, although not having all the attraction of forbidden fruit, was nevertheless good and savory, very different from that which, four years later, he was to pick up in the ashes of Sedan.

It is true that the governments of France and Austria did not mean to make a gratuitous gift; it was understood that, in exchange for these very large concessions in the Orient, they should obtain the support of the cabinet of St. Petersburg in the menacing complications of the Occident, and many circumstances seemed to plead in favor of such a combination. After all, and exclusive of the vengeance taken on "the ungrateful" empire of the Hapsburg, Russia could not greatly rejoice at the work of M. de Bismarck. Without mentioning several relations of the imperial family whom the Hohenzollern dethroned and despoiled with firmness tempered with a few tears, there was in general in the proceedings and principles inaugurated on the Elbe and the Main a strong revolutionary taint which could hardly please a court which did not cease to protect the shadow of Nicholas. The gravest, however, was that the victory of Sadowa had just brusquely disturbed and even threatened to ruin entirely the secular system of the Russian policy in regard to the affairs of Germany.

In fact, since Peter the Great, especially since Catherine II., Russia had always labored to obtain a preponderant influence among the different German courts: its czars have more than once acted with a high hand and used high words in the Teutonic troubles. "The Romanof enjoys with us a birthright acknowledged by his brothers, our sovereigns of the *Bund*," a celebrated publicist of the other side of the Rhine exclaimed with bitterness one day, and the attitude of the secondary States during the Crimean war truly did not weaken the justice of this expression. But it was this work of several reigns, and of a thought hitherto immutable, that Russia saw placed in question by the foreseen results of the campaign of Bohemia. The North of Germany was already escaping its influence, and the "*naïf*" ones alone could deceive themselves on the fortune reserved for the South in a very near future. "From the month of September, 1866, the cabinet of Berlin had, in a circular which was designedly made public, claimed for the confederation of the North and the States of the South alone, to the exclusion of all the other Powers, without excepting Austria, the right to bind their relations as closely as they wished, thus giving to Article IV. of the treaty of Prague, an interpretation of which it did not admit. In the speeches which he had delivered at the opening of the Prussian chambers and of the Northern parliament, the king himself, while addressing them *to Germany, to the brotherly peoples, to the country which the Alps and the Baltic bound*, had given utterance to allusions which made, according to the expression of the official journals, the hearts of all patriots tremble."[104] On his part, M. de Bismarck had cried out in the midst of the same parliament, using these gambling terms which are so common in his language and so characteristic of his temperament: "Our stake has become greater in consequence of our victories; we have now more to lose, but the game is still far from being completely won!" By means of a combined and resolute action of Europe; the absorption of all Germany by Prussia was only a question of time and of management; Russia, even less than France, would find its reward in it. France only saw uniting in a more compact and menacing body a confederation of kingdoms and principalities which already before had been either hostile, or at least opposed to it. Russia, on the contrary, lost an entire league of states, whose fidelity and devotion had never wavered, who formed for it a sort of continuous *enceinte* on the side of an occasionally unsympathetic Occident; in their place was to arise a formidable Power, restless and invading from the very start, called sooner or later by the necessity of history, by the fatality of race, to represent and to oppose the Germanic to the Sclavic idea. At every other epoch of the empire of the czars, in the good old time of Count Nesselrode, for instance,—when, in place of a policy of spite and propaganda on the banks of the Neva, they maintained a policy of conservation and equilibrium,—the conduct of a Russian chancellor in such an occurrence would not have been doubtful: a coalition of Russia, of France, and of Austria would have been formed on the day after

Sadowa for the safety of Europe, and it is not saying too much to affirm that, in the spring of the year 1867, Alexander Mikhaïlovitch held in his hands the destinies of the world.

Thus compelled to make his choice, Prince Gortchakof was unwilling to decline the French and Austrian advances in the question of the Orient; on the contrary, he hastened to echo them loudly, and sometimes even rose on this occasion to a lyricism not often heard in the chancellors' offices. He was charmed with the new minister of Austria, and filled all the country with a rather forced enthusiasm. "M. de Beust," he wrote to his ambassador in London, "inaugurates a new era in the policy of Austria, an era of large and elevated views; he is the first statesman of this country and of our epoch who courageously endeavors to leave the ground of petty rivalries." As regards France, he endeavored especially to indicate plainly that the initiative came from it, and "while begging the Emperor Napoleon III. to recall the interviews which the Emperor Alexander had had with him at Stuttgart" (in 1860), he seemed to wish to assign to the present conferences an extraordinary character of gravity and generality. "His imperial majesty," continued the Russian chancellor, in his dispatch of the 16th November, 1866, to M. de Budberg, "has received with satisfaction the overtures which M. le Marquis de Moustier has made us in view of an understanding between the French cabinet and ours on the eventualities which might arise in the Orient. The general principles which the French minister of foreign affairs has propounded, the assurances which he has given us, have in the eyes of our august master a very especial value, since they emanate from the direct thought of the Emperor Napoleon, and since it was by the express order of his majesty that M. le Marquis de Moustier has broached these questions." The animation and spirits of Alexander Mikhaïlovitch increase daily: he even ended by talking Latin and by confounding the poor Turkish envoy with a classical quotation. "Here," he wrote in the month of February, 1867, "is what I have said to Comnenos-Bey: the isle of Crete is lost to you; after six months of such a bitter struggle, reconciliation is no longer possible. Even admitting that you succeeded in reestablishing there for some time the authority of the sultan, it would only be on a heap of ruins and a mountain of corpses. Tacitus long ago told us of the danger there is in this reign of silence which succeeds devastation: *Solitudinem faciunt, pacem appellant.*"

Unfortunately it did not take long to see that while holding out hopes to France and Austria for the success of their Oriental movement, and even endeavoring to compromise them in this direction as much as possible,[105] the Russian chancellor was extremely careful to maintain his intimate accord with his former colleague of Frankfort, and not to oppose him in his ideas in the affairs of the Occident. Very ardent for the cause of the plebiscite in Crete, he showed on the contrary an absolute indifference on the subject of an analogous cause on the Eider, otherwise legitimate, however, guaranteed by solemn treaties,[106] and which interested to such a high degree the noble and unfortunate country of the future empress. He preserved a not less significant silence as regarded the publication made in the month of March, 1867, by M. de Bismarck, of the conventions with the Southern States, conventions which bound to Prussia the military forces of Germany, and abolished, in fact, "the international independent situation" which the preliminaries of Nikolsburg had stipulated for Bavaria and Würtemberg.[107] Alexander Mikhaïlovitch held Würtemberg as cheaply as Denmark, the throne of Queen Olga, as the cradle of the Princess Dagmar. In the mean time the affair of Luxemburg arose, and the French government could measure the degree of benevolence with which it had succeeded in inspiring the cabinet of St. Petersburg by its "heroic remedies" as regards Turkey. The Russian chancellor was surely right and very sincere in his desire for peace, but he had not for the position of France the regards which England itself thought just to show it; he seemed, above all, engaged in not giving umbrage to his illustrious friend of Berlin. While also glorifying M. de Beust for his "courageous endeavor to have done with petty rivalries," the Russian government did not fail to encourage at the same time, in the most dangerous and provoking manner, the violent Sclavic opposition in the empire of the Hapsburg by means of that famous *congress* of Moscow, of which we shall speak later. Other deceptions still, less known to the public, but not less sharp, probably added to all these disappointments, for Austria as well as France did not delay in making their retreat from this shifting ground of the Orient and joining in with England in thenceforward firmly maintaining the rights of the sultan. The "consultation of doctors" had a final end, and the legendary *sick man* was none the worse for it; but all was then decided for the terrible eventualities of the future.

"There exists an understanding between St. Petersburg and Berlin," M. Benedetti again avowed in the year after (5th January, 1868), while speaking of the so often mentioned mission of General Manteuffel as the point of departure of this agreement which did not cease to harass him. "Was it not, in fact, from this moment," he asked, "that the two courts indicate more plainly their policy, Russia in the Orient and in the Sclavic Provinces of Austria, Prussia in Germany, without even a cloud arising between them? Firmly united on all questions, they have, each for itself, pursued their designs with a confidence which proves that they have stipulated mutual guarantees." And the ambassador adds that this conviction begins to impress itself on many minds, especially on Lord Loftus, his English colleague, for a long time very incredulous on this matter. "His manner of seeing is sensibly modified, and he is not less persuaded than other members of the diplomatic corps that final arrangements had been made between the two governments of King William and the Emperor Alexander. I have, for my part, found the permanent demonstration of it, if I may so express myself, in the firmly fixed resolution, which has never changed, of the cabinet of Berlin, to inaugurate German unity for its own especial benefit, without allowing itself to be moved for an instant by the possibility of a conflict with France. I have also seen the proof of it in the care with which M. de Bismarck avoids explaining himself on the question of the Orient. When one asks him, he replies that he never reads the correspondence of the ministers of the king at Constantinople; and your excellency will not have forgotten with what complaisance he has always lent himself to the views of Prince Gortchakof." M. Benedetti also notices "the new impulse given since last summer to the Pan-Sclavic propaganda;" he shows very clearly the vast designs and far-reaching hopes of the cabinet of St. Petersburg, in its connivance with Prussia, and gives a higher and juster idea in general of the Russian policy at this epoch than certain ill-advised panegyrists of our day, who, to prove that Prince Gortchakof has filled his *rôle* as completely as possible, and with all desirable success, can devise nothing better than to lessen and depreciate this part.

II.

It is the characteristic of all conventional praise to exaggerate not only the tone, but even to deceive itself sometimes in the amount; there is perfume and ashes in incense, said the ancients, and there is something equivocal also in the usual manner of congratulating the Russian chancellor on his "triumph" in the question of the Euxine. To pretend that Prince Gortchakof did not favor the audacious designs of Prussia in order to free Russia from its bonds in the Black Sea, that he delivered Europe in advance to Prince Bismarck in the sole hope of some day repudiating to his advantage the act of 1856, is in truth to pay as little honor to his genius as to his patriotism. Certainly the eminent statesman whose "prophetic glance" the grandchildren of Washington[108] celebrated at St. Petersburg in the year of Sadowa, supplicating the eternal God, "who had made the sun stand still for Joshua," also to suspend the course of life for Alexander Mikhaïlovitch, "so that the eyes of the world might long remain fixed on him,"[109] the consummate diplomat who, in the spring of 1867, slighted the important advances made by the cabinets of Vienna and the Tuileries,—certainly this minister did not fail at this moment to put aside with a disdainful smile, the petty hypothesis, that in the approaching and foreseen overturning of Europe, there would be assigned to Russia as its sole victory and conquest, the abolition of any wounding article of a treaty which events had long before rendered "invalid." It was not for such a "plate of lentils," to use the language of M. de Bismarck, that Prince Gortchakof intended to cede to the Hohenzollern the fixed *birthright* of the Romanof; he did not think of abandoning the Occident for such a ridiculous price: he looked higher, and expected to have the lion's share in the quarry to come. Fortune has deceived his hopes, defeated his calculations, and forced him to bend to many unforeseen necessities; but, if it is puerile to allow him to have made virtues of all these vexatious necessities, and to form for him a sort of aureole of lightnings and thunderbolts of the war of 1870, history, in its impartiality, must not the less take into consideration the intentions of Prince Gortchakof, which were as great as the events themselves, and, without denying his defeat, nevertheless accord him the full benefit *in magnis voluisse*.

They cherished, in fact, great, gigantic projects on the banks of the Moscova and the Neva, in all this agitated and feverish epoch which separated Sedan from Sadowa; they deluded themselves with enchanting dreams; they divided the world between Sclavians and Germans, and the "national" minister responded to the ardent wishes of the entire nation in making the Prussian alliance the pivot of its policy, in seeing in it the absolute condition and the sure pledge of a future of glory and prosperity for Russia. We must look back on the universal mental agitation in consequence of the equally prodigious and unforeseen victory of Prussia in 1866, on the innumerable fantastic plans which were then suddenly formed for the reconstruction of empires and races; it is necessary to recall this endless flight of Minervas all armed, whom the blow of the German Vulcan's hammer caused to spring forth from so many cracked heads who thought themselves Olympian,—the general *remoulding* which our poor philosophy of history, at once so cutting and so malleable, undergoes in the twinkling of an eye,—to appreciate justly the current of strange and impetuous ideas which then seized the people of Peter the Great and of Catherine II. "An irresistible power forces the people to reunite in great masses, making the secondary States disappear, and this tendency is perhaps inspired by a sort of providential prevision of the destinies of the world." This, on the day after Sadowa, was the expression of an official document of incontestable authority, a diplomatic manifest which announced *urbi et orbi* the profoundest thoughts of the imperial government of France.[110] How can one be astonished, then, that the children of Rourik followed the same reasoning, and asked themselves with candor if the battle of Koenigsgraetz did not entirely deliver Central Europe to the Hohenzollern and Oriental Europe to the Romanof? After some moments of hesitation and surprise, Muscovite patriotism resolved therefore, to take no umbrage at the ambition of King William I., but it immediately proclaimed that Russia also had a mission to fulfill, an "idea" to realize, and that the sun of national unities and grand combinations shone for all the world.

There was in the old capital of the czars a celebrated journal whose power has since greatly declined, and which, although now an ordinary paper only, but still important, then exercised a preponderant, tyrannic influence, from the Dwina to the Ural: it was occasionally called, and without malice, "the first power in the state after the emperor." From the time of the fatal insurrections of Poland, the "Gazette of Moscow" was in truth the monitor of the popular passions of Holy Russia, the office from whence the word of command for public opinion went forth into the vast empire of the North, and it often issued formal instructions for the directing ministers at St. Petersburg. Even at this time the all-powerful organ of M. Katkof made itself the mouth-piece of the nation, and imperiously traced the programme of the policy of the future. Only a short time after the conclusion of the peace of Prague, the journal of Moscow laid down "as an incontestable truth, that the march of events has produced interests which invite the two Powers of Russia and Prussia to ally themselves still more actively than in the past;" it affirmed, moreover, that overtures on this point had been made by M. de Bismarck, "overtures the more acceptable as Prussia has no interests in the Orient; on this question, the cabinet of Berlin could take, in concert with Russia, such an attitude as suited it." The theme was again taken up and developed under many a form and in many an article, until a leader of the 17th February, 1867, impressed on it the great consecration of a speculative and humanitarian principle.

"The new era is at last sketched," one reads there, "and for us Russians it has a peculiar bearing. This era is truly ours; it calls to life a new world kept until now in the shadow and expectation of its destinies, the Græco-Sclavic world. After centuries passed in resignation and servitude, this world at last reaches the moment of renovation; what has so long been forgotten and down-trodden, comes back to the light and prepares for action. The present generations will see great changes, great facts, and great formations. Already on the peninsula of the Balkan, and under the worm-eaten couch of Ottoman tyranny, three groups of lively and strong nationalities are being formed, the Hellenic, Sclavic, and Roumanian groups. Closely bound among themselves by the commonalty of their faith and their historical destinies, these three groups are equally connected with Russia by all the ties of religion and national life. These three groups of nations once reconstructed, Russia will reveal itself in an entirely different light. It will no longer be alone in the world; in place of a sombre, Asiatic power, as it now seems to be, it will become a moral force indispensable to Europe, a Græco-Sclavic civilization completing the Latin-German civilization, which without it would remain imperfect and inert in its sterile exclusiveness." Soon after descending from these rather abstract heights to the more practical ground of ways and means, the fiery apostle of the *new era* exclaimed on the 7th April: "If France sustains by arms and by its political influence the *renaissance* of the Latin races, if Prussia acts in the same manner *vis-à-vis* to Germany, why, then, should not Russia, the only independent Sclavic Power, sustain the Sclavic races, and should it not prevent foreign Powers from placing obstacles in the way of their political development? Russia should employ all its powers to introduce in its neighbors of the South a transformation similar to that which took place in Central and Occidental Europe; *vis-à-vis* the Sclavians it should take, without the least hesitation, the rôle which France has taken in regard to the Latin races and Prussia *vis-à-vis* the German world. The task is a noble one, for *it is exempt from egotism*: it is beneficial, for it will achieve the triumph of the principle of nationalities, and will give a solid basis to the modern equilibrium of Europe; it is worthy of Russia and of its greatness; it is immense, and we have the firm conviction that Russia will fulfill it."

It was under the stimulant of such theories, hopes, and passions, that, in the spring of the year 1867, the strange *ethnological exposition of Moscow*[111] was instituted, which soon became the pretext for a great demonstration from without, sufficiently inoffensive in appearance to remove all diplomatic embarrassment, well calculated, however, to produce its effect on *naïf* and inflammable minds, to fascinate unfortunate, disinherited people, richer in imagination than in culture. Certainly, true science would draw very little profit from this projected reunion in the *manége* of Moscow of all the Sclavic "types" with their costumes, their arms, their domestic utensils, and their flora; but the undertaking was considered not the less worthy of the most august protection. The emperor and the empress offered considerable sums to defray the costs of the work, the Grand Duke Vladimir accepted the honorary presidency of it, the high dignitaries of the court and the church charged themselves with its direction. Warm appeals were addressed to the Sclavians of Austria and Turkey, to their different historical, geographical, or other learned societies, to add by numerous contributions to the magnificence of the exposition, and a cloud of emissaries collected in the countries of the Danube and of the Balkan in search of adhesion, samples, and "types." Committees were formed in different parts of the empire, in order to worthily prepare the reception of the "Sclavic guests," who did not fail to swarm to the "national jubilee," and soon a *congress* was spoken of, in which should be discussed the wants and the interests of so many "brother peoples," the hopes and the griefs of the great common country, of the *ideal* country. It was the moment, it is necessary to recall it, when the Cretan insurrection, always persistent, stirred up by Greece, and exaggerated by the journals too little or too well informed, kept the Christian populations of Turkey in alarm and on their guard; the moment, also, when the Czechen of Bohemia; urging on in consequence almost all the Sclavians of Austria, protested against the Cisleithan constitution, and refused to sit in the representative chambers of the empire. The *Kremlin* thus became the *mons sacer* of the *intransigeans* of the two banks of the Leitha, the *congress of Moscow* had all the appearance of an *opposition parliament* opposed to the Reichsrath of Vienna, and the language held by the authorized organs of the cabinet of St. Petersburg was not calculated to calm the susceptibilities of the interested governments, nor to dissuade vexatious manifestations. Speaking of the pious *pilgrims* of Turkey and Austria who were preparing to visit Moscow, "that holy Mecca of the Sclavians," the "Correspondance Russe," the ministerial journal *par excellence*,[112] thus expressed itself in the month of April, 1867: "One cannot reasonably demand of us that we abjure our past. We will let, then, our guests believe that they have come to a sister nation *from whom they have everything to expect* and nothing to fear; *we will listen to their grievances*, and the recital of their evils can only tighten the ties which unite us with them. If now they intend to establish a comparison between their political state and ours, *we will not be foolish enough* to prove to them that they are in the most favorable conditions of Sclavic development. These conditions, we believe, on the contrary, to be bad; we have said so a hundred times, and we can well say so again."

Without doubt the Russian intrigues in the countries of the Danube and the Balkan were not of very recent invention; they even dated back very far in the past, from the reign of the great Catherine. Underhandedly and secretly, the Pan-Sclavic propaganda had been encouraged or protected for nearly a century; but it was for the first time, in this summer of 1867, that the government of St. Petersburg thus loftily assumed the responsibility of such a propaganda, and unfurled in its states the flags of Saints Cyrille and Methode. In an empire where all is watched, regulated, and commanded from the throne, where nothing is done spontaneously, where all is arranged and *devised*, "foreign Sclavians," subjects of two neighboring and "friendly" Powers, were admitted, encouraged to come to expose their grievances, to bring complaints against their respective governments, to demand assistance and deliverance in the name of a new right of nations, of a principle lately discovered of great combinations and national unities. *They were not foolish enough* to dismiss these foreign "deputies," to counsel reason and resignation to them; on the contrary they spoke to them of a "better and approaching condition," they took them through all the cities of the empire amidst enthusiastic manifestations directed by the colonels and archimandrites, they overwhelmed them with testimonies of sympathy, ovations and demonstrations, in which the army, the magistrates, and all the higher official world took part. Generals, admirals, and ministers presided at banquets where the disaster of Sadowa was celebrated as a providential and happy event by the subjects of the Emperor Francis Joseph, where appeals were addressed to the czar "to revenge the secular outrages of the White Mountain and of Kossovo, and to plant the Russian banner on the Dardanelles, and on the basilica of St. Sophia." The shock given by such demonstrations to a whole race, to a whole religious world, was profound and prolonged, and certainly the contemporaneous annals have rarely known a period as *incorrect* in point of view of international right and of the usages of the chancellors' offices as that which had for its starting point the congress of Moscow and for its end the conference of Paris on the subject of Greece. It was a strange one in truth, this epoch, with such presidents of the council as Ratazzi, Bratiano, Koumondouros, with generalissimos like Garibaldi, Pétropoulaki, and "Philip the Bulgarian;" with these expeditions of Mentana, of Sistow, of the *Arcadion* and *Enosis*; with these agitations, to mention all, German, Italian, Czech, Croatian, Roumanian, Servian, Bulgarian, Grecian, and Pan-Sclavic. Without entering farther into the tiresome history of these complex and not yet explained events, it suffices, in order to appreciate the general character of them and to comprehend their close ties, to re-read with all the attention which it merits the report, already mentioned, of the ambassador of France to the court of Berlin, dated the 5th January, 1868. "M. de Bismarck must have," wrote M. Benedetti, "a disturbed Italy, in permanent disagreement with France, to constrain us to maintain forces more or less considerable in the States of the Holy See, to be able, if necessary, to excite, by the aid of the revolutionary party, a violent rupture between the government of the emperor and that of King Victor Emmanuel, to neutralize, in a word, our liberty on the Rhine.... And I would not be surprised if M. de Bismarck were the instigator of the new impulse given since last summer to the Pan-Sclavic propaganda; he finds in it the immediate advantage of disturbing Austria by Russia. Russia will assuredly show itself less enterprising, and Prussia on its part will not encourage it (Russia) to renew the question of the Orient, for the simple reason that it itself (Prussia) would gain no advantage in it, if it did not think it indispensable to pay with this price for the liberty which it claims in Germany. The uncertainty of the situation only tightens every day the ties which unite Prussia with Russia and solidifies the ambitions of the one in Germany with those of the other in the Orient."

A permanent committee for the interests of Sclavic unity was formed on the day after the congress of Moscow, under the auspices of a grand duke, and his action was not slow in making itself felt among the Ruthenes, the Czechen, the Croatians of Austria; but it was especially in the tributary or subject provinces of the Ottoman Porte that the agitation became as chronic as it was perilous. The unfortunate Turk was assailed on all sides: one day it was the Vladika of Montenegro who demanded of him in a menacing tone some port of the Adriatic, another day the Prince of Servia demanded the evacuation of some fortress, enforcing his request with extraordinary armaments. Numerous convoys of arms arrived from Russia in the Danubian Provinces under the false designation of material for the construction of railroads,[113] while the Greek ships of war did not cease to wish to rekindle with all their strength in the isle of Crete an insurrection about to be extinguished and which, in truth, never was of very great extent. It was the epoch of "committees of aid" and "liberating bands" now overrunning the States of the Pope with the cry "*Roma o Morte!*" now making incursions in Thessaly to revenge "the outraged manes of Phocion and Philopœmon," or again freeing five times in the space of a year the Danube from the side of Roumania only to awaken in the

Balkans "the lion with the golden mane!" "To-day it is our duty, brothers, to prove to European diplomacy that descendants of the terrible Krum still exist; the lion with the golden mane and the trumpet of war call you." Thus read in the month of August, 1868, a proclamation dated from the "Balkans," and signed "*Provisional Government.*"[114] "It is a fact," wrote on the 6th February, 1868, in a curious report addressed to Count de Beust by the agent of Austria in the Principalities, Baron d'Eder,—"it is a fact that at Bucharest, as in the different cities on the banks of the Danube, there exist Bulgarian committees; their object is to provoke troubles in Bulgaria, to aid them, to give them more extended proportions than those of the past year. Only quite lately they were persuaded here that on the return of pleasant weather serious complications would break out in Occidental Europe which would permit Russia to declare war against Turkey, and, foreseeing these events, they have made preparations to influence with energy the Bulgarian rising. Although the government of the Principalities is in the hands of a party (radical) traditionally hostile to Russia, it has nevertheless for some time inclined towards this Power, and expects from it the realization of its efforts and its hopes. The journals of the opposition (conservative) combat these Russophile tendencies of the government; they reproach it with acting in concert with Prussia and with preparing difficulties for Austria in case of a conflict between France and Prussia. The journals of the government reply by saying that the national party is from principle the adversary of no Power, and that there is no reason for combating Russia from the moment that this Power defends the cause of right and of oppressed nationalities."

Assuredly it would be unjust to throw on the Russian government the responsibility of all the disorderly agitations of this epoch in the Sclavic-Græco-Roumanian world, but it is not the less true that it did nothing to stop or even disown them. In looking over the parliamentary documents of this time,—the different blue, red, green, and yellow books of the years 1867-1869,—one is struck at meeting at every step repeated and energetic representations, addressed by the cabinets of London, of the Tuileries, and of Vienna to Servia, Roumania, and to Greece concerning their military preparations, the clandestine shipments of arms and marauding bands, while the cabinets of St. Petersburg and Berlin carefully abstained from any proceeding of this sort. By a piquant change of things here below, which must have astonished the Nesselrode and the Kamptz in their heavenly abode, the Occidental Powers now, England and France, to whom also Austria joined itself, denounced to the world the revolutionary practices of the European demagogic party, while Prussia kept silent, and Russia refused to deny the fact or to plead extenuating circumstances for it. The excuses for the government of Athens Prince Gortchakof kindly found in the Hellenic constitution: "This constitution," said he, "gives to all Greeks full liberty to leave their own country and to take part in any conflict such as existed in

Crete;"[115] and that was truly an original spectacle, that of a minister of an autocracy displaying before an old whig like Lord Clarendon the inexorable conditions of a parliamentary and legal *régime*. The Porte, it will be remembered, wished to know nothing of a legality which destroyed it; it ended by losing patience, by addressing an *ultimatum* to the government of Athens, and a conference assembled at Paris "to seek for means to smooth over the difference between Turkey and Greece." Some good people apprehended an embarrassed attitude on the part of the Russian chancellor before such areopagus, they even believed him capable of trammeling the labors of this reunion: this was to ignore the resources of a mind as crafty as cultivated, and which profited by the occasion to venture his famous *mot* on Saturn. "I remember," he wrote to Baron Brunnow, at London, 13th January, 1869, "that there are some persons who accuse Russia of wishing to render the conference abortive. One is not ignorant that the conference emanates from the mind of the emperor. The fable of Saturn has no application in the wanderings of the policy of the imperial cabinet." Alexander Mikhaïlovitch was not at the end of his boldness; he became bitter, almost aggressive; he spoke of the "excitement from without," of a "process of progress," of the "distrust which was attached to every step of Russia," and went so far as to denounce a great conspiracy contrived by the Occidental Powers against the peace of the Levant. "It is impossible for us not to remark," he said, in a dispatch to Baron de Brunnow, of the 17th December, 1868, "that this discordant note is not the only one which has come to *disturb the echoes of the Orient*. It is thus that we have first seen Servia become the end in view of an agitation which, originated with the press, ended by gaining over diplomacy; Prince Michael Obrenovitch was suspected, and nothing less than his tragic end was necessary to disarm the hostilities directed against him. Soon after, accusations were directed against the government of the united Principalities: the Bulgarian bands became a motive for incrimination, it was reproached with having tolerated them, it was accused with having encouraged them. This complication was scarcely removed, before a new crisis arose in the relations of Turkey with Greece, a crisis still more grave and more dangerous to the general peace." Decidedly, in absence of the "fable of Saturn," that of the wolf and the lamb had its application in the wanderings of the policy of the imperial cabinet of St. Petersburg.

The conference of Paris succeeded, nevertheless, in its efforts; the Græco-Turkish difference was smoothed over, and with the spring of the year 1869 the cold wind of the propaganda whistled less strongly in the valleys of the Danube and the gorges of the Balkan. There was a sort of lull; but the combustible matters still remained heaped up, ready to catch fire from the first spark. The radicals of Roumania were not the only ones to foresee an offensive action of Russia in the Orient as soon as serious complications should break out in Occidental Europe; that was an almost universal conviction, and one which the children of Rourik shared the very first. The end of the year 1869 was signaled by an incident which did not fail to gravely impress all serious minds. They celebrated at St. Petersburg the centennial of the institution of the Order of St. George, the great military order of Russia, and of which the first class is only conferred on him who gains a brilliant victory. The Emperor Alexander II. sent this distinction to King William I., to the conqueror of Sadowa and the former champion of 1814. "Accept it," he telegraphed him, "as a new proof of the friendship which unites us, a friendship founded on the souvenir of that great epoch when our united armies fought for a sacred cause which was common to us." And the King of Prussia soon replied by telegraph: "Profoundly touched, and *with tears in my eyes*, I thank you for the honor which you have done me, and which I did not expect; but what pleases me still more are the expressions by which you have announced it to me. I see, in truth, in these expressions a new proof of your friendship and your remembrance of the great epoch when our united armies fought for the same sacred cause."[116]

At the commencement of the same year, and while the conference of Paris was still sitting, there died at Nice a faithful servant of the sultan's, one of the last great statesmen of Turkey. Before descending into the tomb, Fuad-Pacha traced with a faltering hand a memorial for his august master, which he said was his political testament. The document was to remain secret, and, in fact, only came to light quite recently.[117] "When this writing is placed before the eyes of your majesty," one reads in it, "I will no longer be in this world. You can therefore listen to me without distrust, and you should imbue yourself with this great and grievous truth, that *the Empire of the Osmanlis is in danger.*" And after having reviewed the different states of the Continent, and marked out the conflict more or less near, but inevitable, between France and Prussia, Fuad-Pacha concluded by these words: "An intestine dissension in Europe, and *a Bismarck in Russia*, and the face of the world will be changed."

III.

God alone could contemplate his finished work, and say "that it was good;" our poor humanity rarely tastes such a pure enjoyment, and the *party of action* in the councils of the second empire scarcely experienced it in consequence of the events of 1866, which it had so powerfully contributed to create. The ambassador of France at the court of Berlin was among the number of the disabused; the achievement of Italian unity only consoled him, very imperfectly in truth, for the profound blow which the calamity of Sadowa had given his own country. His disenchantment was great; but there is nothing like a great and grievous deception to sharpen and refine a mind naturally sagacious; and if Pascal has spoken of a second ignorance, that which comes after knowledge, there is also for certain diplomats a second knowledge, and like a second sight after a passing blindness. One cannot praise too highly the eminent qualities of observation and of judgment which M. Benedetti showed during the last four years of his embassy at Berlin, and, for this epoch of 1867 to 1870, history will fully confirm the testimony which he once thought proper to testify of himself, while protesting before his chief,[118] that during his mission in Prussia he had been "an active, correct, and far-seeing agent."

From 1867, in fact, the ambassador worked with patriotic zeal to enlighten his government on the state of affairs in Europe, and to advise it to make a strong resolution, either to resign itself frankly to the inevitable, or to prepare in good time for a conflict very imminent and full of great perils. He represented Prussia as working without cessation to unite all Germany, at the risk of provoking a conflict with France, inclining only too often to consider such a conflict as the surest and most direct means of arriving at its ends. In such a case, he guarded against giving them the least hope from the *particularists* of the South. "At the beginning of a national war," he said, "the most obstinate among them will only be extinguished by the masses who will regard the struggle, whatever may be the circumstances in the midst of which it will break out, as a war of aggression of France against their country; and if the fortune of arms were favorable to them, their demands would know no limits." He also noticed "the most active propaganda" which M. de Bismarck maintained in the countries the other side of the Main: "With the exception of some journals in the pay of the governments (of Munich and Stuttgart), or belonging to the ultra-radical party, the press seconds him in all the Southern States." He also sent word to Paris that the minister of William I. continued his negotiations with the revolutionary party in Italy; that he received agents of Garibaldi, unknown to the regular government of King Victor Emmanuel, the personal friend of the Emperor Napoleon III., who, at the time of the complications of Mentana, had only sounded Prussia in order to know "in what measure it could lend it its aid."[119] He was also the first to give warning concerning the shadowy practices with Prim and the Spanish candidature of the Hohenzollern. Lastly, one has already seen that he had recognized from the beginning the alarming character and true bearing of the mission of General Manteuffel to Russia.

"However difficult it may be for a great country like France to trace in advance its line of conduct in the actual state of things," said M. Benedetti to his government at the beginning of the year 1868, "and however great may be the part which it expects to take in unforeseen contingencies, the union of Germany under a military government strongly organized, and which in certain respects has of parliamentary *régime* only external forms, constitutes, however, a fact which touches too closely our national security to allow us to dispense with preparations, and to solve, without longer delay, the following question: Would such an event endanger the independence or the position of France in Europe, and would not this danger be conjured up only by war? If the government of the emperor thinks that France has nothing to fear from such a radical alteration in the relations of the states situated in the centre of the Continent, it will be desirable, in my opinion, in the interest of the maintenance of peace and public prosperity, to shape entirely and without reserve our attitude according to this conviction. If the contrary opinion is entertained, let us prepare for war without cessation, and let us be well assured in advance of what aid Austria can be to us; let us shape our conduct so as to solve one after the other the questions of the Orient and that of Italy; all our united forces will not be too great to render us victorious on the Rhine."

Especially in his manner of judging of the accord established between the two courts of Berlin and St. Petersburg, M. Benedetti showed a justness and superiority of judgment truly remarkable. He had the merit of foreseeing the understanding from the first moment, and of positively believing in it until the last. In the month of September, 1869, the Emperor of the French had thought of appointing as ambassador to the czar one of his most intimate friends, one of his most devoted coöperators of the 2d December, a general renowned for his bravery and intelligence, a grand equerry. It was sufficient to indicate that they wished to enter into relations as intimate and direct as possible, and in spite of the exchange of telegrams at the festival of St. George, they were already, at the beginning of the year 1870, full of hope; they believed that *the affair was progressing of itself*.[120] The French general, an able man, however, was very quickly taken to the bear hunts, to journeys on sledges, and shown many other marks of august kindness, which he had the modesty to credit to the policy of his master, in place of attributing them with much more reason to his very real and in truth very fascinating personal charms. The conviction of the grand equerry was shared by those surrounding him, especially by his aides-de-camp, who did not delay to praise in their confidential letters addressed to Paris, "the great results obtained" by their chief, and to speak of "his growing favor with the Emperor of all the Russias," in terms very strong and much more military than diplomatic.[121] Without being imposed upon by all these recitals, full of cheerfulness, M. Benedetti did not the less persist in his well founded conviction; even on the 30th June, 1870, on the very eve of the war, he expressed it in a lucid dispatch, from which we will have more than one instructive passage to quote. Speaking of the recent interview (1st-4th June) of the Emperor Alexander and the King of Prussia at Ems, the ambassador supposes that M. de Bismarck had shown himself then, as generally, on one side favorable to the policy of the cabinet of St. Petersburg in the Orient, and that on the other he endeavored to excite the susceptibility of the czar in the questions which agitate the national sentiment in Russia as regards Austria, Galicia, etc. "While the minister will have undertaken to reassure the emperor on the first of these two points and to alarm him on the other, the king will have displayed that good grace of which he has always known how to make such a marvelous use to capture the sympathies of his august nephew, and I do not doubt, for my part, that they have left impressions in conformity with his desire. But whatever may have been the means which they employed, their object must have been to strengthen the emperor in the sentiments which they have been able to inspire in him, and they have attained it more or less."

M. Benedetti was, however, far from admitting an official arrangement drawn up in due form between the two courts, and above all far from believing that the minister of Prussia had in all sincerity and candor made the cession and abandonment of the Oriental heritage to the hands of his former colleague of Frankfort, and it is precisely in such estimates that the uncommon perspicacity of the French diplomat shows itself. M. de Bismarck could for the necessities of the moment, simulate indifference regarding the affairs of the Levant, affirm that he "never read the correspondence of Constantinople," and even consider the pretensions of Russia "to introduce a certain unity in the intellectual development of the Sclavians, legitimate;"[122] but the extreme care which he used at the same time to maintain the most intimate relations with the Hungarians, his allies of 1866, should have already enlightened the zealots of Moscow concerning the inanity of their dream of a division of the world between the sons of Teut and those of Rourik. "The Hungarians regard us, us Prussians, as their mediate protectors against Vienna in the future," wrote, in a confidential dispatch, Baron de Werther in the month of June, 1867, on his return from the coronation of Buda, to reassure the cabinet of Berlin on the recent enthusiasm of the Magyars reconciled with their "king;" it is not only against Vienna, it is still much more against Moscow and St. Petersburg, against any Sclavic preponderance on the banks of the Danube, that the children of Arpad will in the future have aid from the Hohenzollern. "Prussia has no rightful interests in the Orient," M. de Bismarck was pleased to say in the years 1867-1870, and the organ of M. de Katkof did not cease to repeat this remark so often commented on; but from the day when Prussia identified itself with Germany, or rather incorporated itself in it, it remained charged, under pain of forfeiture, with the Germanic interests and influences in the countries of the Danube and of the Balkan, and the interest then became greater, much greater, than that of France and England.

All this was very well understood by the ambassador of France to the court of Berlin, and from time to time keenly exposed in the dispatches which he addressed to his government during the last years of his mission in Prussia. Writing, in his report of the 5th January, 1868, of the complaisance with which the chancellor of the confederation of the North always lent himself to the views of Prince Gortchakof, M. Benedetti added, however: "He (M. de Bismarck) persuades himself without doubt that other Powers have an interest of the first order in preserving the Ottoman empire from the covetousness of Russia, and he abandons the care of it to them; he knows, moreover, that *nothing can be definitely accomplished there without the aid or the adhesion of Germany, if Germany is united and strong*; he believes, then, that he can, for the present, and without peril, himself sharpen the ambition of the cabinet of St. Petersburg, provided that he obtains in return for this condescension a kind withdrawal from everything which he undertakes in Germany."

"In the Orient," wrote the ambassador some time after (4th February, 1868), "M. de Bismarck is careful to preserve a position which does not bind him in any way, and permits him, according to the necessities of his own designs, to give the hand to Russia, or to ally himself with Occidental Powers; but he can only preserve this position by abstaining from any proceeding which would compromise him with the friends or the adversaries of Turkey." This reasoning was not long in being fully justified by the attitude of Prussia, during the conference of Paris, on the subject of Greece (January, 1869). The cabinet of Berlin did not share in the ardor of Alexander Mikhaïlovitch; it did not defend, as he did, persecuted innocence in the person of "the young Roumania," and of the Servian *Omladina*, and above all was careful to denounce the great conspiracy of England, France, and Austria against the peace of the Levant. In reality the minister of Prussia did not wish the death of the just Osmanli, still less the collapse of Hungary, the advance guard of the Germanic "mission" in the East;[123] and his sympathies for a "certain ideal unity" of the Sclavians grew cold in proportion as the hour of the real unity of Germany approached. "Any conflict in the Orient will put it under the influence of Russia," wrote the French diplomat the 27th January, 1870, "and he will seek to excite it; he tried it last year at the beginning of the Græco-Turkish trouble. *Russia is a card in his game* for the eventualities which may arise on the Rhine, *and he is particularly careful not to change the rôles*, not to become himself a card in the game of the cabinet of St. Petersburg."

Some months after, on the very eve of the war with France (30th June, 1870), M. Benedetti, while thinking that the ties between Russia and Prussia could only have been drawn closer in the recent interview of Ems, concluded by the following observations: "It must not be supposed, however, that M. de Bismarck thinks it opportune to connect his policy closely with that of the Russian cabinet. In my opinion, he has not contracted and is not disposed to make any engagement which might, while compromising Prussia in the complications of which Turkey will become the scene, draw France and England closer together, and create difficulties for him or weaken him on the Rhine. The kind feelings of the chancellor of the confederation of the North for Russia will never be of a nature to limit his liberty of action; *he promises in fact more than he means to do*, or, in other words, he seeks the alliance with the cabinet of St. Petersburg to gain for himself the benefit of it in case of a conflict in the Occident, but with the well-fixed resolution never to engage the resources or the forces of Germany in the Orient. I have also always been persuaded that no official arrangement has been concluded between the two courts, and we can certainly believe that they did not consider that at Ems."

Everything, in fact, leads us to believe that neither a treaty was signed there, nor conditions discussed; the commonalty of views and the harmony of hearts dispensed with a fatiguing discussion of details. Moreover, it would have been very difficult, in all the useless cases, to make stipulations *en règle* for the eventualities, the time of whose appearance is not known, of which it is impossible to calculate the distant consequences, or even the immediate effects. They contented themselves with the conviction that they had no opposite interests; that, on the contrary, they were congenial and sympathetic, and that it was understood that at the propitious moment each one would be for himself and God for all. It must also be acknowledged that the Russians, in their views concerning the Orient, are not exempt from certain *mirages*. Europe credits them with much more method than they have in reality: the sentiment is profound and tenacious, but the plans are as wavering as they are different and vague. One might say that this great people suffer in this regard rather from a fascination and almost a fatality which prevents them from pursuing a systematic conquest; it advances on the phantom which possesses it only to make it recoil. It is a matter worthy of notice that Russia is never so far removed from the goal as when it undertakes to force the *dénoûment*. In 1829, a few halting places only separated its armies from Constantinople, and they turned back. It lost, in 1854, all the fruit of its campaign in Hungary, and of its ascendency in consequence of the catastrophe of February, while its prospects were never as brilliant as on the day when the treaty of Paris expected to close the Black Sea to it. It lost Sebastopol, but it gained the Caucasus and a whole world on the banks of the Amour and the Syr-Daria. The temptation became then very natural in presence of the formidable conflict which since 1867 was preparing in the centre of Europe, rather to await events than to wish to regulate them and to prescribe their course. In a war between the two strongest Powers of the Continent, which promised to be as long as desperate, and which in the end might well equally exhaust the two adversaries and draw several other states into the lists, Russia—thus they surely thought on the banks of the Neva—would always find the opportunity and the means of saying its word and securing its booty. Such a line of conduct seemed entirely marked out for a chancellor to whom so much good fortune had already come while "meditating;" it recommended itself to a policy which only measured the infinity of its aspirations by the uncertainty of possible events. The infinity of desires accommodates itself in case one can do nothing better with the indefinite in the designs, and nothing at times gives such a false impression of depth as emptiness.

It was cruelly ironic of the founder of German unity to choose in each of his successive enterprises an accomplice who was to become his victim in the following undertaking; but he showed, also, his great superiority in having had each time a very clear aim, a well-defined object marked out, and, so to speak, tangible, while his partners allowed themselves to be drawn in, one after the other, in the perilous game, under the impulse of abstract principles, vague desires, and cloudy combinations. At the time of the invasion of the Duchies and his first attempt against the equilibrium of Europe, M. de Bismarck was certainly not at a loss to show his aim: the prey was in reach of his hands, and the roadstead of Kiel spread itself in all its splendor before whoever had eyes to see; but M. de Rechberg is still seeking for it to-day, and to make the motives of his coöperation in this work of iniquity acceptable. "He tried to master the demagogic passions, to gain the ascendency over the revolution,"—these are the pompous and sonorous phrases taken from the "doctrine" with which later the former Austrian minister was to seek to cover up before the Austro-Hungarian delegations his fatal and pitiful policy of 1863. At Biarritz, the president of the Prussian council demanded in very clear terms the line of the Main for his country, while the dreamer of Ham recommended "the great war for the German nationality," and let his undecided glance fall first on the right bank of the Rhine and Mayence, then on the limits of 1814, and only fixed it on the winged lion of St. Mark. From 1867 to 1870, the chancellor of the Northern Confederation resolutely made preparations for the unification of Germany and the conquest of Alsace and Lorraine, leaving to his former colleague of Frankfort perfect leisure "to awaken the echoes of the Orient," and to demand of them the key to the approaching destinies of Russia. In each of these fatidical circumstances, the same great *realist* is always leading the ideologists to different degrees and to different titles: it is always the same Fortinbras of Shakspere,—the *fort en bras* of Germany,—proclaiming his dominion where the doctrinary, melancholy, or word-making Hamlets have only lost their way in chimerical and puerile machinations, and, before a "murder which cries out to heaven," find no other words than,—the time is out of joint!

"Russia cannot feel any alarm at the power of Prussia,"[124] said Prince Gortchakof, in reply to the representations which were made him from the beginning of the Hohenzollern affair on "the danger which would result to Russia from the aggrandizement of Prussia, and from the extension of its influence in Europe." As to the Spanish candidature of the Prussian prince, the chancellor recalled that "when Prince Charles of Hohenzollern became (in 1866) sovereign of Roumania, with the support of France and in spite of

Russia, this latter had limited itself to remonstrances, and had then accepted the fact, he did not see why to-day Prussia could be more responsible for the election of another member of the royal family to the throne of Spain." Thus spoke the minister of the czar at the very beginning of the conflict, the 8th July, 1870, before the renunciation of Prince Anthony, before any exhibition of anger on the part of the cabinet of the Tuileries, and at the moment when Europe still thought well of the legitimate susceptibilities of France. However, when the hour of blindness and giddiness came, and when the government of Napoleon III. lost all the profit of a great diplomatic success by its provoking language before the legislative body, by its demands of Ems, and its fatal declaration of war (15th July), illusions could no longer be cherished concerning the true sentiments of the cabinet of St. Petersburg. "With all due deference to General Fleury," wrote with humor M. de Beust to Prince de Metternich, the 20th July, "Russia perseveres in its alliance with Prussia so far, that in certain eventualities the intervention of the Muscovite arms must be looked upon not as probable, but as *certain*." Soon after the declarations of war of the 15th July, the Russian government had addressed to Vienna the very clear and categorical notice that it would not allow Austria to make common cause with France. General Fleury was even soon to think himself lucky with having at least made sure that this invalidating clause touching the empire of the Hapsburg was not explicitly mentioned in the declaration of neutrality which the Emperor Alexander II. published the 23d July.[125]

"Russia has done us much harm," said the Duke de Gramont, in regard to this interdicting command to Austria.[126] It weighed equally on the court of Copenhagen and forced it to neutrality, in spite of all the enthusiasm of the unfortunate Scandinavian people for an alliance with which was connected a French plan of a landing in the North, an enterprise of the greatest strategical interest, General Trochu said, who was to have taken part in it. "Russia," thought with an official journal of the country, the ambassador of the United States at St. Petersburg, "has contributed more to the neutrality than any other nation; by its menaces it has forced Austria not to move, and it has succeeded, by the influence of the emperor and the hereditary prince, in hindering Denmark from taking part with France."[127] England, it is just to add, powerfully seconded in all this the Russian chancellor. It was more prejudiced than ever against France, thanks to the recent and terrible revelations of M. de Bismarck concerning the *dilatory negotiations* in August, 1866, on the subject of Belgium. It was evident that for the pleasure of Prince Gortchakof the conflagration came much too soon. The military preparations of Russia were not made; even the perfectly "moral" action on the Sclavic world had undergone a rest since the conference on the subject of Greece. M. de Bismarck had not exactly consulted the convenience of his colleague on the Neva. As M. Benedetti had predicted, he had taken care not to invert the *rôles* and thought only of his own convenience and opportunities; but Alexander Mikhaïlovitch did not the less apply himself to play his *rôle* according to his strength. A sagacious observer, the ambassador of the United States, already mentioned, wrote about this time from St. Petersburg to his government: "The general opinion here seems to be that, if Russia were ready, it would declare war and try to gain certain advantages from it.... The government is making great efforts to prepare for future events. The cartridge factories work night and day. An order for a hundred Gattling cannon has just been sent to America." They armed, they deterred or intimidated the probable allies of France, thinking thus to equalize for the moment the chances between the two belligerents,[128] and they still hoped to find more than one favorable opportunity in the midst of the numerous events of a war which Napoleon III. himself proclaimed must be "long and difficult."

The terrible disasters of France in the beginning of the campaign suddenly arrested the imaginations in their flight and dissipated the sublime vision of a "new Græco-Sclavic world," which since 1867 had haunted the minds of those on the banks of the Moscova and the Neva. With the marvelous political and *realistic* aptitude which distinguishes it, the Russian nation soon understood that for the moment any crusade in the Orient was impossible, that the destiny of the world was being decided at the foot of the Vosges, and that it must attend to the most urgent and reasonable claims. A curious phenomenon, the peninsula of the Balkan was never as relatively quiet, as little tormented by the "great idea" as during these years 1870-1871, during this "intestine dissension in Europe" which Fuad-Pacha when dying had so feared for the empire of the Osmanlis. Towards the end of the month of August, still before the catastrophe of Sedan, public opinion in Russia cared only for the displeasing article of the treaty of Paris on the subject of the Euxine. "Russia," said an influential journal of St. Petersburg,[129] "has not hindered the forced unification of Germany, and, in its turn, *it does not dream of the forced unification of the Sclavians*; but it has the right to demand that its position on the Black Sea and the banks of the Danube be ameliorated. We hope that its legitimate demands will be taken into consideration in the European congress which will probably follow the present war." A European congress! that was in truth the only logical issue, however unreassuring in such grave events, disturbers of the equilibrium of the world; and it must render this justice to the greater part of the Russias, that they have the true appreciation of the situation, and aspire to a *rôle* as legitimate as honorable. They wish to attain a satisfaction of *amour-propre*; but they did not wish to sacrifice France and the general interests of the Continent to it; the little question was in their eyes only the corollary of the great. At Constantinople one did not augur otherwise from the line of conduct which the cabinet of St. Petersburg undoubtedly pursued, although dreading it. On the 2d September, Mr. Joy Morris, minister of the United States to the Porte, wrote to his government that the general conviction on the Bosphorus was that Russia would profit by the crisis to bring about the revision of the treaty of 1856. "It would be strange if it did not succeed in it," added the "Yankee" diplomat, "seeking, as it will, to obtain honorable conditions of peace for France, and exercising a dominating influence on the regulations of the terms of peace." Unfortunately, and for the first time in his long and popular reign at the chancellor's palace, the "national minister" divorced himself on this occasion from the sentiment of the nation, and in place of acting as "a good European," according to the favorite expression of M. de Talleyrand, he sought above all to show himself the good friend of his former colleague of Frankfort. He took care to renounce the question of the Black Sea,—he owed his country this little consolation after such great mistakes,—but he resolved to separate two causes which public opinion in Russia demanded to have united; and it demanded it with an idea much more politic than generous, in an instinct much more sensible for the vital interests of the future than for the satisfaction more or less lively of the present moment. He thought that he could not better serve the Russian cause on the Euxine, than in injuring as much as possible the cause of Europe in Alsace and Lorraine, and he endeavored above all to let France and Prussia fight out their quarrel in single combat. Immediately after the first French disasters, he seized with *empressement* the ingeniously perfidious idea of the *league of neutrals*, originally an Italian idea, naturalized in England by Earl Granville, and soon became in the hands of the Russian chancellor, as was very acutely remarked, the most efficacious means to "organize impotence in Europe." M. de Beust had vainly essayed, *while adopting the principle* of the English proposition (19th August) to change the character of it, to make it the point of departure of a concerted intervention; he demanded "efforts not separated, but common in view of a mediation," in place of a ridiculous conception which only "leagued" the states to prevent any collective proceeding. "The combination which the minister of Austria then suggested," wrote on this subject a judicious historian, "was repeated again and again by him during the whole duration of the war. If it had been adopted, it would have changed the course of things. One can say that it is for this reason that Europe did not adopt it."[130]

It is for this reason that Prince Gortchakof especially opposed it from the first day to the last. There was a moment when England itself felt some qualms of conscience and showed a wish for mediation. That was at the beginning of the month of October, after a circular of M. de Bismarck had announced to Europe the conditions of peace of Germany, which were Alsace and Lorraine. "The ambassador of Prussia communicated this circular to the Russian government, and Prince Gortchakof abstained from making his impressions known. Sir A. Buchanan said to him then, that at London they were disposed to be governed in a certain measure by what was done at St. Petersburg. The chancellor replied simply that Prussia, not having asked of him his opinion, he had not given it.[131] Earl Granville had the, for him, extraordinary courage to return again to the charge, and Sir A. Buchanan read to the Russian chancellor a memorandum timidly asking "if it would not be possible for England and Russia to arrive at an agreement concerning the conditions under which peace could be concluded, and then to make, with the other neutral Powers, an appeal to the humanity of the King of Prussia, also recommending moderation to the French government." Prince Gortchakof gave to those overtures a dry and disdainful reception. Prussia, said he, has indicated its conditions of peace; a victory alone can modify them, and this victory is not probable. Confidential conversations between England and Russia will be then without object; common representations would always have a more or less menacing character. Isolated action of each of the neutral Powers before the King of Prussia is preferable.[132] Isolated action! Alexander Mikhaïlovitch was not moved, and for Russia this action was summed up in several personal letters addressed by the august nephew to his royal uncle, very charming letters, which recommended peace, justice, humanity, and moderation, and to which the conqueror of Sedan always replied affectionately, with a moved heart and with tears in his eyes, pleading his duties to his allies, his armies, his people, and his frontiers.[133] It was this "policy of euphemism," as the historian has so well called it, which they did not cease to practice, during the entire war, on the banks of the Neva, towards General Fleury as well as towards M. Thiers and M. de Gabriac, and the last word as well as the first thought of "action" of Prince Gortchakof was to leave France alone with its conqueror, alone till exhaustion, *usque ad finem*. It is known in what terms this end was announced at St. Petersburg. "It is with inexpressible feeling and returning thanks to God," the Emperor of Germany telegraphed from Versailles to the Emperor of Russia, on the 26th February, 1871, "that I announce to you that the preliminaries of peace have just been signed. Prussia will never forget that it owes to you that the war has not taken extreme dimensions. May God bless you for it. Your grateful friend for life."

"Long and disastrous" was this war, alas! as the unhappy Cæsar had well predicted, long enough at least to let Europe measure all the depth of its abasement, and "to give it all the time to blush at nothing," according to the strong expression of the poet. Still more humiliating, perhaps, than this abasement, is the thought of the perfect similarity of the two terrible catastrophes which succeeded one another in the interval of scarcely four years; in producing its second tragedy so soon after the first, destiny was sufficiently disdainful to our generation not to even change the procedure or bestow any care on the imagination. The work of 1870 was only the exact copy of that of 1866. You will take the Orient, M. de Bismarck said at St. Petersburg, through General Manteuffel, as on the shore of Biarritz he had told the Emperor Napoleon III. to take Belgium, always making the same gift of the property which did not belong to him, the same gracious gift of the fruit defended by the dragon. The dreamers of Moscow believed in a *new era*, in a new "Græco-Sclavic-Roumanian world," as Napoleon III. had thought of a Europe remodeled after the principle of nationalities. "Russia will not feel any alarm at the power of Prussia," Prince Gortchakof declared at the beginning of the Hohenzollern affair, exactly as the zealots of the *new right* had affirmed of France on the eve of the campaign of Bohemia. In both of the terrible years they had counted on the events and opportunities of a war, slow and of divers fortunes; they had even made it a study to derisively equalize the chances of the belligerents, and the surprise and the fright were not less great at St. Petersburg after Reichshoffen and Sedan than it had been at Paris after Nahod and Sadowa. The military preparations were wanting in Russia in 1870, as in France in 1866, and after the one as after the other of the calamities which desolated and overturned the world, they had only egotistical and petty thoughts; they prevented designedly any collective intervention, they aided Prussia in *freeing itself from all European control*; in a word they sacrificed the policy of justice, preservation, and equilibrium to a calculation as false as sordid, and which the great humorist of Varzin had one day called the *politique de pour-boire*.

The Russian chancellor, it is just to acknowledge, was happier after Sedan than Napoleon III. had been after Sadowa: he had his Luxemburg, he could proclaim the abrogation of Article II. of the treaty of Paris, "the abrogation of a theoretical principle without immediate application," as he himself said in an official document.[134] One knows the judgment which at that time the cabinets gave on this "conquest" purely nominal in reality, and extremely small in any case in proportion to all those which Alexander Mikhaïlovitch had allowed to his former colleague of Frankfort. He succeeded, but not by legitimate means, by that action of *éclat* and equity which one had hoped for in Russia, dreaded at Constantinople; he did not provoke the revision of the treaty of 1856, in "seeking to obtain honorable conditions of peace for France and in exercising a dominating influence on the regulation of the terms of peace."[135] He chose precisely "the psychological moment" of the defeats of France, of the disorder of Europe and of the gloomy shock to public right, to give it in his turn a humiliating blow, a *telum imbelle*, but not *sine ictu*. He freed himself and his own chief from an engagement contracted with the Powers, as he had freed his friend of Berlin from any control of Europe. "The procedure of Russia," said Earl Granville, in his remarkable dispatch of the 10th November to Sir A. Buchanan, "breaks all the treaties: the object of a treaty is to bind the contracting parties one to the other;

according to the Russian doctrine, each party submits all to his own authority, and holds himself bound only to himself."

At the beginning of the year 1868, an eminent man whom the disasters of his country were soon to restore to the political life which the second empire closed to him, rose even here[136] with passionate eloquence against "the growing mistrust of this elementary right which honor and good public sense have called the faith of treaties." "We see," said he, "creating itself every day under our eyes, a fruitful jurisprudence whose rapid development does not astonish those who know what force false principles borrow from and lend in turn to the passions which they favor. Only a few years ago they imposed on this unilateral resilition of reciprocal treaties some conditions which made the usage of them more legitimate, or at least more rare and less perilous. They still wished greatly to admit that, in case one state should want to repudiate a treaty signed by representatives regularly accredited, it should be necessary that in its interior one of those great overturnings of institutions, persons, and things should be effected which is called a revolution. A revolution was a sheriff's summons by which a nation made known to whom it should concern its intention to put itself into bankruptcy and to no longer pay its debts. This was, it seems to me, a sufficiently great facility, but the last form of new right does not find it sufficient to its taste. The formality of a revolution is embarrassing and costly to carry out. A change of ministry, or, better still, a vote of parliament causes less inconvenience. Nothing more will be necessary henceforward in order that a convention in which God, honor, and conscience have been taken to witness the past year be trampled under foot the following year."

Well! we have lived through enough, since the time when an honest conscience uttered this cry of alarm, to see foreign jurisprudence arise without even the formality of a revolution, of a change of ministry or a vote of parliament, to hear it proclaimed by the minister of a regular absolute monarchy, by a Russian chancellor. It is true that the Italians also then hastened to profit by the misfortunes of France, to break in their turn a solemn engagement made with it in a public document, that in 1870 they had even anticipated Prince Gortchakof in a proceeding well known to them; but it was not from a government born yesterday that the successor of Count Nesselrode should have borrowed the procedures. There was a day when Alexander Mikhaïlovitch reproached this very government with *moving with the revolution to reap the heritage of it*.[137] Since then he has also moved with the revolution,—with one of the most audacious, most violent revolutions which has ever overturned thrones and kingdoms; he has reaped no heritage from it, it is true (it is only too often so in life, as one knows), he only accepted from it a gracious legacy, a legitimate donation, a modest gift in fact, and out of proportion to services rendered, but which was not the less sullied with undue influences, and which injured the right of the third parties, the right of nations.

How otherwise great and glorious might have been the "conquests" of Alexander Mikhaïlovitch, if, inspiring himself, in the month of October, 1870, with the legitimate ambition of the Russian people, the "national minister" had brought about a concerted action of Europe in order to produce peace between France and Germany, and to regulate the troubled affairs of the Continent! "We have always been of the opinion," wrote M. de Beust, on the 10th September, to St. Petersburg, "that it is for Russia to take the initiative." Its great influence abroad, its security in the interior, its good relations with the conqueror, assigned to it in truth such an initiative, and certainly neither Austria, Italy, nor England would have hesitated to range themselves under its banner. There was no necessity for a menacing intervention, nor even for that armed neutrality which M. Disraeli recommended:[138] the wish firmly expressed by all the Powers of the Continent would have fully sufficed. They could have thus limited the losses of France, given to Germany a less formidable organization, more in harmony with the aspirations and liberal occupations of our century,—the great vassals of the new emperor would not have failed to lend their aid to it,—a general disarmament would have given to a generation cruelly tried, and which now cannot even rest in its sterility, a reparative and a fruitful work. And who would dare to doubt that after such services Russia would not have obtained of Europe the grateful abrogation of that onerous article of the treaty of 1856? France would certainly not have thought of opposing it; Austria would not have maintained a clause which it had combated from the beginning, and which, four years before, it had solemnly declared to be "only a question of *amour-propre*," whose gravest interests demanded the sacrifice; as to England, it is well known that in course of time it accommodates itself to everything. How much such a benefit procured for humanity by a monarchical government, absolute indeed, would have given force to the cause of order and preservation, of rejuvenation of monarchical principles! with what prestige it would have surrounded the Russian people; what imperishable splendor it would have attached to the name of Alexander II! The call of destiny was very manifest; the *rôle* as plain as easy: the successor of Count Nesselrode shrunk from it. It was only a sin of omission, if you will, but of that sort which the sublime lover of justice Alighieri did not pardon when they were committed against his ideal of *justitia et pax*. On such a sin he inflicted the name of *il gran rifiuto*.

VI.

TEN YEARS OF ASSOCIATION.

On the 9th January, 1873, Napoleon III. passed sadly away from the land of exile at Chiselhurst, and a short time after, the 27th March, William I. entered on the sixty-sixth year of a life in which assuredly the most extraordinary favors of fortune have not been wanting. Germany celebrated the *fête* of its new emperor with transports of joy, the more noisy and sincere since the monarch had waited for this anniversary to ratify a last convention with the government of Versailles, a convention which assured the anticipated payment of the fifth milliard of the French ransom, and the very early return of the troops of occupation from the other side of the Vosges. The great accounts with *the hereditary enemy* thus definitely settled, the conqueror of Sedan thought, on his part, of acquitting himself of a little debt of the heart: he resolved to carry to the Emperor Alexander II. the expression of his lively gratitude for the loyal aid which he had lent him during a memorable period of trials and combats. Long foreseen, from time to time announced and put off, the journey to St. Petersburg was at length undertaken at the beginning of pleasant weather, and M. de Bismarck took care to state precisely on this occasion the date as well as the character of the close association of interests established between Russia and Prussia, and which became so fatal to the Occident. "The commonalty of views,"—thus the official organ of the German chancellor expressed itself,[139]—"which brought about the alliance of Prussia and Russia in 1863, at the time of the Polish insurrection, was the point of departure for this present policy of the two states, which, on the occasion of the great events of the last years, has affirmed its power. Since the attitude of Russia in the question of Schleswig-Holstein, up to the important proofs of sympathy given to Germany by the Emperor Alexander during the last war, all has concurred to render this alliance still more firm."

By a sort of historical fiction which confounds the reason not a little, but which a sovereign will imposes on acts and even public monuments in Russia, the campaign of 1870 did not cease to be exalted in the official spheres of the empire of the czars as the continuation of the work of 1814, as the final episode of "that great epoch when the united armies of Russia and Prussia fought for a sacred cause which was common to them both."[140] At the Kremlin, in the splendid hall consecrated by the Emperor Nicholas to the military glories of the country, and which is the *arc de l'Etoile* of Holy Russia, the foreign tourist is astonished to see glittering now in letters of gold on the marble the names of Moltke, of Roon, and other captains of Germany who shone in the last war against France.[141] And the conqueror of Sedan might imagine that he was still in the midst of his subjects in traversing in 1873 the vast Muscovite plains: from the frontier to the Gulf of Finland the journey was an uninterrupted succession of triumphs and ovations. At each depot where the imperial train stopped a guard of honor was in waiting, and played the German national song; the czar came to meet his august guest to Gatchina, and the 27th April the two sovereigns entered the capital of Peter the Great. The skies were gloomy and cold, and the sun refused to lighten "the city of wet streets and dry hearts," as one of its poets has called it; but human industry did all that was possible to supply the place of nature, and make amends for the irreparable outrage of the climate. "All the greenhouses of the capital, without excepting those of the imperial gardens," says an eye-witness,[142] "were literally devastated to improvise around the gates and windows a spring which, retarded in our North, only arrived with summer," and the rich carpets suspended from the ledges or stretched along the edifices gave to the boreal city the joyous aspect of the city of lagoons. "The perspective of Izmaïlovsky, the perspective of Voznessensky, the Grande-Morskaïa, formed a sort of continuous alley of draperies of the Russian, German, and Prussian colors. On a great number of balconies, one saw in the midst of the verdure and the flowers the busts of the two monarchs crowned with laurel. The façade of the great stable Préobrajensky was ornamented with a number of standards surrounding a colossal cross of that military order of Saint George of which his majesty the Emperor William is the oldest knight and the only grand ribbon." The crowd pressed close to the passage of the guests from Berlin; the unreserved Prince de Bismarck and the taciturn Count de Moltke especially attracted the eyes of the spectators.

For twelve days there was an endless succession of reviews, parades, tatoos, illuminations, balls, *raouts*, banquets, concerts, and gala representations. Among the latter, the chroniclers mention the two splendid ballets of the "Roi Candaule" and "Don Quixotte." The people had also their part in the rejoicings, especially on the evening of the 29th April, at the gigantic festival of the Place du Palais. The two sovereigns were present at the immense balcony concert above the piazza of the castle. "On their arrival, five electric suns all at once lighted the square with such intensity that one could distinguish the features of all the spectators, and the orchestra struck up the national Prussian hymn. The total number of musicians was 1,550, in addition to 600 trumpets and 350 drums. After the hymn the "March of King Frederick William III." was played; then came a whole series of military marches, the "March of Steinmetz," the "Watch on the Rhine," the "March of the Garde of 1808," to the music of which the Russian regiments returned to St. Petersburg after the campaign of Eylau, and the "March of Paris," which the allied armies heard in olden times at the time of their triumphal entry into the capital of France. The military prayer, "God is great in Zion," also produced an immense effect." One can hardly explain how, in the midst of music entirely consecrated to the gods Mars and Vulcan, the sweet romance of Weber, entitled "The Praise of Tears," could be introduced, unless it was a discreet homage rendered to the well known sensibility of the old Hohenzollern, and of which many speeches, letters, or telegrams bear in history authentic traces. This easily impressionable character of the sovereign of Germany was visible as far as was necessary at St. Petersburg; it showed itself especially at the moment when the two monarchs made their adieux in the imperial *salons* of the depot of Gatchina. In order not to succumb to his emotion, William I. had to leave the *salon* brusquely; his head bent forward, his features contracted, he went out with hasty steps and reached the car *without turning round.*

However, if during this sojourn of the Prussian guests on the banks of the Neva all the honors were for the uncle of the czar, the curiosity of the public, panting and almost feverish, willingly turned, one may be sure, to the extraordinary minister whose uniform of the white curassiers set off his imposing stature—to this chancellor of Germany who, in the short space of a lustrum, had founded an empire on the ruins of two others. One had not had time to forget at St. Petersburg the grumbling diplomat, who from 1859 to 1862 astonished and amused the Russian society by his slanders against his own court, by his pleasantries on the "old fogies of Potsdam" and the "Philistines of the Spree," and who occasionally repeated the famous *mot* of M. Prudhomme—the *mot*: "*If I were the government!*"—he who was to laugh at it the first. He was the government at this time, he was even the master of Europe; and his star had dimmed the star of a Hapsburg, of a Napoleon! The subject gave rise to more than one touching reconciliation, to many a *piquant* reminiscence, and there was room also for futile remarks for the *plerisque vana mirantibus* of which the immortal historian speaks in presence of any prodigious change of fortune. In presence of the man of the five milliards, the great ladies at the winter palace remembered a certain ambassadress ten years before, who one day boldly declared that she could not pay forty silver roubles for early asparagus, who another day avowed in all candor that she owed her new diamond ear-rings only to the exchange of a valuable snuff-box, an old gift of the Prince of Darmstadt.[143] The ambassadress was the wife of Prince de Bismarck, then baron, prince to-day, a good prince too, and having lost nothing of his former affability. He was easy, playful, earnest, as at the time of his mission in Russia; he inquired for friends, acquaintances, small or great people whom he had known formerly, and seemed to renew relations and conversations as if interrupted only yesterday. The statesman disappeared entirely, to show only the courtier and the man of the world, and it was only in his relations with Prince Gortchakof, a sagacious observer tells us, that he laid aside the foreign minister, and only appeared as the companion, almost as the compatriot. He showed him the deference of an affectionate friend towards his elder,—of a disciple towards the master, said the flatterers, without thinking of evil, without thinking, above all, on the *discipulus supra magistrum* of whom Alexander Mikhaïlovitch, a good Latinist himself, perhaps thought.

They often appeared thus in public, at numerous *fêtes* and receptions, side by side, the one towering above the crowd with his strongly-marked head, the other also easily recognizable by his fine, *spirituel*, and rather sharp features. According to that ingenious court etiquette of which the good Homer has given the first precept, in making Diomede and Glaucus exchange their brilliant armor, the Russian minister wore the insignia of the black Eagle of Prussia, and the Prussian minister the insignia of St. Andrew of Russia,—and this exchange of ribbons involuntarily recalled the commonalty of ties which had for so long united these illustrious diplomats. Such a cordial, unalterable understanding between two statesmen directing two different empires, was assuredly a rare phenomenon, well calculated to excite attention, and which, during the pompous solemnities of St. Petersburg, did not cease, in fact, to occupy reflective minds. They sought in vain in the past for the example of a harmony of action as constant and glowing: certain political friendships celebrated in history, those among others of Choiseul and Kaunitz, of Dubois and Stanhope, or yet of Mazarin and Cromwell, were only evoked an instant to be immediately recognized as deceptive souvenirs, apparent analogies only. No one, however, disregarded the considerable, decisive influence which the accord between the two chancellors has had on the recent destinies of Europe; nor did any one doubt the prodigious benefit which M. de Bismarck has been able to draw from this juncture in his bold enterprises: the opinions began to differ only when there was a question of settling the accounts of Russia, of fixing well the profits brought to the empire of the czars by this association of ten years, the most turbulent ten years which the Continent has known since the day of Waterloo.

According to the ideas of some, there was only advantage and gain for the people of Rourik, in the situation created by the immense events of Sadowa and Sedan. They showed the humiliating treaty of 1856 torn up, Austria punished for its "treason" at the time of the Crimean war, France sunken and weakened, England a resigned spectator of the progress of General Kaufman at Bokhara, and Russia recovering its ancient prestige, tasting in all quiet the vengeance, that pleasure of the gods and of the great favorites of the gods like Alexander Mikhaïlovitch. Is there not in truth, was said, a marvelous fortune, an imposing unity in the career of this minister who, at the conference of Vienna, had sworn to take revenge for the abasement of his country, and who has so well kept his word? Is there not a grand Nemesis in the successive chastisement of these proud "allies" who, in 1853, had undertaken the defense of the crescent against the cross of St. Andrew, who, ten years later, had dared to raise the question of Poland? At the present time Austria and France are rivals in flattering, obsequious conduct before the so decried "barbarian of the North," England solicits of him a *modus vivendi* in central Asia; and this enviable and glorious position Russia has obtained without conflict, without sacrifices, only by *meditating*, developing its interior prosperity, and letting its neighbor act alone, its secular, tried friend, whose devotion has never been doubted. It is only just that Prussia should reap the fruits of its valor and its fidelity, and the well known sentiments of the Emperor William towards the czar, the family ties which have so long united the two courts; lastly, the destinies, so distinct and yet so connected, of the two states, are certain gages of a future, permanent, and immovable understanding. How many times has Prussia solemnly declared that it has no interest in the Oriental question. The day when the question of the succession of the Osmanli arises, the Hohenzollern will prove his gratitude to the Romanof. The little jealousies and the little rivalries have had their day, like the little states and the little artifices of influence and of the balance of power: the future is for a rational policy based on the nature of things, the reality of geography, the homogeneity of races; and this policy assigns to Russia and Germany their respective *rôles* and corollaries. In point of view of general principles, we can only rejoice that the sceptre of the Occident has escaped a turbulent, volcanic nation now making Jacobin, now ultramontane propaganda, but always revolutionary, to pass into the hands of a well-ordered, hierarchical, and disciplined state, as it is. Lastly, Sadowa and Sedan were Protestant victories over the first two Catholic Powers, and the contest in which M. de Bismarck engaged against the Roman Curia is only the logical consequence of this great fact of history; but without even sharing certain ideas, widely spread however, of a possible fusion of the Protestant and Orthodox beliefs, it is not for the church of Photius, in any case, to take umbrage at the mortal blow given to the Vatican.

To such justifications, in which neither convincing arguments nor sharp touches were wanting, those dissenting opposed objections inspired by a patriotism equally sincere, but much less hopeful. Also admiring the facility and promptitude with which Russia has arisen from its great disaster of the Crimea, they pretended only that this great result had been obtained long before the advent of M. de Bismarck, long before any association with him, and that from the year 1860 the empire of the Rourik had retaken the great position which it deserved in Europe, when the sovereigns of Austria, Prussia, and so many of the princes of Germany had come to salute the czar at Warsaw, to recognize his moral supremity, and that Napoleon III. on his part sought his friendship and accepted his arbitration. The great ability with which Prince Gortchakof used the "French cordiality" for the good of Russia, without giving up any essential interests, and without compromising the conservative and traditional principles of his government, always remained one of his greatest claims to the gratitude of his country, and it would have been desirable had he preserved the same moderation, the same reserve, later in this intimacy with Prussia, which on the occasion of the Polish insurrection had replaced the former understanding with the Tuileries. The successor of Nesselrode exaggerated, without doubt, the bearing and the danger of the famous *remonstrances* on the subject of Poland, as well as the nature of the services, very selfish as a whole, which his friend of Berlin then rendered him; in any case, that was certainly not a reason to pout at Europe after the affair had turned out to the striking advantage of the Russian government, to pout at it during long years, to wish no other ally than Prussia, and to persist, in respect to this last Power, in the constant policy of let-go, let-do, and let-take.

This was in general the profound misfortune of the fifteen or twenty last years,—thought these enlightened patriots,—that rancor and bad humor had played such a great *rôle* in the grave affairs of the world: sad sentiments surely, and from which the present chancellor of Germany has alone been able to preserve himself! It was through anger at the conduct of the cabinet of St. Petersburg in the Italian question, that Austria took under its protection the insurgents of Poland; it was through bad humor towards England in the question of the congress that Napoleon III. abandoned the cause of Denmark, and Alexander Mikhaïlovitch yielded to such motives more than to any others; he was the first to practice this "policy of spite" with his imaginary grievances against Austria in the war of the Orient, as he was also not the last to cherish a certain "*policy de pour-boire*" with his *league of the neutrals* which hindered any concerted action of the Powers. What happy opportunities for the preservation of Europe, for the glory of his nation and the splendor of his august master, has not the Russian chancellor let pass through love for Prussia: in the spring of 1867, when France and Austria offered him such large concessions in the Orient; in the autumn of 1870, when England and Austria solicited him to take the initiative in the work of peace! What illusions also in that belief, that Prince Gortchakof has sacrificed nothing during those ten years of association with his formidable colleague! Was the port of Kiel, the key of the Baltic, delivered into the hands of the Germans, nothing? Was that nothing, the dismemberment of the Danish monarchy, the country of the future empress? Was the vassalage of Queen Olga nothing? The overturning and spoliation of so many reigning families allied by blood to the House of Romanof, the loss of the independence of these secondary States always so devoted and so faithful to Russia? Lastly, was this profound overturning of the ancient European equilibrium, and the unmeasured, gigantic aggrandizement of a neighboring Power, nothing?

"Greatness is a relative thing, and a country can be diminished, while remaining the same, when new forces accumulate around it."[144] These words, which Napoleon III. heard on the day after Sadowa, Russia could well apply to itself, since the day of Sedan, for assuredly no one would wish to pretend that the abolition of Article III. of the treaty of Paris is the equivalent of the forces accumulated by Prussia in the centre of Europe. As to the *hopes* in the Orient, they are very contingent, like every speculation of heritage: the *sick man* has already so many times deceived the expectations of his doctors, one can no longer count the mortal crises which should have carried him off, and perhaps it is not Russia that should complain of this prolongation of the agony. It is still a question in truth if Russia is now in a position to take care of the succession, if it is sufficiently supplied with implements for such a vast establishment; if, in a word, it has all its military and financial strength, as well as all the administrative *personnel* indispensable to advantageously occupy the domains as various as extended. It cannot take possession of European provinces like the countries along the Amour and Syr-Daria; it runs the risk of finding more than one ungovernable Poland among those peoples of the Danube and the Balkan; and the unity of the law, the uniformity of the *svod*, will not be so easy to establish in the countries where, side by side, the most incongruous institutions have flourished from the *régime* of the cimeter to that of the parliament. Will not the transformation of Turkey transform, however, in turn the Muscovite people, and will not history on this occasion be careful to repeat the great and pathetic lessons of *Græcia capta*? Will Russia still be Russia the day when it rules the Oriental peninsula, and can an empire bathed by the blue waves of the Bosphorus preserve its capital on the icy banks of Finland? Grave and obscure problems before which it is allowable to stop, to conceive apprehensions and doubts. What is not doubtful, on the contrary, is that at the destined hour Prussia will make its conditions and will stipulate its compensations. It will not be a debt of gratitude which it will think of paying then, it will be a new bargain which it will make. Will it demand as the price of its consent, Holland, Jutland, or the German territories of Austria? the frontier of the Vistula, or the provinces of the Baltic?

But who knows if this prolonged drama of Turkish decadence is not yet destined to receive a *dénoûment* little or not at all foreseen, yet very original and nothing less than illogical. The publicists and the patriots of Berlin do not speak to-day of the mission of Austria in the countries of the Danube and the Bosphorus, which they say is called by Providence to strengthen in these countries German interests, to bring there "German culture." Since the great day of Sedan, especially, exhortations and summons are not wanting to this Power "to seek its centre of gravity elsewhere than at Vienna," in short, to justify its secular name of *Ostreich*, and to become an empire of the East, in the true meaning of the word. A monarchy constantly menaced with the early loss of its Germanic possessions on the Leitha may at length be brought to try the experiment, when, above all, care is taken to present to it this experiment as a necessity and as a virtue; a state which has never been strongly centralized, and which has always oscillated between dualism and a federal system more or less definite, will even have a great chance to appear to Europe as the most proper outline of this medley of races, of religions, of institutions, which stretches from the Iron Gates to the Golden Horn. An *empire of the East* of Germanic traditions and influences on the Bosphorus, more to the South a kingdom of Greece enlarged by Thessaly and Epirus, lastly, in the North a Germany completed in its unity by the Cisleithan provinces,—that will be something to fully content the world, not excepting England. We must acknowledge, one solution of the formidable Ottoman question is like another, and every hypothesis, every fantasy, has the right to appear, when one touches this fantastic world of the Orient, and that world not less mysterious and terrible which the great recluse of Varzin carries in his head.

What, in any case, is not within the domain of hypothesis and fantasy, what unfortunately is only a too evident and palpable reality, is, that in place of this "combination purely and exclusively defensive," as Prince Gortchakof one day so justly called the old *Bund*,—in place of a league of peaceful states, all devoted friends of Russia, and forming for it a continual succession of ramparts,—the empire of Alexander II. now sees before it, firmly settled all along its frontier, a formidable Power, the strongest Power of the Continent, ambitious, avaricious, enterprising, and having henceforward the undoubted mission of defending against it what they have agreed to call the *interests of the Occident*. This Power can always excite the Polish question, if it wishes to, according to its wants, and quite differently than the cabinets of Paris and London would do it: has not the argument for such a "*coup au cœur*" been very warmly sustained in 1871, by certain Hungarian statesmen in the confidence of the Prussian minister? The conduct of the government of Berlin at the time of the last insurrection of Warsaw did not injure it in the future: the passionate speeches of M. de Bismarck in 1849 against the revolt of the Magyars did not prevent him from arming, many years later, the legions of General Klapka. We cannot at least deny the Prussian plans in 1863 on the left bank of the Vistula, "the natural frontier;" now, do not the friends of Berlin occasionally insinuate that this would be the most efficacious means to end the spirit of Polonism? They do not speak of the provinces of the Baltic, as before Sadowa they repudiated all thoughts of ever wishing to free the Main; but the Teutonic effervescence from Courland and Livonia goes on increasing, and to what grievous sacrifices will the Hohenzollern not resign himself when he thinks that he hears a voice from above, the voice of "German brothers?"

Certainly it would have made the prince regent tremble in 1858, if any one had spoken to him then of a war against a Hapsburg, and of a companion in arms named Garibaldi; he ended, however, by accepting the hard necessity, and he gave the signal for a fratricidal combat, with grief in his soul and tears in his eyes. Is it not puerile, however, to measure the destinies of nations by the life, more or less long, of this or that sovereign? An emperor can reign in Germany who has neither affection for, nor the remembrance of Alexander II.; he can raise up "a Pharaoh who knows not Joseph," to speak with Holy Writ, and then there is something stronger in the world than czar and emperor: the necessity of history, the fatality of race. A formidable race that of these conquerors of Sadowa and Sedan, whose invading and conquering minds have from the beginning survived all transformations and accommodated themselves to all disguises! Humble, and at the same time presumptuous, temperate and prolific, expansive and tenacious, practicing with persistence their old proverb, *ubi bene, ibi patria*, and nevertheless always preserving a rough attachment for the *mother country*, the Germans infiltrate every country, penetrate all regions, disdain no corner of the habitable world. They have their friends and relations on all the thrones and in all the offices of the world; they people the industrial centres of Europe and the solitudes of the far West; they decide the presidential elections in the United States; they furnish the largest contingent of the high administrative *personnel* in the empire of the czars, and the remembrance is still recent of that statistic of the Russian army, which, in 100 superior officers, counts eighty of German origin.[145] So Germany appeared before the great strokes of fortune of 1866 and of 1870, before the era of *iron and blood*, before M. de Bismarck had awakened in it the secret of its strength, had said to it the magic word, *tu regere imperio populos*! Is it necessary to recall now the hatred which the Germans have always borne against the Sclavic name, the extermination which they lately vowed on the Elbe and the Oder; and does not the mind recoil in terror before a new conflict of the two races, to-day more probable than ever? It is allowable to treat all these apprehensions as boyish dreams, hollow thoughts of *literati* and professors; but the eminent men, the serious men, the *augures* and *aruspices* of politics, have they in our day treated otherwise many a formidable problem? Have they not used the same language on the question of Schleswig-Holstein and the German pretensions to Alsace, in regard to the unity of Italy and the plans of the *National Verein*? That would be a curious chapter of contemporaneous history to write, that of the *Diplomats and Professors*, and which could well show that of these two respectable bodies the most pedantic and the most ideological is not exactly the one which a vain people thinks.

Is there not,—the same persons continue, more careful of the interests of the present and the future than of the unseasonable reminiscences of the past,—is there not ideological force, for instance, in the manner of assimilating the two epochs of 1814 and 1870, and of saluting in Field Marshal Moltke the continuator of the work of Koutouzof? At the time of the memorable war of which the burning of Moscow had given the heroic signal, it was all Europe that arose against an insolent master and bore deliverance to states trodden and ground down by a universal dominion. Was it the same in the last conflagration? and can one not rather say that it was France, on the contrary, that fought at this moment for the equilibrium of the world and the independence of kingdoms, trying to repair by a tardy and badly conceived effort a series of culpable errors, but from which it was not the only one to suffer? Different in their motives, the two epochs scarcely resemble each other more as to ways and means. It was "a war by means of revolutions" that the Prussian minister had early announced to M. Benedetti, and he has kept his word; he had regards, attenuations, *comprehensions* for the *commune* difficult to justify; now he openly protects the Republican *régime* in France against any attempt at restoration, thus sacrificing the monarchical principle and the highest considerations of European order to a purely selfish and vindictive calculation. That is not the spirit which animated the allies of 1814; the magnanimous Alexander I. especially understood differently the duties of sovereigns and the solidarity of conservative interests. And what a severe judgment would the Emperor Nicholas have given on every *ensemble* of the policy of Berlin, on that regeneration of Germany which has not ceased to be the revolution from above, from the federal execution in Holstein up to the arrest of the syndics of the crown; from the destruction of the *Bund* up to the overturning of the dynasty of the Guelphs; from the formation of the Hungarian legions and the close relations with Mazzini to the *Kulturkampf* against the Catholic Church!

That we may not be deceived in fact, we can still say it is the revolution alone which finds its profit in the war made to-day in Germany on Catholicism, and very great, very *naïve* is the illusion of those who flatter themselves with seeing Protestant or Orthodox ideas, the religious spirit in general, benefited by the losses of Papacy. It suffices to cast a glance on the great battalions of the *Kulturkampf* to recognize their God; they bear on their banners very clearly the sign under whose name they expect to conquer. Are these sincere Protestants, these *evangelical men* for whom the Gospel is a truth, who first rush to the assault or who only follow it with their wishes and their prayers? Assuredly not; all those who from the Reformation have not kept the name in vain, but the strong doctrine, openly repudiate this dissension, while sighing in their souls. They have the just feeling that in our epoch, so overturned, so profoundly disturbed by the genius of negation, religious interests are conjointly responsible between them just as well as conservative interests. Those eager for the combat, the zealots "filled with the divine spirit," are precisely those who admit neither divinity nor spirit, who have no other positive religion than positivism; and it is not in them surely that Luther resuscitated would wish to recognize his children. The great adversary of Rome in the sixteenth century held on to the revelation, he held on to his Bible, to his dogma of pardon: are not all these things very "old-fashioned," and very laughable in the eyes of the disciples of Strauss and Darwin? The apostle of Wittemberg believed in justification through faith; the apostles of Berlin believe in justification through success.

It is a grave matter,—at length conclude these men, alarmed in their patriotism and in their conservative sentiments,—an extremely perilous matter for a great state to abandon, in its relations with the Powers, certain established maxims, certain rules of conduct tried by long experience, become in a manner the *arcana imperii*, and Napoleon III. has just paid dearly for such a rupture with the ancient traditions in the exterior policy of France. Russia had also, in regard to Europe, sacred traditions, which have made the greatness and the strength of the preceding reigns; under these reigns, they were jealous in defending the liberty of the Baltic, they watched over the maintenance of the equilibrium of strength between Austria and Prussia, they appreciated the friendship and the devotion of the secondary States of Germany, and they caused the monarchical principle to be everywhere respected as opposed to revolution. Then Russia never had to repent at having turned aside from the ways hollowed out by the triumphal car of Peter the Great, of Catherine II., of Alexander I., and of Nicholas!

Thus spoke the independent minds on the banks of the Neva while the official world there displayed all the northern magnificence in honor of William the Conqueror: however, they only lent a reasoning and touching language to a vague, but intense and profound sentiment which agitated the very soul of Russia. With that habit of obedience and discipline that one can often accuse of a servile instinct, but which with this people is also sometimes a great and admirable patriotic instinct, the children of Rourik were careful not to cross the government in the brilliant reception which it gave the Prussian; they limited themselves to remaining impassible witnesses of a spectacle which did not appeal to their inmost feelings. The press showed itself abstemious of descriptions, more sparing still in reflections during these days of *fêtes* and festivals; the officials of Berlin only praised them with having maintained a *decorous* tone. Such was also the tone of Russian society taken as a whole; the beautiful *perspectives* of the imperial residence appealed to the moral as well as to the physical man; flowers from hot-houses on the first floor, ice under foot! The guests were not the last to see the contrast: with the exquisite perfumes of exotic plants, they breathed from time to time the sharp air of the country, the rough North wind, and it was not M. de Bismarck himself who did not seem to feel the circumambient atmosphere. One found in him more vivacity and enjoyment than of dash and warmth; his words preserved a measuredness which was not usual with him, and seemed to designedly avoid all *éclat* and all light. A curious matter, during this sojourn of two weeks in the capital of Russia, the former grumbling diplomat did not let any of his sallies and jokes escape, of which he is generally so prodigal,—none of those amazing indiscretions which are at once the amusement and the horror of the *salons* and the chancellors' offices. They only gleaned a single sensational expression fallen from those lips which have so often pronounced the decree of destiny, the expression "that he could not even admit the thought of being hostile to Russia." The declaration seemed explicit and reassuring, and like a discreet reply to an apprehension which did not dare to show itself openly. The incredulous or fretful souls could not, however, desist from observing that only ten years before such an assurance given to the empire of the czars by a minister of Prussia, would have seemed very superfluous, would have even provoked smiles.

Here ends the task which was imposed on us in undertaking this study. The meeting of the two chancellors in the capital of Peter the Great, in the spring of 1873, was like the epilogue of a common action which has lasted ten years, and which has contributed so much to change the face of the world. Since this epoch, Europe has known no tempest, although occasionally menacing and threatening clouds have not ceased to traverse its still obscured horizon. There were even glimmerings and indications that the old and fatal agreement between the cabinets of Berlin and St. Petersburg was no longer as absolute as in the past, that it admitted certain intermissions, or at least certain differences of opinions and appreciations. It is thus that the government of the czar refused to follow the chancellor of Germany in his Spanish campaign, in his feverish adhesion to the presidency of Marshal Serrano, and it did not seem doubtful that the personal intervention of Alexander II., strongly supported by England in the past year, turned from France an iniquitous aggression and a terrible calamity. Since that epoch, also, the adhesion of Austria to the official policy of the two Northern states has come—we cannot emphasize it too much—either to complete or to complicate an association in which it becomes difficult to discover any common interests, and which, up to this day at least, has only found harmony in silence. The future alone can unveil the importance and the virtue of this extolled alliance of three empires, as badly known as it is badly conceived, perhaps; but one will scarcely be deceived in supposing that to-day, in this double and troubled household, it is M. de Bismarck who can think himself the happiest of the three.

APPENDIX.

LETTER FROM M. BENEDETTI TO THE EDITOR OF THE "REVUE DES DEUX MONDES." REPLY OF M. KLACZKO.

PARIS, *24th September*, 1875.

TO THE EDITOR,—You published in the last number of the "Revue des deux Mondes," an article by M. Klaczko, which forces me to ask you for an opportunity for a short explanation. I surely would not wish to contest with any one the right of estimating the events of which this author has undertaken the anecdotal history, and of judging, as best one can, of the part which I took in them; I call, on the contrary, with all my heart, in my own interest as well as in that of the government which I have had the honor to serve, for the examination and the discussion; for it, as for me, I can only be satisfied with the light which already flashes from it, and with the errors which have been dissipated; but the discussion is serious and useful only if it is loyal, and it is loyal only when recounting fixed and undeniable facts.

Now, here is what I read in the article of M. Klaczko: "Certainly the ambassador of France at the court of Berlin had, in this year 1866 a very difficult and painful position, we had almost said a pathetic one. He had worked with *ardor*, with *passion*, to bring about this *connubio* of Italy and Prussia, which seemed to him to be an immense good fortune for the imperial policy, a brilliant victory gained over the old order of things to the profit of the 'new right' and Napoleonic ideas. In the fear, very well founded besides, of seeing this work miscarry and Prussia draw back, if one spoke to it of eventual compensations and preventive engagements, he had not *ceased to dissuade* his government from any attempt of this kind." Pp. 210, 211. Already, at p. 206, in a note, M. Klaczko had said: "M. Drouyn de Lhuys, who had already obtained from Austria the cession, in any case, of Venetia, insisted at this moment more strongly than ever, that they should also take pledges in advance from Prussia, 'the most formidable, the most active of the parties.' M. Benedetti *did not cease to oppose* such a proceeding, fearing that Prussia would renounce in this case all idea of war against Austria."

Now, these allegations have no meaning, or they signify that I was the real inspirer, if not the negotiator, without the knowledge of my government, of the treaty of alliance concluded in 1866 between Prussia and Italy; that I, moreover, turned, by incessant efforts, M. Drouyn de Lhuys from his intention of demanding of the Berlin government, before the war against Austria, the pledges eventually necessary for the security of France.

M. Klaczko neither corroborates these assertions by any known fact, nor by the extract from an official document; he gives no proof of them in any degree or in any way.

As to what concerns the Prusso-Italian treaty, he was informed, however, since he continually quotes the publication which I made in 1871, under the title, "My Mission in Prussia," that I repudiated any participation in this act; he knew that I had claimed to have shown it, and it is not sufficient to contradict me; in such a case it is necessary to prove the contrary, to establish that, far from having remained ignorant, as I maintained, of the accord between Prussia and Italy, I had been the principal instigator of it.

It is of importance to me that the readers of the "Revue des deux Mondes" be enlightened; they have seen the article of M. Klaczko, it is just to place under their eyes some words only from the dispatches which I published.... I wrote on the 14th March, 1866: "The early arrival of an Italian officer, General Govone, is announced, who comes to Berlin charged with an important mission; this news ... has caused considerable emotion. If it is confirmed, one will not fail to believe that Prussia and Italy are negotiating a treaty of alliance."

The third day after, I added: "General Govone arrived day before yesterday at Berlin. According to Count Bismarck and the Italian minister, he is charged with a military mission, and his journey will have simply for its object the study of the perfection arrived at in the instruments of war."

Two days later, I was in a position to inform my government exactly, and I said: "I wrote you, announcing the arrival of General Govone, that, according to M. de Bismarck and the Italian minister, this envoy of the cabinet of Florence was simply charged with studying the military condition of Prussia. Forgetting, without doubt, what he had told me on this point, M. de Bismarck informed me yesterday that General Govone was authorized to conclude arrangements with the Prussian government. The communications which he has made to the president of the council substantiate this." In closing this dispatch, I added: "The legation of Italy observes toward me absolute reserve. I do not know whether to regret it. The confidences of M. de Bismarck, which I cannot, however, decline, already place me in a sufficiently delicate position."

At last, on the 27th March, when the plenipotentiaries had already held several conferences, I wrote to M. Drouyn de Lhuys: "(M. de Bismarck) has spoken to me of his conferences with General Govone and the Italian minister, ... and I am so much the better in a position to inform you that M. de Barral, Italian minister, *has* AT LAST *decided on his part not to hide from me entirely his proceedings and the intentions of his government.*"

One of two things, either M. Klaczko admits that my correspondence was sincere, or he supposes that it was drawn up with the design of dissimulating my conduct and the part which I clandestinely took in the negotiation. In the first case, no one will conceive how he can pretend that I labored *with ardor and with passion to bring about this connubio of Italy and Prussia*. In the second hypothesis matters are changed, and I shall expect that M. Klaczko will be explained as far as he goes by the expression of my opinion.

For the moment, I will invoke the only testimony that no one can suspect, that of the Italian plenipotentiary. The correspondence of General Govone was published after his death and subsequently to "My Mission in Prussia," through the efforts of General La Marmora, who has omitted nothing. In this correspondence, where all is told in detail, my name is quoted twice, the first time in a telegram of the 28th March, twelve days after the arrival of the Italian plenipotentiary at Berlin, and here is what he says as regards me: "I think that I ought to announce to you that the president (M. de Bismarck) keeps M. Benedetti exactly advised."

In the letter in which my name appears for the second and last time, dated the 6th April, on the very eve of the signing of the treaty (the dates are valuable, and it is well to retain them), General Govone mentions a visit which he paid me, the first since his arrival at Berlin; and what did I say to him concerning these negotiations? I quote literally: "Yesterday, after my visit to M. de Bismarck, I saw M. Benedetti; he thought that it was preferable for us to sign no treaty, but only to have a project all discussed and ready to sign when the mobilization of Prussia should be achieved."

Do these two extracts, Mr. Editor, authorize the belief that I was the confidant and the counselor of the Italian envoy? Do they not confirm, on the contrary, from point to point the sincerity of my correspondence? In what has M. Klaczko sought, where has he seen that I labored for the accord between Italy and Prussia? Should he not have told us before making such a grave assertion? Does he think to reproach me for having endeavored to keep myself informed as to what was passing, and for having instructed my government exactly?

As to the assertion of M. Klaczko, twice repeated in his article, that I did not cease, before the war, to dissuade M. Drouyn de Lhuys from speaking at Berlin of eventual compensations and preventive engagements, from fear of seeing Prussia give up the combat with Austria, I will reply by the following extract from a letter which M. Drouyn de Lhuys himself addressed to me on the 31st March, during the negotiation opened between the two cabinets of Berlin and Florence: "I have read with pleasure," said he to me, "the private letters which you have written to me during the present month. I beg leave to express to you all my thanks for them. If I have received them without replying immediately, it was because I had nothing to modify *in the instructions* which I have given you on different occasions. We are still of the same opinions. While recognizing the gravity of the new crisis in which we participate, we see, in the contention which presents itself to-day, no sufficient motive for us to depart from our attitude of neutrality. We have explained ourselves frankly to the court of Prussia. When we have been asked by the cabinet of Vienna, we have firmly declared to it, that we wish to remain neutral, although it has observed to us that our neutrality was more favorable to Prussia than to Austria. *We await, then, the armed conflict*, if it must break out, in the attitude in which we really are. The king himself has acknowledged that the present circumstances do not offer the bases of accord that his majesty desires. The course of events, the nature and the bearing of the interests which are involved, and the dimensions which the war will take, as well as the questions which it will give rise to, will *then* determine the elements of the understanding which can exist between Prussia and us."

In this same letter, the whole of which can be read on page 77 of "My Mission in Prussia," M. Drouyn de Lhuys wished moreover to indicate to me the consideration which obliged us to observe a reserved attitude in view of the efforts made by Prussia, and by Italy, to act in concert, and he added at the close: "That is the whole truth concerning our opinions. I approve, however, completely of your attitude and your language, and I trust that you will continue to keep me equally well informed of all the details of this crisis."

Would M. Drouyn de Lhuys have acknowledged the receipt of my correspondence in these terms, if it was intended to deter him from any plan of contracting eventual engagements with Prussia, if there had existed between the minister and the ambassador the disagreement the whole responsibility of which M. Klaczko wishes to throw on me? I dwell no longer on this subject, leaving to the penetration of your readers the task of seeing things more clearly; I only wish you to remark that, if M. Klaczko, as I suppose, has seen that letter before writing his article, it becomes impossible to explain the errors of it.

I regret to say, however, that I should have to criticise almost all his work, if I wished to correct the defective parts of it; but I do not intend to abuse my right of reply, and I will go no farther. I will rectify, however, another error on account of its particular importance. Replying to a telegraphic question of M. Drouyn de Lhuys, I wrote him on the 8th June, 1866, that no one in Prussia, from the king to the most humble of his subjects, with the exception of M. de Bismarck, would consent, in my opinion, to abandon to us any part of the German territory on the Rhine. After having quoted an extract from my dispatch, M. Klaczko adds: "And this is the same diplomat who had so well appreciated the situation before the campaign of Bohemia, it is the same ambassador *who now undertakes* to present to M. de Bismarck the demands of the cabinet of the Tuileries, who went so far as to submit to him, on the 5th August, a plan of a secret treaty implying the abandonment to France of the whole left bank of the Rhine, without excepting the great fortress of Mayence!"

M. Klaczko mistakes. I did not take upon myself to make this communication, and his allegation, deprived, moreover, of all proof, astonishes me the more as he could have seen in "My Mission in Prussia," that affairs were not conducted in that manner; that, on the contrary, while pointing out the serious and new difficulties which seemed to oppose this project, I demanded time to previously go to Paris to confer with the government, and that I was *ordered* to proceed. Did I do well or badly in obeying? That is another question; but M. Klaczko should all the more abstain from presenting this incident in such a manner as to emphasize the consequences of it, which have been grave and gloomy, as he is careful to remember.

If it is thus that M. Klaczko understands the duties of the historian, I can only express my surprise at it. He, doubtless, did not perceive that party spirit and personal sympathies have suggestions which loyalty disavows. I regret it for a publicist who had accustomed the readers of the "Revue des deux Mondes" to better prepared and more impartially written studies. As far as I am concerned, you will understand, Mr. Editor, that I could not sanction by my silence assertions so destitute of foundation, and that M. Klaczko has forced me to protest in spite of my very sincere desire to avoid any polemics, and to maintain a reserve from which it is painful for me to depart. This letter, however, has no other object, and while asking you to insert it in the next number of the "Revue," I beg you to accept the assurance of my highest regard.

BENEDETTI.

M. Benedetti's letter was communicated to M. Julian Klaczko, who returned it to us with the following observations:—

M. le Comte Benedetti confounds two very different negotiations which have been spoken of in our work, as well as the two very distinct estimations of which they have been the object on our part. It was only in the affair concerning the treaty on Belgium, in the month of August, 1866, that the conduct of M. Benedetti toward his minister seemed incorrect to us; we have not passed the same judgment on his attitude in the months of March and April of the same year, as regards the secret treaty negotiated between M. de Bismarck and General Govone; still less have we reproached him with having been the inspirer of this treaty *without the knowledge of his government.* We have only affirmed that his dispatches at that time were of a nature to deter the French government from any attempt at a prior engagement with Prussia in view of the eventualities of the war.

M. Benedetti in truth did not cease to represent the court of Berlin as inaccessible to any overture of this sort. Even on the 8th June, 1866, on the eve of the war, he wrote: "The apprehensions which France inspires everywhere in Germany still exist, and they will reawaken unanimously and violently at the slightest indication which could reveal our intention to extend ourselves toward the East.... The king, like the most humble of his subjects, would not listen at this moment to the possibility of a sacrifice (on the Rhine). The crown prince, profoundly sensible of the dangers of the policy of which he is the witness, declared, not long ago, to one of my colleagues, with extreme vivacity, that he preferred war to the cession of the little county of Glatz." "My Mission in Prussia," pp. 171-172. In his other reports, as well as throughout his whole book, M. Benedetti always returns to this circumstance, that he never "encouraged hopes" on this side, and that he "sufficiently indicated that one would not obtain in any case, with the consent of Prussia, territorial concessions on the frontier of the East." ("My Mission," p. 176).

That was, however, not the sentiment of the Italian negotiators at the court of Berlin. M. de Barral, in a telegram addressed the 6th May to General La Marmora, thus expressed himself: "They are busily occupied with negotiations, we are assured, which are taking place between France and Austria to indemnify Italy, and which will have gone as far as the line of the Rhine to France. To the observation which I made on the danger of such an offer by a German Power, Bismarck replied to me by shrugging his shoulders, indicating very clearly that, should the case occur, he would not recoil from this means of aggrandizement!" On his side, General Govone, in his very minute report of the 7th May, relates the same incident in a fuller and much more explicit manner. "M. de Bismarck wishes to know the intentions and desires of the emperor; he has spoken of them to M. de Barral; he told him to try to learn something about them through M. Nigra; he has even given them cause to believe that he will be disposed to abandon to him the banks of the Rhine, having been informed by his agents that the emperor was negotiating with Austria, and that Austria would cede to him, so he believes, Venetia, and would even invite him to take possession of the left bank of the Rhine." M. de Barral, to whom he spoke, cried out: "But Austria should not thus compromise itself with Germany while sacrificing countries which belong to the confederation!" M. de Bismarck made a gesture which seemed to say: "I too would cede them." Lastly, in his report of the 3d June, five days before the dispatch of M. Benedetti concerning "the king and the most humble of his subjects," General Govone quotes the following reply of M. de Bismarck to his demand whether one could not find "some geographical line" to indemnify France? "There will be the Mosel (said M. de Bismarck). I am, he added, much less German than Prussian, and I would have no difficulty in conceding to France the cession of all the country between the Mosel and the Rhine: the Palatinate, Oldenburg, a part of the Prussian territory, etc. But the king will have great scruples, and can only decide in a supreme moment when it is a question of losing or winning all. At any rate, to bring the mind of the king to any arrangement with France, it will be necessary to know the minimum (*il limite minimo*) of the pretensions of this Power." La Marmora, "Un pó più di luce," p. 211, 221, 275.

Thus the Italian negotiators differed notably from M. Benedetti in their opinion on this very grave point; in all the confidential and evidently sincere relations which they had with their own government, they considered a territorial and previous arrangement between France and Prussia as a very difficult thing, without doubt, but not impossible. We have not discussed in our work the question whether it was General Govone or M. Benedetti who had judged the situation best; we have not even mentioned this divergence of opinions: we have only asked how M. Benedetti could have believed that after Sadowa and Nikolsburg he would find Prussia accessible to arrangements which it had not wished to accept before its immense victories and in the midst of an extremely perilous crisis? How could he have undertaken on this 5th August[146] to demand of M. de Bismarck for France all the left bank of the Rhine without excepting the great fortress of Mayence, when on the 8th June he was persuaded that one could not obtain from Prussia even a territory of the value of the county of Glatz? We have given the only possible explanation of this contradiction, the only one, we dare affirm, which has presented itself to the minds of all those who have studied these events. Before the campaign of Bohemia, we said, M. Benedetti did not think it possible to obtain territorial concessions from Prussia, and had shown all the more plainly the difficulties of such a demand which he feared to see Prussia refuse and thus render its *connubio* with Italy abortive, if they insisted prematurely, too firmly on the point of compensations. He desired rather to count on the military events to procure advantages for his country, on "the necessities to which the war might reduce the Prussian government" ("My Mission," p. 172), for he did not expect any more than the most ordinary of mortals the startling blow of Sadowa. After Sadowa he was dismayed at the success of the Hohenzollern; patriotic anguish for France succeeded in his heart to the generous sympathies for Italy, and, as he himself says, "in view of the important acquisitions of Prussia he was of the opinion that a territorial remodeling was henceforward necessary for the security of France." ("My Mission," p. 177). This remodeling he had *at first* hoped to find on the Rhine, "provided that the language of his government was firm and its attitude resolute" (p. 178); he had then sought it on the Meuse and the Escaut, and had allowed himself to be drawn into that secret negotiation on Belgium which was to be so fatal to France.

It was probably not the *patriotic anguish* attributed by us to M. Benedetti on the day after Sadowa, that could have wounded his feelings. Could it be the Italian sympathies with which we have credited him that awakened his susceptibilities? But the pronounced liking for the country and the cause of M. de Cavour has been the principal and marked characteristic of the political life of the former ambassador of France to the court of Berlin; in sight, and with the knowledge, of every one, M. Benedetti has always been reckoned among the most distinguished members of a party which had great influence in the councils of the second empire, a party which considered Italian unity as the most glorious work of the reign, the most useful for France, and, in its eyes, the *connubio* of Italy and Prussia seemed an immense good fortune for the imperial policy, a brilliant victory gained over the old order of things, to the profit of the "new right" and Napoleonic ideas! The diplomatic career of M. Benedetti, even presents in this respect a character of unity and indivisibility which will arouse the eternal admiration of all Italian patriots. In 1860 he had negotiated and brought to a successful end the treaty on Savoy and Nice, in exchange for which the imperial government tore up the treaty of Zurich, and sanctioned implicitly the annexations of Tuscany and Emilia. In 1861 he was made minister plenipotentiary of France to Turin, as if to console Italy for the recent death of M. de Cavour, to reëstablish in any case beyond the Alps the friendly relations which the invasion of the kingdom of Naples had for a moment strongly compromised. In the summer of the following year (August, 1862), the harmony between France and Italy was again troubled in consequence of Aspromonte, and of the circular of General Durando, of the 10th September, which demanded the evacuation of Rome. M. Thouvenel was then obliged to leave the Hotel of the Quai d'Orsay, giving place to M. Drouyn de Lhuys; and M. Benedetti, as well as his colleague of Rome, M. de La Valette, hastened to give his resignation, in order to mark with *éclat* his disapprobation as regarded a system become less favorable to the aspirations of Italy. He did not reënter the career until two years later, the 7th October, 1864, after the convention of the 15th September had given satisfaction to the wishes of the cabinet of Turin concerning Rome, also after M. de Bismarck had passed by Paris and had placed there the first beacons of the great combination against Austria. The post at Berlin was then raised to an embassy, and M. Benedetti became the holder of it. His former colleague of Rome, M. de La Valette, did not delay to sit in the councils of the empire, and at the same moment General La Marmora, well known for his *Prussomania*, undertook the direction of affairs at Turin. And from the beginning of the year 1865, M. de Bismarck engaged in his first campaign against Austria concerning the Duchies, and made his first proceedings at Florence to combine an understanding with Italy. The *connubio* was not definitely consummated until April, 1866, under the eyes of M. Benedetti.

No one that we know (and we less than any one) has reproached M. Benedetti with having favored this *connubio without the knowledge of his government*; but M. Benedetti will doubtless not pretend that this understanding between Italy and Prussia did not have all his sympathies. General Govone had no confidences for him at Berlin, perhaps; it was M. Benedetti, on the contrary, who made the Italian negotiator precious confidences,—that one among others, "that M. de Bismarck was a sort of *maniac*, whom he (Benedetti) knew and had *followed* for nearly fifteen years."[147] He had advised him, also, "not to sign any treaty, but only to have a project thoroughly discussed and ready to sign when the mobilization of Prussia should be achieved." Would M. Benedetti seek to persuade that by this advice he had wished to hinder the *connubio*? No, assuredly, by such advice M. Benedetti told General Govone to act only in earnest. It was good counsel that he gave him. Now one does not give good counsel for an affair which one wishes to see go under. Moreover, it was not the Italians that it was necessary to render favorable to the *connubio*; they inclined to it naturally: the important part was to gain over the court of Berlin, to triumph over its scruples, to reassure it, above all, as to the intentions of France. "I think that I should announce to you," the Italian negotiator telegraphed on the 28th March to General La Marmora, "that the president (M. de Bismarck) keeps M. Benedetti exactly informed."[148] M. de Bismarck would certainly not have thought of keeping M. Benedetti so exactly informed, if he had credited him with an aversion or even a lukewarmness for the Italian marriage. Then, as since, in France as well as abroad, in the eyes of the publicists as well as in the eyes of his own chiefs (as we are going to prove immediately), the former ambassador of France to the court of Berlin has always passed for the agent of the imperial government who wished most ardently for the success of the Italo-Prussian combination, and the book, "My Mission in Prussia," has not succeeded at all in shaking a conviction which we do not fear to call general.

We would never have thought of intruding in such an important debate our obscure person and our humble writings; but, since M. Benedetti has kindly wished to recognize in the works previously published by us in the "Revue des deux Mondes," "studies better prepared and more impartially written," we feel less hesitation in quoting one of those pages which we consecrated even here seven years ago to that pathetic episode of contemporaneous history. Speaking in our "Preliminaries of Sadowa," of the treaty negotiated between M. de Bismarck and General Govone in the spring of 1866, we expressed ourselves as follows: "There was only one strong mind like M. de Bismarck to enter into a compact with this secretary of the dreaded kingdom who assisted his colleague the Count de Barral; in the depths M. Benedetti appeared from time to time. In this respect, we involuntarily stretch our hand toward that volume of Machiavelli; we are seized with a desire to re-read a chapter from the "Legazioni." How happy he would have been, the great Florentine, to contemplate his three compatriots fighting with a *barbarian*! At Paris, one only saw (in this treaty) the single, prodigious fact of a pact concluded between a monarch by the grace of God, and a king of the national will, and one went into ecstacies over the skill of M. Benedetti. There was only one diplomat of the new school who could perform such a miracle!" Lastly, at the beginning of the same study, in relating the circumstances which in 1864 had brought on the political stage those formerly disgraced by the affair Durando, we said: "Without doubt it cost M. Drouyn de Lhuys something to accept as a colleague M. de La Valette, who made no secret of his desire to take his department from him; it cost him still more, probably, to allow such an open adversary as M. Benedetti to be imposed on him as principal agent. Two years later, after Sadowa, and on the day when he gave up his portfolio, the same minister was yet to countersign another decree which raised M. Benedetti to the dignity of the grand cross. Who knows, however, whether, in the mind of M. Drouyn de Lhuys, this second signature was not destined to avenge somewhat the first? In truth, perhaps that was a peculiar trait of mind, a Parthian trait, to distinguish so highly an agent for having only too well served a policy the responsibility of which he not the less repudiated."[149]

Did the former chiefs of the ex-ambassador of France to the court of Berlin judge otherwise of it? M. Benedetti himself furnishes us on this point with valuable testimony, which we will take care not to neglect. He says ("My Mission," p. 148) that in January, 1870, M. Daru, then minister of foreign affairs, had made, in a letter, allusion to the events of 1866, in terms which could not but strongly affect the ambassador: "The territorial state of Prussia," M. Daru had written him, "results from events which *perhaps* it has not depended on you to bring about." Thus, even four years after Sadowa, they did not cease to attribute to M. Benedetti, to the bureaux of the Quai d'Orsay, a notable part in these gloomy events. The ambassador found it opportune to enlighten his new chief on "the *rôle* which he played in this circumstance," by a private letter dated the 27th January, 1870. "I am not ignorant," we read there, "of all that has been said on this point; but, by a feeling which you will appreciate, I do not doubt, I have never thought of declining the share of responsibility which has been cast on me, and, for this purpose, to set at right the errors too easily gathered by a badly informed public." He affirmed, therefore, that he was then "an active, correct, foreseeing informer," and he appeals to his correspondence deposited in the archives of foreign affairs. "I should add that I never, *and in none of the missions which I have fulfilled,* have undertaken other correspondences than those whose marks exist in the department, or in the hands of your predecessors, and that I never had, *in all the epochs of my career,* other orders to execute than those that have been given me directly through them." ("My Mission," pp. 148-149). Yet that is not sufficient for M. Benedetti, and in publishing this letter he accompanies it (p. 150) with a triumphant commentary: "I have affirmed a fixed and indubitable fact in mentioning, in my letter (to M. Daru), that I did not have the honor, *on any occasion* (these words are underlined by M. Benedetti himself), to sustain a direct and confidential correspondence with the emperor. He has deigned to grant me his confidence, and occasionally to testify to me his satisfaction; he has never ceased to transmit to me his orders by the mediation of his minister of foreign affairs, with whom I have exclusively corresponded. No one will suppose, I think, that I would affirm this in such absolute terms as I have in writing to M. Daru, my immediate chief, if I had not been fully authorized."

Unfortunately some pages beyond (p. 194), M. Benedetti is forced to acknowledge that, in his negotiation concerning the secret treaty on Belgium, he exchanged a correspondence which did not pass through the department for foreign affairs, and which the directing minister of this department did not know of. "I thought it fitting," we read there, "to address to the minister of state, M. Rouher, the letter in which I announced my interview with M. de Bismarck, and which accompanied the plan of the treaty relating to Belgium. M. Rouher did not lay before the ministry, not having then undertaken the direction of it, the correspondence which during several days I exchanged with him." It is true that, in order to palliate this very grave irregularity, M. Benedetti pretends that M. Drouyn de Lhuys had offered his resignation toward the middle of August: "At this moment there was no minister of foreign affairs;" but we have proved to him that M. Drouyn de Lhuys did not lose his portfolio until the 1st September, 1866. Up to that date, M. Drouyn de Lhuys had not ceased to direct the department, with the desire of remaining there, and of preventing the complete abandonment of the traditional French policy. The ambassador himself quotes in his book several dispatches exchanged with him on grave questions, up to the date of the 21st and 25th August (pages 204 and 223); but M. Benedetti thought *proper* to be silent to his immediate chief concerning the negotiation on the subject of the treaty on Belgium, and only to inform the minister of state. This negotiation not only had its beginning, but also its end (it was broken off by M. de Bismarck the 29th August), *during the ministry of M. Drouyn de Lhuys, and without his knowledge.* This was then *one occasion* when M. Benedetti did not exclusively correspond with the minister of foreign affairs! There was then *one epoch in the career* of M. Benedetti when he received orders which did not pass through the Quai d'Orsay! And how suppose of the honorable M. Daru that what had happened in the month of August, 1866, could have also taken place in the months of March and April of the same year?

M. Benedetti completely ignores in his protest this incident of the treaty concerning Belgium; it is, however, the culminating point, in fact the only grave point of the debate, and the only one concerning which we allowed ourselves to reproach him with having acted *without the knowledge*, not of his government, but *of his minister.* Would M. Benedetti perhaps find that this is an anecdotal incident, incompatible with the dignity of history? He had in fact first tried, in his letter published in the "Moniteur," the 29th July, 1870, to give to this deplorable event an entirely anecdotal turn, to assign to the compromising document a, so to say, spontaneous generation; he would have wished to give only an exact account of the ideas of M. de Bismarck, and "consented to transcribe them in a manner under his dictation." He could not long persist in such trifling; he had to avow in his book that he had entered on a veritable negotiation, and M. de Bismarck has since then taken malicious pleasure in casting light on the different phases of this negotiation, by different extracts taken from the papers of Cerçay and published in the "Moniteur prussien," in reply to the book of M. Benedetti. "During my long career," says M. Benedetti, in the preface of his book (p. 4), "I have been charged only on three different occasions with opening negotiations having a fixed object, and leaving me with an initiative part proportionate to the responsibility." He enumerates these three negotiations and proves that he conducted them all to a good end, but he takes good care not to include in the number his negotiations on Belgium, in which he was given an initiative part, and in which we will also give him his proportional part of the responsibility.

We will also leave him the tone of his polemics; it is like his diplomacy, *sui generis*, and we can say with M. de Bismarck: "M. Benedetti is too clever for us."

JULIAN KLACZKO.

THE MISSION EXTRAORDINARY OF MR. FOX.

On Monday, the 16th April (according to the Russian calendar, the 4th), 1866, an attempt was made on the life of Alexander II., Emperor of Russia. The would-be assassin was a Russian named Dmitry Karakozoff, a member of the order of the Nihilists. The rescuer of the Czar was a newly-emancipated serf, Ossip Ivanovitch Komissaroff by name. The facts of the attempted assassination are as follows: In the morning of that day Komissaroff started for the chapel built by Peter the Great on an island in the Neva. The bridge between the main bank and the island had, however, been removed, and he therefore turned toward the palace quay. On approaching the Summer Garden he joined the crowd of people waiting to see the Emperor pass. While trying to secure a favorable position, Komissaroff was attracted by a stranger who was attempting to force his way to the front, and who kept his right hand constantly in his coat pocket.

When the Emperor appeared, the man beside Komissaroff drew a pistol and aimed it at his Majesty. He stood so near that the shot would undoubtedly have proved fatal, had not Komissaroff struck up his arm and caused the weapon to be discharged in the air. Karakozoff was seized, and after trial, was executed on the 15th September. Komissaroff was made a nobleman, and had gifts and orders showered on him by the score. Mr. Clay, our minister to Russia, delivered a congratulatory address to the Emperor at a special audience, and the Emperor returned his thanks to the President and the people of the United States.

In the mean time, Congress, remembering that Russia had given our nation its warmest sympathies and aid in our hour of peril, introduced a joint resolution, relative to the attempted assassination of the Emperor of Russia. The resolution was approved by President Johnson, and it was then resolved to send a special envoy in a national vessel to carry to the Emperor of Russia the congratulations at his providential escape. For this delicate mission the Hon. Gustavus Vasa Fox, the Assistant Secretary of the Navy, was chosen. At his own request it was determined to send him in a monitor, a class of vessel which had never crossed the Atlantic, but in whose seaworthiness Mr. Fox trusted implicitly. For this purpose the *Miantonomoh*, a two-turret monitor, to be accompanied by two wooden men-of-war, was selected. On June 5, 1866, Mr. Fox left St. John, N. B., for Queenstown, arriving there on June 16th. Mr. Fox then left the *Miantonomoh*, and made short trips through England, Ireland, and France. He rejoined the squadron at Copenhagen on Saturday, July 21st, and after having been hospitably entertained by the king, left on August 1st for Cronstadt. He arrived there on August 5th, and on the following day he went to St. Petersburg and paid his respects to Mr. Clay, the United States Minister there. On the 8th the mission was received at Peterhof by the Emperor, assisted by Prince Gortchakof. Mr. Fox addressed the Emperor, who replied to him through Prince Gortchakof. On August 9th his Majesty visited the ships at Cronstadt.

For more than a month a series of dinners and balls were given in honor of the mission, and Mr. Fox's progress throughout the country was a perfect ovation. He was made honorary citizen of all the large cities; he received delegations of peasants, and was honored with rich presents from the

Emperor. The tact and eminent social qualities which he displayed, made this altogether unique mission successful, and greatly strengthened the warm ties which exist between the two countries. It will be seen that M. Klaczko erroneously calls Mr. Fox "assistant secretary of state."

FOOTNOTES:

[1] Plutarch, Theseus, *initio*.

[2] *Aus der Petersburger Gesellschaft*, vol. ii. p. 156.

[3] Expressions from the Russian circular of the 6th July, 1848, addressed by Count Nesselrode to his agents in Germany.

[4] The Germanic Confederation was formed in 1816. Frankfort was chosen as its seat, whither delegates were sent from all the States of Germany retaining sovereign rights. These delegates formed the assembly called the Diet.

The assembly was composed of seventeen envoys, presided over by the representative of Austria. There were however thirty-one States exclusive of the free cities, represented in the last period of the Diet's existence. The Diet was so constituted that each of the following States or combination of States had one representative: Austria; Prussia; Bavaria; Kingdom of Saxony; Hanover; Württemberg; Grand Duchy of Baden; Electorate of Hesse; Grand Ducal Hesse; Denmark, for the Duchies of Holstein and Lauenburg; The Netherlands, for Limburg and Luxemburg; The Duchies of Saxe-Meiningen, Saxe-Coburg-Gotha and Saxe-Altenburg; Brunswick and Nassau; The two Mecklenburgs (Schwerin and Strelitz); Oldenburg, Anhalt and two Schwarzburgs (Rudolstadt and Sonderhausen); Lichtenstein, Reuss, Schaumburg Lippe, Lippe Detmold, Waldeck and Hesse Homburg; The free cities, Lubeck, Frankfort, Bremen and Hamburg.

The votes were equal. Sittings were secret.

On important occasions the assembly was resolved into what was called the *plenum*, in which a greater number of votes were assigned to the chief States, and the total number of voices was then increased to seventy. In these cases a majority of three fourths was necessary for any question to be carried.

The leading idea with the founders of the Diet was the preservation of internal tranquillity, the next, the formation of a league which should inspire other nations with respect.

Ambassadors were accredited to the Diet.—TRANSLATOR.

[5] Russian circular of the 27th May, 1859, concerning the war in Italy.

[6] This young lieutenant was M. de Bismarck. The *Landwehr* is divided into two levies. The soldier belongs to the first levy seven years, to the second levy for a like period.—TRANSLATOR.

[7] A writer in a position to be well informed, a former under secretary of state in the ministry of Prince Schwarzenberg, thus narrates the origin of Russian intervention in Hungary, tracing it back to 1833, to the celebrated interview of Munchengraetz between the Emperor Francis I. of Austria and the Czar Nicholas. In one of the confidential conversations, Francis spoke with sadness and apprehensions of the sickly and nervous state of his son and prospective successor, and begged the czar to maintain towards that son the friendship which he had always had for the father. "Nicholas fell on his knees, and raising his right hand to heaven, swore to give to the successor of Francis all aid and succor he should ever need. The old Emperor of Austria was profoundly touched, and placed his hands on the head of the kneeling czar as a token of benediction." This strange scene had no witness, but each of the two sovereigns narrated it some months later to a superior officer who then commanded the division of the army stationed at Munchengraetz. This superior officer was no other than the Prince of Windischgraetz, who, later, in 1848, nominated and made generalissimo of the Austrian army at the critical moment of the Hungarian insurrection, took upon himself to recall to Nicholas, in a letter, the pledge formerly given at Munchengraetz. The czar replied by placing his whole army at the disposition of his imperial and apostolic majesty.—Cf. Hefter, *Geschichte Oesterreichs*, Prague, 1869, vol. i. pp. 68-69.

[8] Session of the Prussian chamber of the 6th September, 1849. This speech is not reproduced in the official collection of the *speeches* of M. de Bismarck published at Berlin.

[9] The battle of Sadowa, or as it is more commonly called in Germany, the battle of Königsgrätz, was fought on the 3d of July, 1866, and decided the result of the conflict between Prussia and Austria.—TRANSLATOR.

[10] We take the liberty of citing on this subject a piquante *scène d'antichambre* which has its instructive side. There was then at Vienna, in the ministry of foreign affairs, a very original figure, an usher, the memory of whom is not effaced at the Ballplatz. He bore the uncouth name of Kadernoschka; placed in the large waiting room before the cabinet of the minister, it was his duty to introduce the different visitors to the chief. This M. Kadernoschka was an usher of great style: he had been trained by the old Prince Metternich himself and loved to recall that he had "exercised his functions" from the time of the famous congress of 1815! One day, after a long interview with Prince Gortchakof, Count Buol sees this good Kadernoschka entering with a more than usually solemn air. He had a communication to make to his

Excellency "in the interest of the service!" And Count Buol learns that the Russian envoy, after having left his Excellency, had appeared entirely overcome and suffocating with anger,—that he had asked for a glass of water; that for half an hour he had walked up and down in the waiting room, gesticulating with violence, talking to himself, and crying from time to time in French: "Oh! some day they shall pay me well for that, they shall pay me for that!"

[11] Protocol of the conference of the 17th April, 1855.

[12] A religious ceremony which, in the Protestant Church, corresponds in a certain degree to the first communion in the Catholic Church.

[13] Referring to Henry IV., Emperor of Germany from 1056 to 1106, who humbled himself before Pope Gregory VII. at Canossa in 1077.—TRANSLATOR.

[14] Referring to the closing words of Cato's speeches: *Cæterum censeo Carthaginem esse delendam*.—TRANSLATOR.

[15] Treaty of Gastein, 14th August, 1865, between Austria and Prussia on the one side and Denmark on the other.—TRANSLATOR.

[16] *Sturm and Drang-Periode*, first period of Goethe and Schiller.

[17] Varzin, the Tusculum of the German chancellor, is situated in Pomerania, to the right of the Stettin-Danzig road, and about ten miles from Schlawe. The comfortable dwelling-house is almost surrounded by a magnificent park of beech and oak trees. Varzin has been in M. de Bismarck's possession since 1867.—TRANSLATOR.

[18] In the popular edition of the book of M. Hesekiel, this scene is *illustrated* by a vignette.

[19] Berlin is situated on the river Spree.—TRANSLATOR.

[20] Session of the chamber of the 15th November, 1849. One knows that the chancellor of Germany has lately enacted a law which institutes civil marriage in Prussia. However, none of the speeches which have been cited is found in the official collection of the *speeches* of M. de Bismarck published at Berlin.

[21] Session of the chamber of the 21st April, 1849. See also the interpellation of M. Temme in the session of the 17th April, 1863.

[22] A circular of Prince Schwarzenberg, made public by a calculated indiscretion, after having related the incident of the telegraph, and the desperate course of M. de Manteuffel as regards the Austrian minister,

added: "His majesty the Emperor thinks it his duty to comply with the desire of the King of Prussia, *so modestly expressed.*"

[23] Shakspere, *Henry IV.* part I. act iii. scene I.

[24] It does not, however, fail to be interesting, and to even have a very piquant side. Still full of the conviction that they had made on Denmark a war "eminently iniquitous, frivolous, and revolutionary," the Prussian plenipotentiary to the *Bund* labored, in 1852, very actively in dissipating for the future a possible cause of perturbation, and negotiated an Esau bargain with the Duke Christian-August Augustenburg, the former upholder of *Schleswig-Holsteinism*, and eventual pretender to the Duchies. Thanks to the intervention of M. de Bismarck, the old duke signed for the sum of one million and a half rixdalers given by the government of Copenhagen, a solemn act, by which he bound "*himself and his family*, on his princely word and honor, to undertake nothing which could disturb the tranquillity of the Danish monarchy." That did not prevent the son of Christian from impudently insisting on his pretended rights in 1863, nor even M. de Bismarck from supporting them for a certain time, up to the moment when the famous syndics of the crown cast the doubt in the soul of the first minister at Berlin and proved to him that the Duchies, belonging by right to no one, belonged to King William by the fact of conquest.

[25] The minister of Nassau, Baron Max de Gagern was at the head of this deputation.

[26] "Austria is not a state, it is only a government."

[27] As well as the Germans born or naturalized in Russia who encumbered the different branches of the state service, and occupied in general a very large and important position in the administration of the empire. On his accession to the ministry, Alexander Mikhaïlovitch loudly signified his intention of "purging" his department of all these "intruders." Routine, however, and above all Sclavic idleness (which willingly leaves to foreigners and to "intruders" all work demanding perseverance and application) were not slow in triumphing over the principle of nationality; the palingenesis of the minister, announced with so much fuss, ended in a very insignificant change in the *personnel* of the lower order, and the chancellor found among these Germans his two most devoted and capable aids: M. de Westmann, deceased last May at Wiesbaden, and M. de Hamburger, quite recently made secretary of state.

[28] Letter of M. de Cavour to M. Castelli-Bianchi, *Storia documentata*, vol. viii. p. 622.

[29] See, for this and all that follows concerning the relations of France and Russia in the years 1856-63, *Two Negotiations of Contemporaneous Diplomacy; the*

Alliances since the Congress of Paris, in the *Revue des deux Mondes*, of the 15th September, 1864.

[30] It is true that, in a circular of the 27th May, 1859, the Russian vice-chancellor took care to give a commentary to his proposition, and to prove that the congress which he had planned looked to nothing chimerical. "This congress," said he, "*did not place any power in presence of the unknown*: its programme had been traced in advance. The fundamental idea which had presided at this combination, *prejudiced no essential interest. On one side, the state of territorial possession was maintained*, and on the other there could come from the congress *a result which had nothing excessive or unusual in the international relations.*" It would be well to re-read this remarkable circular, and to weigh every word of it. One will find in it the most curious and substantial criticism, made, so to speak, by anticipation, of the different projects of the congress, those which later the Emperor Napoleon III. was to present to Europe, especially the eccentric project which surprised the world in the imperial speech of the 5th November, 1863.

[31] Massari, *Il Conte Cavour*, p. 268.

[32] *Aus der Petersburger Gesellschaft*, vol. ii. p. 90.

[33] In 1862, at the moment of definitely leaving his post at St. Petersburg, M. de Bismarck received the visit of a colleague, a foreign diplomat. They were speaking of Russia, and the future chancellor of Germany said, among other things, "I am in the habit, when leaving a country where I have lived long, to consecrate to it one of my watch charms, on which I have engraved the final impression which it has left me; do you wish to know the impression which I carry from St. Petersburg?" And he showed to the puzzled diplomat a little charm on which these words were engraved: "*Russia is nothingness!*"

[34] M. de Bismarck has since presented these quadrupeds to the zoölogical garden of the former free city of Frankfort.

[35] Constantin Roessler, *Graf Bismarck und die deutsche Nation*, Berlin, 1871.

[36] Frederick William IV. having died the 2d January, 1861, the prince regent took from that day the name William I.

[37] See the remarkable pamphlet entitled *Europa's Cabinete und Allianzen*, Leipzig, 1862. It is the work of a Russian diplomat, celebrated in political literature, the same whose book on the *Pentarchie* had such a loud echo under the monarchy of July.

[38] See in the *Revue des deux Mondes* of the 1st October, 1868, *Les Préliminaires de Sadowa*.

[39] See the celebrated circular dispatch of M. de Bismarck of the 24th January, 1863, in which he gives an account of the curious interviews which he had with the ambassador of Austria, Count Karolyi, in the last months of the year 1862, soon after his accession to power.

[40] "Why, then, should not representative institutions be accorded at the same time to the kingdom of Poland and to the empire of Russia?"—Dispatch of Lord John Russell to Lord Napier, 10th April, 1863.

[41] "This *connivance* of Austria was not the least remarkable event in the history of this insurrection."—Confidential dispatch of M. de Tengoborski to M. d'Oubril, 4th February, 1863.

[42] "The Polish insurrection, on which its duration impressed a national character," the Emperor Napoleon III. said in his speech of the 5th November, 1863.

[43] "On former occasions, M. de Bismarck always spoke to me of the probability that the Russian army would be too weak to suppress the insurrection."—Dispatch of Sir A. Buchanan, 21st February, 1863. He uses the same language to the Austrian minister, Count Kavolyi. On his part, the director of the diplomatic chancellor's office of the Grand Duke Constantine wrote on the 4th of February, at the first news of the envoy of the Prussian generals for the conclusion of a military convention: "While recognizing the courtesy of the mission of these gentlemen, we cannot give an exact account of what has influenced it. There is no *pericolo* (*sic!*) *in mora*, and we have no need of it for the coöperation of foreign troops.... The Prussian government paints the Devil much blacker than he really is."—Confidential dispatch of M. de Tengoborski to M. d'Oubril, Russian minister at Berlin.

[44] The German papers at this time published this interview after the narration of M. Behrend, who did not deny it. See, among others, the *Cologne Gazette* of the 22d February, 1863.

[45] Dispatch of M. Buchanan of the 17th October, 1863. Inclosure. Minute of conversation between M. de Bismarck and Sir A. Buchanan.

[46] Seeking an issue, however dishonorable to the campaign so foolishly undertaken, the chief of the foreign office had decided towards the end of September (after the speech of Blairgowrie) to declare the Emperor Alexander *deprived of his rights over Poland*, "for not having fulfilled the conditions in virtue of which Russia obtained this kingdom in 1815." France was to make an analogous declaration, but M. Drouyn de Lhuys, become prudent, and with reason would not send his note until after that of England had reached Prince Gortchakof. Lord Russell then wrote his dispatch; it was read at the council, approved by Lord Palmerston, and a copy of it was given to the minister of foreign affairs of France. Lord Napier had already been

advised to inform Prince Gortchakof of an "important communication" which he would soon have the honor to transmit to him, and the Duke of Montebello was also instructed by the French government to support his colleague of Great Britain in his solemn declaration; already the debated document had left for its destination, and was on its way to St. Petersburg, ... when suddenly, and to the unspeakable astonishment of the persons initiated, a telegram brusquely stopped in Germany the bearer of the note; another telegram informed Lord Napier that no further attention should be given to the "important communication." For during the interval Count Bernstorff had read at the foreign office a Prussian dispatch in which M. de Bismarck advised the principal secretary of state to take care how he proceeded,—for, if the czar were declared deprived of his rights over Poland for his violation of the treaty of Vienna, the German governments could also declare on their part the King of Denmark deprived of his sovereignty over the Duchies of the Elbe for not having fulfilled all the engagements of the treaty of London. Lord John Russell recalled the courier and tore up the note.—*Vide* in the *Revue des deux Mondes* of the 1st January, 1865, "Two Negotiations of Contemporaneous Diplomacy; M. de Bismarck and the Northern Alliance."

[47] "In 1848 Denmark had demanded the protection of France; M. Bastide, then minister of foreign affairs under the republic, took its part warmly, and there was even an idea of sending 10,000 men to assist the Danes in the defense of their country."—Dispatch of Lord Cowley of the 13th February, 1864. See also the curious dispatches of M. Petetin, then envoy of the republic at Hanover.

[48] The official journals of Berlin have renewed this reasoning in their recent discussions on the laws of guarantee accorded to the Holy See. The Pope, they argue, cannot be treated as a sovereign, as reprisals cannot be exercised against him by seizing his states.

[49] See the *Revue des deux Mondes* of the 1st October, 1868, *Les Préliminaires de Sadowa*, as well as the instructive work of General La Marmora, *Un pó più di luce*, Firenze, 1873.

[50] It is not useless to mention, *en passant*, the circumstances in the midst of which these new candidatures were produced. Summoned by the conference of London to present his pretensions, M. de Bismarck (28th May, 1864) could not do otherwise than to follow Austria, and to pronounce himself for the Duke of Augustenburg. The 2d June, at the reunion succeeding the conference (the telegraph had had time to work), the Russian plenipotentiary declared unexpectedly that the emperor, his august master, "desiring to facilitate as far as he could the arrangements to be concluded," had ceded his eventual rights, as chief of the House Holstein-Gottorp, to his relative, ... the

Grand Duke of Oldenburg! The 18th June, another relative of the Emperor Alexander II., Prince Frederick William of Hesse, also asserted his rights to the succession at the conference of London. This is an example of the numerous and discreet services which Prince Gortchakof knew how to render to his friend of Berlin in the sad campaign of the Duchies.

[51] Verse of a German song.

[52] We have taken care to preserve in the translation the character of edifying obscurity which distinguishes the original.

[53] "What can one say now, if France had shown itself opposed to these proceedings (the treaty of Italy with Prussia), we could not run the risk of finding ourselves face to face with an Austro-Franco alliance. Prussia was as solicitous as we, perhaps even more, with the attitude which France would take in case of a war of Prussia and Italy against Austria."—La Marmora, *Un pó più di luce*, p. 80. Three days before the signing of the secret treaty with Italy, M. de Bismarck said to General Govone: "*All this, let it be well understood, if France wishes it, for, if she shows ill will, then nothing can be done.*"—Dispatch of General Govone to General de la Marmora of the 5th April, 1866. *Ibid.* p. 139.

[54] Letter of the emperor to M. Drouyn de Lhuys of the 11th June, 1866. It is from this letter, solemnly presented to the legislative body, that the quotations which follow are taken.

[55] He used this expression more than once, and in a very convincing tone, in the council of ministers before 1866. It was not till later, after Sadowa and the affair at Luxemburg, that he at times seemed to yield to the "party of action" in his views concerning Belgium, without, however, ever giving his full acquiescence.

[56] Dispatch of M. Nigra of the 8th August, 1865. La Marmora, p. 45.

[57] Dispatch of General Govone of the 17th March, 1866. La Marmora, p. 90.

[58] It was on his return from Biarritz that M. de Bismarck said to the Chevalier Nigra, these significant words: "If Italy did not exist, it would have to be invented." La Marmora, p. 59.

[59] Dispatch of General Govone, of the 6th April, 1866. La Marmora, p. 139.

[60] *Est aliquid delirii in omni magno ingenio.*—BOERHAAVE.

[61] At the moment when hostilities commenced; dispatch of M. de Barral of the 15th June, 1866. La Marmora, p. 332.

[62] Dispatch of General Govone of the 2d April, 1866. La Marmora, p. 131.

[63] Dispatches of General Govone of the 2d April and 22d May 1866. La Marmora, pp. 131 and 245.

[64] George Hesekiel, iii. p. 271.

[65] *E la vipera avrà morsicato il ciarlatano.* Dispatch of General Govone of the 15th March, 1866. La Marmora, p. 88.

[66] It was the Queen Augusta who affirmed it in a letter to the Emperor of Austria, saying that on this matter she had received the word of honor of her royal spouse. See the curious dispatch of M. Nigra of the 12th June, 1866, as well as the telegram of General La Marmora of the same day. La Marmora, pp. 305 and 310.

[67] After the death of the great Italian agitator, the journals of Florence published his letters to M. de Bismarck during the years 1868-1869. In case of a war between France and Germany, Mazzini suggests the plan of overthrowing Victor Emmanuel, if this latter allied himself with the Emperor Napoleon III.

[68] It is necessary to observe that the strategical part of the note of d'Usedom was an *almost literal* copy of an article of Mazzini published in the *Dovere* of Genoa, the 26th May, 1866.

[69] See the notes of M. d'Usedom of the 12th and 17th June, as well as the dispatch of Count de Barral of the 15th June. La Marmora, pp. 316, 331, 345-348.

[70] In a dispatch of the 1st March, 1866, M. Nigra informs General La Marmora that, conformably with his authorization, he endeavored to broach the question of the exchange of the Danubian Principalities for Venetia. He showed the advantages which this solution would have for France and England, who would thus see the two programmes of the wars of the Crimea and Italy peacefully accomplished. The minister adds that the Emperor Napoleon III. was *struck with this idea.* La Marmora, p. 119.

[71] Dispatch of General Govone of the 3d June, 1866. La Marmora, p. 275.

[72] Telegrams of Count de Barral of the 7th April and the 1st June, 1866. La Marmora, pp. 141 and 266.

[73] Telegram of M. de Launay, from St. Petersburg, of the 1st June, 1866. La Marmora, p. 266. One can see in the same work with what *empressement* M. de Bismarck used this opinion of the Russian chancellor, and transmitted it by telegraph to the different cabinets.

[74] Telegrams of M. de Barral. La Marmora, pp. 248 and 294.

[75] Benedetti, *Ma Mission en Prusse*, pp. 99 and 254.

[76] This detail, as well as those which follow, are taken from the narration made by M. Thiers himself, some days later, to the diocese of Orleans, and gathered together by M. A. Boucher in his interesting *Story of the Invasion* (Orleans, 1871), pp. 318-325.

[77] "He (M. de Bismarck) only goes out accompanied, and agents of French police will come as far as the frontier to follow him during the whole journey," announced M. de Barral from Berlin, the 1st June, 1866, three days after the assault by Blind. M. Jules Favre (*History of the Government of the National Defense*, vol. i. p. 163-164) speaks of the uneasiness manifested by the minister of William I. at the interview at the castle of *Haute-Maison*, at Montry: "We are very badly off here; your *Franc-tireurs* can take aim at me through the windows." One can also recall the language of the German chancellor in the Prussian chambers concerning the assault by Kulmann.

[78] According to the analysis of Lord Lyons, to whom M. de Chaudordy communicated this telegram.—Dispatch of Lord Lyons, of the 6th October, 1870. It is curious to compare with this singular telegram of M. Thiers the opinion expressed by Prince Gortchakof before the English ambassador, "that the conditions indicated in the circular of M. de Bismarck of the 16th September could only be modified by military events, and that nothing authorized such a conjecture."—Dispatch of Sir A. Buchanan of the 17th October. Now the conditions indicated in the Prussian circular of the 16th September were already *Alsace and Metz*.

[79] Confidential note of M. Magne for the emperor.—*Papers and Correspondence of the Imperial Family*, vol. i. p. 240.

[80] The letter addressed to the minister of France at the Hague and placed under the eyes of the emperor, was re-found at the Tuileries after the 4th September.—*Papers and Correspondence of the Imperial Family*, vol. i. p. 14.

[81] This, however, was only a short desire on the part of Prince Gortchakof, a design without consequence, and of which we find the only authentic trace in an obscure phrase of a dispatch of the French ambassador at Berlin. Vide Benedetti, *My Mission in Prussia*, p. 226.

[82] Dispatch in cipher intercepted by the Austrians and published in connection with the war of 1866 by the Austrian staff.

[83] *Papers and Correspondence of the Imperial Family*, vol. ii. pp. 225, 228. The editors pretend that this letter was addressed to M. de Moustier, which is entirely erroneous, M. de Moustier being then at Constantinople. We are inclined to believe that the receiver was M. Conti, who had accompanied the emperor to Vichy. It will be remembered that Napoleon III., very unwell and

suffering during this whole epoch, had gone the 27th July to Vichy, where M. Drouyn de Lhuys went to see him for a short time; the chief of the state could not, however, prolong his sojourn in the watering-place, and returned to Paris on the 8th August.

[84] "For some time it has been too often said that France *is not ready*."—Confidential note of M. Magne of the 20th July (*Papers and Correspondence of the Imperial Family*, vol. i. p. 241). M. de Goltz had early discovered this secret, and had not ceased to recommend to M. de Bismarck a firm attitude as regarded France.

[85] *My Mission in Prussia*, pp. 171-172. M. Drouyn de Lhuys, who had already obtained from Austria the cession, in any case, of Venetia, insisted at this moment more strongly than ever that they should also take pledges in advance from Prussia, "the most formidable, the most active of the parties." M. Benedetti did not cease to oppose such a proceeding, fearing that Prussia would renounce in this case all idea of war against Austria, and this dispatch of the 8th July was in reality only a new plea in favor of the *laisser-aller* without conditions which should be granted to M. de Bismarck.

[86] Benedetti, *My Mission in Prussia*, pp. 177 and 178. *Moniteur prussien* (*Reichsanzeiger*) of the 21st October, 1871.

[87] *My Mission in Prussia*, p. 181. This assertion of M. Benedetti is fully confirmed by the note found among the papers of the Tuileries, of which we will speak farther on.

[88] "Prussia will disregard what justice and foresight demand, and will give us at the same time the measure of its ingratitude, if it refuses us the guarantees which the extension of its frontiers obliges us to claim."—Dispatch of M. Benedetti, the 5th August, 1866, found at the castle of Cerçay among the papers of M. Rouher, and published in the *Moniteur prussien* of the 21st October, 1871. Towards the same epoch, they spoke also of the ingratitude of Italy. "The unjustifiable ingratitude of Italy irritates the calmest minds," wrote M. Magne in his confidential note by order of the emperor, dated the 20th July. The cabinet of Florence in truth created in France at this moment unheard of embarrassments by susceptibilities and demands which, to say the least, were very ill-timed. After having been beaten on land and sea, at Custozza and at Lissa, and having received as a recompense the magnificent gift of Venetia, the Italians made pretensions to Tyrol! There was even an instant when the emperor thought "of renouncing the fatal gift made him, and of declaring, by an official act, that he gave back to Austria its parole." See the curious note of M. Rouher written by order of the emperor, *Papers and Correspondence of the Imperial Family*, vol. ii. pp. 229 and 23.

[89] La Marmora, *Un pó più di luce*, p. 117. Report of General Govone, 3d June, 1866. *Ibid.* p. 275.

[90] "All the efforts which he (M. de Bismarck) has without cessation made to bring about an agreement with us prove sufficiently that, in his opinion, it was essential to indemnify France."—*My Mission in Prussia*, p. 192. Thus thought the ex-ambassador of France, even in 1871!

[91] *Papers and Correspondence of the Imperial Family*, vol. i. pp. 16, 17. The editors thought that they recognized in this note the handwriting of M. Conti, chief of the emperor's cabinet.

[92] "On my departure from Paris, towards the middle of August," says M. Benedetti, in his book, *My Mission in Prussia*, p. 194, "M. Drouyn de Lhuys had offered his resignation, and I supposed that his successor would be M. Moustier, who was then ambassador at Constantinople. At this moment there was no minister of foreign affairs. In this state of things, I thought it *proper* to address to the minister of state, M. Rouher, the letter in which I announced my interview with M. de Bismarck, and which accompanied the plan of treaty relative to Belgium." M. Drouyn de Lhuys had not tendered his resignation towards the middle of August; right or wrong, he believed at this epoch that he was "doing an act of honesty and disinterestedness in remaining," and his portfolio was not taken from him till 1st September, 1866. Up to that date M. Drouyn de Lhuys had not ceased to direct the department; the ambassador himself quotes in his book several dispatches exchanged with him, on grave questions, dated 21st and 25th August (pp. 204, 223), and M. Benedetti has singular ideas on the hierarchical duties, believing that it is *proper* for an agent to evade the control of his immediate chief in view of his near retirement. The conclusion of the passage quoted in the book of M. Benedetti is not less curious: "M. Rouher," says he, "has not laid before the ministry, having never taken the direction of it, the correspondence which I, during several days, exchanged with him. If I gave it here, I should not know how to refer the reader, that he might verify the text of it, to the depot of the archives, as I am authorized to do with all the documents which I put before his eyes." What of that? Once decided to make revelations, M. Benedetti could have well produced this correspondence with M. Rouher on such a disputed subject, while conscientiously warning the reader that he could not find the originals at the depot of the archives. (It is known that the originals were seized by the Prussians, with a great number of other important documents, in the castle of M. Rouher, at Cerçay.) While throwing "a little more light" on all the unnatural obscurities, let us also observe that it is wrongfully, but with a design easy to divine, that the celebrated circular of M. de Bismarck, of the 29th July, 1870 (at the beginning of the war), had assigned to this plan of the secret treaty concerning Belgium a much later date, the year 1867, the epoch

after the arrangement of the affair of Luxemburg. This allegation does not withstand a first examination and a simple comparison of the parts delivered to the public. The shadowy negotiation on the subject of Belgium was held in the second half of the month of August, 1866, as M. Benedetti says.

[93] The *Moniteur prussien* of the 21st October, 1871, gives (from the documents seized at Cerçay) extracts from the instructions sent from Paris the 16th August to M. Benedetti concerning the secret treaty. A passage from these instructions contains "the designation of the persons to whom this negotiation was to be confined."

[94] Quoted from the circular of M. de La Valette of the 16th September, 1862.

[95] These details, as well as those which follow, are taken from the papers seized at Cerçay and published in the *Moniteur prussien* of the 21st October, 1871.

[96] The two plans of the treaties have since been published by the Prussian journals of the 29th July and 8th August, 1870. The Prussian government is now in possession of two French autographs of the plan concerning Belgium; the one which M. Benedetti left with M. de Bismarck in the month of August, 1866, the other likewise from the hand of M. Benedetti, with marginal notes by Napoleon III. and M. Rouher; this latter document was seized at Cerçay. For the description and other details, see the *Moniteur prussien* of the 21st October, 1871, and the article from the *North German Gazette* on the subject of the affair La Marmora.

[97] Private letter from M. Benedetti to the Duke of Gramont, dated 22d August, 1866. *My Mission in Prussia*, p. 192.

[98] Albert Sorel, *Diplomatic History of the Franco-German War*, vol. i. pp. 29, 30.

[99] Papers seized at Cerçay, *Moniteur prussien* of the 21st October, 1871.

[100] Dispatch of Count de Mülinen to Baron de Beust, 30th December, 1866.

[101] Dispatch of M. de Beust to Baron de Prokesch at Constantinople, January 22, 1867.

[102] "What alarms me the most, is the considerable change which the pacification of the provinces of the Caucasus has given to the situation of Russia. I have no doubt that in future possibilities the most serious attacks of the Russians will be directed against our provinces of Asia Minor." Thus Fuad-Pacha expresses himself at the beginning of 1869 in his political testament addressed to the sultan.

[103] Remarks of the Emperor Nicholas to Sir Hamilton Seymour. For the rumors concerning Thessaly and Epirus, see especially the dispatch of Fuad-Pacha to the ambassadors at Paris and London, 27th February, 1867.

[104] Benedetti, *My Mission in Prussia*, p. 249.

[105] "I wish very much that you would send your carriage before my door, but on the condition that you get in at my house," one of the predecessors of M. de Moustier said wittily to M. de Budberg, at the Hotel of the Quay d'Orsay, some years before, but in the same way in which Russia encouraged the advances of the cabinet of the Tuileries, at the same time that it carefully avoided any positive engagement with it.

[106] The preliminaries of Nikolsburg as well as the treaty of Prague had stipulated the retrocession to Denmark of the northern districts of Schleswig after a popular vote. One knows that Prussia up to the present has evaded the execution of this engagement.

[107] M. de Beust wrote concerning these military conventions with a resigned *finesse*: "An alliance established between two states, one of which is weak, the other strong; an alliance which has no particular text, but which should be permanently maintained for all the eventualities of war, is not of a nature to create a belief in an *international, independent existence* of the weak state."—Dispatch to Count Wimpffen, at Berlin, 28th March, 1867.

[108] See Appendix.

[109] Speech of the assistant secretary of state, Mr. Fox, at the banquet given by the English Club of St. Petersburg to the mission extraordinary from the United States in 1866.

[110] Circular of M. de La Valette, 16th September, 1866.

[111] See the *Revue des deux Mondes* of the 1st September, 1867: "The Congress of Moscow and the Pan-Sclavic Propaganda."

[112] It emanated directly from the ministry of the interior, was written in French, and destined to "enlighten" foreign opinion on the facts and deeds of the Russian government.

[113] See, on this subject, the English, French, and Austrian parliamentary documents of the year 1868, and especially the reports of the agents of Austria at Iassy and Bucharest.

[114] Appendix to the dispatch of the Consul de Knappitsch to Baron de Prokesch at Constantinople, Ibraïla, 14th August, 1868.

[115] Dispatch of Sir A. Buchanan to the Earl of Clarendon, 19th December, 1868.

[116] Official journal of the Russian empire, 12th December, 1869.

[117] One can read this remarkable document, which bears the date of the 3d January, 1869, in the interesting pamphlet of M. J. Lewis Farley, *The Decline of Turkey*, London, 1875, pp. 27-36.

[118] Private letter to the Count Daru, 27th January, 1870.

[119] See, on this subject, the curious dispatch of the 10th November, 1867. The correspondence of Mazzini with M. de Bismarck during the years 1868 and 1869, suggesting the plan of overthrowing Victor Emmanuel if this latter became the ally of the Emperor Napoleon III., has been brought to light only very recently, after the death of the celebrated Italian agitator.

[120] Confidential letter of M. de Verdière, St. Petersburg, 3d February, 1870. *Papers and Correspondence of the Imperial Family*, vol. i. p. 129.

[121] "The Emperor of Russia has taken the general in great favor; he takes him continually on bear hunts, and makes him travel with him on a f... in his one-seated sleigh. That is the height of favor, and I think that politics are in a good condition."—Confidential letter of M. de Verdière, 25th January, 1870. *Papers and Correspondence*, vol. i. p. 127.

[122] Expressions of the *North German Gazette* (principal organ of M. de Bismarck) of the 20th July, 1867, on the occasion of the congress of Moscow.

[123] *Drang nach Osten*.

[124] Dispatch of Sir A. Buchanan, St. Petersburg, 9th July, 1870. For the details of these years, 1870-71, we can only refer the reader to the very instructive work of M. A. Sorel, *Diplomatic History of the Franco-German War*, Paris, Plon, 1875, 2 vols. We have only two reservations to make in regard to a book written with as much sincerity of investigation as loftiness of mind. The author shows a pronounced weakness for "the diplomacy of Tours," and limits in much too great a degree the original views of Prince Gortchakof in his connivance with Prussia since 1867.

[125] Dispatches of Sir A. Buchanan of the 20th and 23d July. Valfrey, *History of the Diplomacy of the Government of National Defense*, vol. i. p. 18.

[126] *France and Prussia*, p. 348.

[127] Dispatch of Mr. Schuyler to Mr. Fish, St. Petersburg, 26th August. General Trochu, *Pour la vérité*, p. 90.

[128] Prince Gortchakof was far from having at the beginning absolute confidence in the victory of Prussia; he told M. Thiers more than one *piquant* detail on this subject. Deposition of M. Thiers before the commission of

inquiry, p. 12. In an interview, towards the end of July, with a political personage whom he knew to be in relation with Napoleon III., he even let these words fall: "Tell the Emperor of the French to be moderate." Valfrey, vol. i. 79.

[129] The *Golos*, quoted in the dispatch of Mr. Schuyler, 27th August.

[130] A. Sorel, *Diplomatic History*, vol. i. p. 254. Let us quote the passage from another dispatch of M. de Beust, dated the 29th September, and destined for London: "Let us not fear to say it: what to-day serves powerfully to prolong the conflict to the extreme horrors of a war of extermination, is, on one side illusions and false hopes, on the other indifference and contempt for Europe, spectator of the combat."

[131] A. Sorel, *Diplomatic History*, vol. i. p. 402.

[132] Report of Sir A. Buchanan of the 17th October.

[133] It was only the simple recommendation of an armistice, with no other design of influencing what might be the conditions of peace, that Prince Gortchakof declined to make common cause. M. d'Oubril, his minister at Berlin, found himself at the last moment without instructions on this subject. "It is singular enough," wrote Lord Loftus, on the 26th October, "that Russia, after having in many circumstances, proved its desire for peace, thus stands aside and prefers isolated to common action."

[134] Dispatch of Prince Gortchakof to Baron Brunnow at London, November 20, 1870.

[135] Dispatch of Mr. Joy Morris of the 2d September, quoted above.

[136] See the *Revue des deux Mondes* of the 1st February, 1868 ("The Diplomacy and the Principles of the French Revolution," by M. le Prince Albert de Broglie).

[137] Note to Prince Gagarine at Turin, 10th October, 1860.

[138] Speech on the 1st August, in the House of Commons.

[139] *Provincial Correspondence* of the 1st May, 1873.

[140] Telegram from the czar to King William I. of the 9th December, 1869. Quite recently, at the last banquet of St. George, the Emperor Alexander II. said: "I am happy to be able to state that the close alliance between our three empires and our three armies, founded by our august predecessors for the defense of the same cause, exists intact at the present moment." Official journal of the Russian empire of the 12th December, 1875.

[141] Count Tarnowski, "A Visit to Moscow," *Revue de Cracovie*, November, 1785.

[142] *Ausder Petersburger Gesellschaft.* The other descriptions are taken from the *Journal de St. Petersburg,* and *L'Invalide Russe* of that time.

[143] *Aus der Petersburger Gesellschaft*, vol. ii. p. 89.

[144] Confidential note of M. Magne, 20th July, 1866. *Papers and Correspondence of the Imperial Family*, vol. i. p. 241.

[145] The *Golos*, several years ago, advanced these curious statistics, the effect of which was profound at the time. The name of Kozlof had a moment of celebrity in Russia: hearing it pronounced at the end of a long list of purely Teutonic names, at the presentation of the officers of a grand army corps, the czarovich cried out, "At last! thank God." Fr. J. Celestin, *Russland seit Aufheburg der Leibeigenschaft*, Laibach, 1875, p. 334.

[146] We have said: "How could he undertake to present to M. de Bismarck the *demands of the cabinet of the Tuileries?*" and M. Benedetti sees in the word undertake the insinuation of an initiative. We have, however, very explicitly said, *The demands of the cabinet of the Tuileries*, and we immediately added M. Benedetti's own expressions: "*I have provoked nothing*, still less have I guaranteed the success; I have only allowed myself to *hope* for it." None of our readers could mistake the meaning of our words, nor, above all, see therein the insinuation which M. Benedetti gratuitously credits us with.

[147] "*Del Conte Bismarck dice (M. de Benedetti) che è un diplomatico per così dire* MANIACO; *che da quindici anni che to conosce e lo* SEGUE."—Report of General Govone, 6th April, 1866. La Marmora, p. 139.

[148] La Marmora, p. 110.

[149] See the *Revue* of the 15th September, and the 1st October, 1868.

Milton Keynes UK
Ingram Content Group UK Ltd.
UKHW030853011224
451361UK00001B/53

9 789362 510433